RENEWALS 458-4574
Date Due

WITHDRAWN
UTSA LIBRARIES

Disruption Management
Framework, Models and Applications

Disruption Management
Framework, Models and Applications

by

Gang Yu
University of Texas at Austin, USA

Xiangtong Qi
Hong Kong University of Science and Technology, China

NEW JERSEY • LONDON • SINGAPORE • BEIJING • SHANGHAI • HONG KONG • TAIPEI • CHENNAI

Published by

World Scientific Publishing Co. Pte. Ltd.
5 Toh Tuck Link, Singapore 596224
USA office: Suite 202, 1060 Main Street, River Edge, NJ 07661
UK office: 57 Shelton Street, Covent Garden, London WC2H 9HE

British Library Cataloguing-in-Publication Data
A catalogue record for this book is available from the British Library.

DISRUPTION MANAGEMENT: FRAMEWORK, MODELS AND APPLICATIONS

Copyright © 2004 by World Scientific Publishing Co. Pte. Ltd.

All rights reserved. This book, or parts thereof, may not be reproduced in any form or by any means, electronic or mechanical, including photocopying, recording or any information storage and retrieval system now known or to be invented, without written permission from the Publisher.

For photocopying of material in this volume, please pay a copying fee through the Copyright Clearance Center, Inc., 222 Rosewood Drive, Danvers, MA 01923, USA. In this case permission to photocopy is not required from the publisher.

ISBN 981-256-017-3

Library
University of Texas
at San Antonio

Gang Yu would like to dedicate the book to his parents, Deqian Yu and Junxiu Zhang, who taught him value, integrity, and persistence.

Xiangtong Qi would like to dedicate the book to his family, Jianping and Sophie, for their love and support.

Preface

Uncertainty is an intrinsic and pervasive property that fittingly characterizes the very nature of the world we live in. Uncertainty makes the world dynamic, vibrant, and complex. Uncertainty exists everywhere and it poses tremendous challenges to human decision makers. Uncertainty causes disruptions to an operational plan and it makes the smooth execution of a perfect plan difficult and, perhaps, even to fall apart. Uncertainty is hardly avoidable or preventable. Thus, we must face it. We can hedge against it, design strategies to cope with it, reduce its negative consequences, and even use it to our advantage. Disruption management is a methodology that copes with disruptions in real time.

During the past decade, we have seen a flourish of research and applications in the area of disruption management. The initial value was achieved in the airline industry. The successful implementation and usage of a decision support system for disruption management saved several major airlines in the United States tens of millions of dollars annually together with improved on-time performance and better customer service. Recently more research has been conducted on disruption management in the area of production management, inventory control, supply chain coordination, machine scheduling, telecommunication routing, and project management. These studies have demonstrated that

1) Disruption management has a broad range of applications;
2) Disruption management problems can be effectively modeled and solved; and
3) Disruption management can create remarkable values and impact.

The targeted audiences of our book are researchers in the area of operations research/management and practitioners in charge of operations control. We intend to write every chapter of the book in a self-contained manner so that readers who are interested in specific areas need only read the relevant chapters. We illustrate various concepts and models via simple examples. For each chapter, we include a brief literature review section summarizing the literature relevant to the discussed content. We also list all the references associated with the chapter at the end of each chapter.

The field of disruption management is young, growing, and promising. We hope to use the book to open the door for exploration, to stimulate more interest in research and applications, and to promote the endeavor of advancement of this field.

As disruptions become the norm rather than the exception, the challenges as well as the opportunities are ahead of us. God does play with dice. Let us face it.

Gang Yu
Xiangtong Qi

Acknowledgments

This book is largely based on the many years of collaborative work with prominent researchers and practitioners. Gang Yu would like to thank his friends and co-authors who collaborated with him in the field of disruption management including: Jonathan Bard, Boaz Golany, Panos Kouvelis, Anna White, Ahmad Jarrah, Stephen Gilbert, Chung-Yee Lee, Ming-Hsien Yang, Hanqin Zhang, Chenxiu Gao, Sandy McCowan, Anant Rakshit, Nirup Krishnamurthy, Selcuk Karabati, Zhaohan Sheng, and Tiaojun Xiao. Gang Yu is deeply indebted to his former and current students who wrote their dissertations and/or conducted research in disruption management and its various applications including: Michael Argüello, Mark Song, Guo Wei, Benjamin Thengvall, Songjun Luo, Jian Yang, Xiangtong Qi, Yusen Xia, Guidong Zhu, and Minghui Xu. It is due to the remarkable and continued effort of this elite group together with many others that keeps advancing this research field.

Gang Yu also deeply appreciates the full-hearted support and understanding of his wife, Xiaomei Song, son, Ray, and daughter, Kelley. He certainly hopes that the disruptions to his family life due to writing this book can be well managed by applying concepts from the book.

Xiangtong Qi wishes to thank his Ph.D. supervisors, Professor Gang Yu and Professor Jonathan Bard at the University of Texas at Austin, during his disruption management research. Xiangtong appreciates his friends Jian Yang, Yusen Xia and Guidong Zhu for their friendship and collaboration. Xiangtong is also grateful to his former supervisor Professor Fengsheng Tu from Nankai University for bringing him to the field of operations research.

Xiangtong Qi owes a great debt of gratitude to his wife, Jianping Wang, and daughter, Sophie. Their support was critical for him to complete this book.

We would also like to thank Ms. Kathy Walsh for her professional editing, and Yusen Xia, Tiaojun Xiao, Guidong Zhu, and Yiwei Cai for their careful proofreading that made the book more readable and of better quality.

Gang Yu
Xiangtong Qi

Contents

Preface vii

Acknowledgments ix

1. Introduction 1
   - 1.1 Case Study: Disruption Management at Continental Airlines 2
     - 1.1.1 The Storm of the Century woke Continental Airlines up 3
     - 1.1.2 CALEB Technologies responded to the call . . . 4
     - 1.1.3 Background of Continental Airlines 5
     - 1.1.4 The Go-Forward plan and the CrewSolver project 6
     - 1.1.5 Challenges in modeling, solutions, and real-time technology 8
     - 1.1.6 The payback and the testimonials 10
     - 1.1.7 The vision, the Franz Edelman Award, and the bright future. 14
   - 1.2 General Description of Disruption Management 16
   - 1.3 Approaches to Uncertainties 18

	1.4		General Guidance of Disruption Management	23
	1.5		An Overview of the Book	25
	1.6		Literature Review	27
2.	General Models for Disruption Management			31
	2.1		Introduction	31
	2.2		Goal Programming Models	32
		2.2.1	Goal programming in general form	32
		2.2.2	Goal programming models for disruption management of the shortest path problem	36
	2.3		A Scenario-based Model	40
	2.4		Local Search Methods	45
	2.5		Literature Review	49
3.	Disruption Management for Flight Scheduling			51
	3.1		Introduction	51
	3.2		Flight Scheduling Problems	52
	3.3		Issues in Flight Rescheduling	54
	3.4		Time-Space Network Models	57
		3.4.1	Disruptions and network formulation	58
		3.4.2	Mathematical models	60
		3.4.3	Extensions and discussions	63
		3.4.4	LP relaxations and rounding heuristics	66
		3.4.5	Computational results	69
	3.5		A Time Band Model	70
	3.6		Set Packing Model	73
	3.7		Literature Review	76

4. Disruption Management for Airline Crew Scheduling 79

- 4.1 Introduction 79
- 4.2 Overview of Crew Scheduling Problem 80
- 4.3 Network Flow Formulation 82
- 4.4 A Heuristics Algorithm 85
  - 4.4.1 Discussion on criteria selection 86
  - 4.4.2 Branch and bound algorithm 87
  - 4.4.3 Computational results and impacts 91
- 4.5 Integer Programming Model 94
  - 4.5.1 Integer programming formulation 94
  - 4.5.2 LP relaxation 95
  - 4.5.3 Branching strategies 96
- 4.6 Related Literature 97

5. Disruption Management for Machine Scheduling 101

- 5.1 Introduction 101
- 5.2 Problem Statement and Definitions 102
- 5.3 Disruption Management for an SPT Schedule 105
  - 5.3.1 Post-disruption management for machine disruption 106
  - 5.3.2 Post-disruption management for job disruption 107
  - 5.3.3 Predictive management for machine disruption 109
  - 5.3.4 Predictive management for job disruption . . . 113
- 5.4 Problems with Min-max Deviation Cost Functions . . 117
  - 5.4.1 Post-disruption management for machine disruption 118
  - 5.4.2 Post-disruption management for job disruption 118
  - 5.4.3 Predictive management for machine disruption 120

                5.4.4 Predictive management for job disruption . . . 122
        5.5 Extensions to Parallel Machines 124
                5.5.1 Post-disruption management for machine
                       disruption 125
                5.5.2 Post-disruption management for job disruption 128
                5.5.3 Predictive management for machine disruption 129
                5.5.4 Predictive management for job disruption . . . 131
        5.6 Literature Review 131

6. Disruption Management for Logistics Scheduling   135
        6.1 Introduction 135
        6.2 Problem Description 136
        6.3 Minimizing Total Completion Time and
             Transportation Cost 139
                6.3.1 Problem $P2|D = \infty, t^k, K^k| \sum C_i + TC$ 139
                6.3.2 Problem $Pm|D, t_j = 0, b| \sum w_i C_i + TC$ 142
        6.4 Minimizing Only Job Completion Deviation Costs . . 144
                6.4.1 Problem $P2|D = \infty, t|L_{\max}$ 144
                6.4.2 Problem $P2|D, t|L_{\max}$ 147
                6.4.3 Problem $Pm|D, t_j = 0| \sum w_i U_i$ 148
        6.5 Minimizing Weighted Sum of Job Deviation Costs and
             the Original Objective Function 150
                6.5.1 Problem $P2|D = \infty, t = 0|\alpha \sum w_i C_i + \beta \sum w_i T_i$ 150
                6.5.2 Problem $P2|D = \infty, t|\alpha \sum w_i C_i + \beta \sum w_i T_i$ . . 152
        6.6 Literature Review 153

7. Inventory Disruption Management Based on Economic Production Quantity Models   157
        7.1 Introduction 157

7.2 Problem Formulation 158
    7.2.1 Disruptions and disruption management policies 160
    7.2.2 Deviation cost 162
7.3 Disruption Management with Fixed Setup Times ... 163
    7.3.1 General models 163
    7.3.2 Minor disruptions 165
7.4 Disruption Management with Flexible Setup Times .. 168
7.5 Two-Stage Models 176
    7.5.1 Case for fixed setup times 178
    7.5.2 Case for flexible setup times 180
    7.5.3 Special cases for minor disruptions 181
    7.5.4 Two-stage model with multiple retailers 185
7.6 Related Literature 187

8. Disruption Management for Discrete Production Planning Problems   191

8.1 Introduction 191
8.2 Problem Formulations 193
8.3 Dynamic Programming Algorithm 196
8.4 Case for Convex Cost Functions 197
    8.4.1 Preliminaries 198
    8.4.2 The greedy algorithm 202
    8.4.3 Solving original production planning problems . 209
8.5 Numerical Examples and Computational Experiments 210
    8.5.1 Numerical examples 210
    8.5.2 Computational experiments 213
8.6 Related Literature 216

9. Disruption Management for Supply Chain Coordination 219

9.1 Introduction 219

9.2 Supply Chain Coordination without Disruptions . . . 221

9.3 Centralized Decision Making with Demand
Disruptions 224

    9.3.1 Modeling of disruption management 224

    9.3.2 Optimal policies under a demand disruption . . 225

    9.3.3 Value of disruption management 230

9.4 Decentralized Decision Making after Demand
Disruptions 231

    9.4.1 Case 1 : $\Delta D \geq \lambda_1 k$ 231

    9.4.2 Case 2 : $0 < \Delta D \leq \lambda_1 k$ 233

    9.4.3 Case 3 : $-\lambda_2 k \leq \Delta D < 0$ 234

    9.4.4 Case 4 : $\Delta D < -\lambda_2 k$ 236

    9.4.5 Impact of disruption management on supply
chain coordination 237

9.5 Extension to Nonlinear Demand Functions 240

    9.5.1 Disruption management for centralized decision making 240

    9.5.2 Disruption management for supply chain
coordination 242

9.6 Extensions to a Supply Chain with Two Retailers . . . 245

    9.6.1 Model description 245

    9.6.2 Supply chain coordination 248

    9.6.3 Centralized decision making for demand
disruptions 250

    9.6.4 Supply chain coordination with demand
disruptions 252

9.7 Literature Review 253

10. Disruption Management for Project Scheduling   257

    10.1 Introduction 257

    10.2 Modeling of Disruption Management for Project Scheduling 258

        10.2.1 Types of disruptions 260

        10.2.2 Options for disruption management 262

        10.2.3 Objective function 262

        10.2.4 Disruption management time window 264

        10.2.5 ILP model 264

    10.3 Some Special Cases 265

        10.3.1 Resource-unconstrained case 265

        10.3.2 Case with one non-renewable resource 269

        10.3.3 Case with one renewable resource 270

    10.4 A Hybrid MIP/CP Solution Approach 270

        10.4.1 Procedure 272

        10.4.2 Branch and cut 273

        10.4.3 Constraint propagation 275

    10.5 Numerical Examples 279

    10.6 Computational results 284

    10.7 Literature Review 286

11. Conclusion   289

Index   293

Chapter 1

Introduction

We live in a complex and dynamic world where uncertainty fittingly characterizes its intrinsic nature. In this world, change is constant and everything else is variable.

What is the business environment in this rapidly transforming world? Advanced information technology through global networks has significantly influenced today's business by increasing competition, eliminating boundaries, and improving access to information. The marketplace in the 21st century is technology-driven and fiercely competitive. To succeed, or even just survive in this new era, it is essential to maintain a commitment to effective and scientific management of all available resources. Since our business environment is evolving at a rapid pace, our decisions should also adapt to the change.

Traditionally, people emphasize planning – making a detailed and complete blueprint for actions to gain the highest value. Needless to say that planning is very important. Making a sound plan before taking actions is a fundamental principal that guides peoples' practice in various disciplines. However, a good plan is only half of the process. No matter how superior a plan is, in the execution phase, various unanticipated events will disrupt the system and make the plan deviate from its intended course and even make it infeasible. How to cope with disruptions? How to reach our goals while minimizing all the negative impact caused by disruptions? How to get back on track in a timely manner while effectively using our available resources? These are the essential topics investigated in the field of "disruption management."

Applications of disruption management range from airlines and manufacturing systems, to telecommunications and educational institutions. The value of disruption management has been demonstrated via multiple sources, and has recently been recognized by the OR/MS community. For example, the INFORMS 2002 Franz Edelman Award was given to the work undertaken by Continental Airlines to deal with the problems of crew disruptions (Yu *et al.* 2003). The 2003 IIE Outstanding Publication Award and 2002 IIE Transactions Best Paper Award were given to research conducted by Bard, Yu and Argüello (2001) on reconstructing aircraft routings in response to aircraft groundings delays.

Disruption management is dramatically exemplified by the event that a lightning in March 2000 caused a ten-minute fire at Philips Electronics manufacturing plant in New Mexico, which left the supplier short of a critical chip for several weeks. The two telecommunication companies, Nokia and Ericsson, which directly source from Philips, took different remedial actions. The outcomes were drastically different: Nokia gained 3% of the handset market mostly from Ericsson while Ericsson lost $1.68 billion, largely caused by the event (The Wall Street Journal, 1/29/2001). The other example is the 2003 U.S.-Canada blackout – a massive power outage that occurred in parts of the northeastern United States and eastern Canada on August 14, 2003. It was the largest blackout in North American history, affecting an estimated 10 million people in Southern Ontario, Canada and 40 million people in eight U.S. states. This event severely affected the logistics of the companies residing in the affected area as well as their customers. For example, to reduce loss and ensure operational continuity, a Chinese publishing company in Beijing quickly rescheduled its production and switched its orders on high-quality paper supplies from a US company in New Jersey to a company in Spain.

The following case study gives a thorough coverage of how disruption management concept is applied and what impact it creates.

1.1 Case Study: Disruption Management at Continental Airlines

There is not a single day at any time of the year that airlines are able to operate smoothly and completely as planned. The buzz word "irregular operations" in airlines' terminology usually refers to disrupted operations from the originally planned schedule. The disruptions come from all possible causes, ranging from inclement weather, aircraft mechanical problems, crew sickness, and union strikes, to the now more frequently faced security-related incidents. It might be more proper to define "irregular operations" as regular operations since there has never been a "regular operation" in any day of any airline's history.

Moreover, due to severe competition, airlines' profit margins are sharpened razor thin, with large sums of fixed costs spent on airplanes, fuel, and facilities. In good times, when airlines have stable RASM, or Revenue per Available Seat Miles, they make money in regular operations. But in irregular operations, airlines lose money. So the real trick to making money is to get back to regular operations as quickly as possible, and minimize the loss and negative impact in the recovery process. This is the "disruption management" concept accepted in the airline industry.

1.1.1 *The Storm of the Century woke Continental Airlines up*

The Storm of the Century in 1993 became the catalyst for Continental Airlines to search for new strategies to deal with disruptions. In March 1993, the super blizzard hit the United States, the worst since the legendary blizzard of 1988, claiming 240 lives, affecting 26 states, and causing damages of approximately $1 billion. Twenty inches of snow were dumped in the Southeast, 11 tornadoes were spawned in Florida alone, and hurricane-force winds of over 75 miles/hour resulted in grounded aircraft up and down the eastern seaboard for days. One of Continental's hubs – Newark Airport – was closed for almost two days.

It took Continental five days to dig out from under the storm. Employees located airplanes by brushing the snow off the planes' identification numbers. Crew managers found crews by calling the airports to find out where they had been sent for accommodations. Some crews stayed together and others were dispersed among two or three different hotels. It took days for Continental to figure out the location of all its crews. Most flight crews tried to call in to the operations center but found the phone lines jammed. From an operational standpoint, Continental completely lost control of its operations.

Such a disaster woke Continental up. Continental's management began to reexamine its operational processes. The senior management pulled thirteen employees from their duties in the operations center and formed a taskforce for improving recovery operations. Anna White, director of Crew Technology, set out to find a viable solution to quickly and efficiently get its flight crews in place to fly following a major disruption to operations.

1.1.2 CALEB Technologies responded to the call

Recognizing the immediate need, Continental wanted to buy an off the shelf product to handle major crew disruptions, customize it, and have it deployed in six months. However, it did not quite work out that way. The taskforce visited both domestic and international airlines, to see what software others were using to handle the problem. It turned out that other airlines were looking as well. Then, Continental talked to the major software vendors in the airline industry and found that all the existing software was built on prevailing pairing optimization techniques – suitable for planning optimization but not for real-time disruption management. Dr. Tom Cook, the former President of Sabre Decision Technologies and INFORMS president, acknowledged that people have tried and failed many times to develop such a system, and no similar system existed in the market place at that time. It was not because of lack of interest, but due to the sheer complexity of dealing with a large-scale complex problem, sophisticated government regulations, and complicated disruption scenarios.

Then, through its information technology provider – Electronic Data Systems (EDS) – Continental discovered Dr. Gang Yu, and his newly founded CALEB Technologies. As a professor at the McCombs School of Business at The University of Texas at Austin with strong expertise in operations research, Dr. Yu also had ample airline experience. He had traveled to United Airlines' headquarters in Chicago numerous times and sat in on the System Operations Center. For countless numbers of hours, he observed and investigated how the operations managers handled disruptions. As a result, he helped United Airlines build the airline industry's first disruption management system – the Delay and Swap Advisor in 1991. As Chairman and CEO of CALEB Technologies, Dr. Yu responded to the call and was determined to build a real-time decision support system – CrewSolver – to manage crew recovery under disruptions.

Larry Kellner, President of Continental Airlines, recollected, "We would like to do projects that make good business sense and benefit our employees. Matching crews and aircraft to meet the schedule is always a complex problem. We couldn't find a tool that fit our philosophy and approach, so we partnered with CALEB to build one. We are willing to try innovative techniques and take risks when we see the potential. We saw a huge potential here." With a vision to lead the airline industry, Continental invested in Dr. Yu and his then three-person company. To mitigate risk, Continental also bought an insurance policy for Dr. Yu to protect the potential multi-million dollar losses if Dr. Yu could no longer lead the project due to unforeseen contingency.

1.1.3 Background of Continental Airlines

Continental Airlines, a major United States air carrier, transports passengers, cargo, and mail. It is the fifth largest United States airline and, together with its wholly owned subsidiaries, Continental Express and Continental Micronesia, operates more than 2,000 daily departures to 123 domestic and 93 foreign destinations.

Continental operates its domestic route system primarily through its hubs in the New York metropolitan area at Newark International Airport (abbreviated as EWR), in Houston, Texas at George Bush Intercontinental Airport (abbreviated as IAH), and in Cleveland, Ohio at Hopkins International Airport (abbreviated as CLE). This hub system allows it to provide passenger services between a large number of destinations more frequently than it would by servicing each route directly. Such a system also allows Continental to add service to a new destination from a number of cities, using a limited number of aircraft. Each domestic hub is in a well-populated area and large business center, ensuring a high volume of passenger traffic. Continental serves more non-US cities than any other US carrier, including cities throughout the Americas, Europe, and Asia. It has more than 50,000 employees, including 4,000 pilots and 8,000 flight attendants.

Continental's system operations control center (SOCC) is located at its headquarters in Houston, Texas. At the SOCC, Continental personnel monitor operations, track the execution of schedules, anticipate disruptions, and determine the recovery from disruptions. The SOCC provides a central location for making all decisions affecting airline operations, including customer service, crew scheduling, aircraft routing, maintenance scheduling, and dispatch. When disruptions occur, SOCC personnel change the flight schedule, perhaps canceling or delaying flights, route aircraft to support those changes, and finally reassign crew to fly the new schedule. Although they make these decisions sequentially, they do not make them in isolation. They use advanced systems to view the impact one decision may have on another. The operations managers who change the flight schedule and route the aircraft consider the impact on passengers, crew, and required scheduled maintenance in making these decisions. They confer with customer service representatives, crew coordinators, and maintenance routers when making recovery decisions. After the operations managers determine the new flight schedule and aircraft routings, the crew coordinators take over to assign crew to uncovered flights and recover crew back onto their original schedules.

1.1.4 The Go-Forward plan and the CrewSolver project

Seven years ago, Continental was coming out of bankruptcy. Continental's Chairman and CEO Gordon Bethune actually had to call Boeing and say, remember those deposits we gave you for new airplanes? We need them back to make payroll. That's where Continental was. To get the airline out of bankruptcy, Bethune came up with a Go Forward plan. This plan has four cornerstones: Fund the Future, Make Reliability a Reality, Fly to Win, and Work Together.

Does the CrewSolver fit the Go Forward Plan? Janet Wejman, Continental's Chief Information Officer, and Anna White examined where Continental was from a crew technology standpoint to make sure that CrewSolver was in sync with this Go Forward plan. It was easy to see that Continental needed an operations research tool to Make Reliability a Reality. At that time, Continental was considered the worst airline. As illustrated by Bethune's book, *From Worst to First*, it was quite obvious that Continental was the worst airline so much so that the second worst airline looked good compared to it. What Continental needed was operational consistency, in which crews play a major role. So Wejman approached Bethune, and told him that Continental needed the CrewSolver tool to help them get there, and explained how and why. And even during those bankrupt times, Bethune went for it because he understood the value of making operations run more smoothly.

The next cornerstone of the Go Forward plan is Fund the Future. Continental's management knew that if Continental's operations ran more smoothly, they could put dollars back on the bottom line. Such benefits can be seen in the reduction in hotel stay for crews, crew overtime pay, customer service agents, and reservations agents; in flying the expensive leased aircraft to generate revenue, versus sitting on the ground; and in not canceling flights and potentially losing the high yield revenue passengers, who pay full fares to fly. That is where CrewSolver has enabled Continental to put dollars back to the bottom line, and helped Fund the Future.

The next cornerstone of the Go Forward plan is Fly to Win. Continental's goal is to be in the top 25% of major airlines for reported profit margin. Continental's management knew that CrewSolver could contribute, by helping them maximize completion factor. By successfully crewing all operating flights after a schedule disruption, no additional flight cancellations will be incurred as a result of crew coverage. That, in turn, minimizes lost revenue from additional cancellations.

Working Together is a big component of Continental's Go Forward plan. Continental's Golden Rule is to treat both the internal and external customer, with dignity and respect. Continental believes that both their paying customers and their crew members deserve open and honest communication. CrewSolver allows them to take an irregular crew situation, quickly assess their options, choose the best course of action, and implement that plan in a matter of minutes. This means they can provide consistent and reliable crew information internally, which translates into better communication to both their crews and their customers.

Thus, CrewSolver addresses all the major points that are key success factors in the Go Forward Plan. However, can the system bring the needed return on investment (ROI)? Dr. Yu and his team spent two months building a prototype system and used Continental's MD 80 fleet as the test bed. By comparing the decisions from Continental's crew coordinators and the optimal decisions generated by the prototype system on some typical disruption scenarios, they showed that the ROI should be within eight months. Equipped with all the above, Continental's top management gave the go-ahead.

1.1.5 Challenges in modeling, solutions, and real-time technology

Now the challenge has shifted to Dr. Yu and his CALEB Technologies to build a real-time decision support system to face the complex and dynamic environment, take all the components into account, and handle all the possible scenarios. The Delay and Swap Advisor Dr. Yu helped build for United can only handle aircraft and not crews. The crew recovery problem is several orders of magnitude more complex due to the significantly higher number of crew members than aircraft and a larger quantity of crew restrictions due to safety considerations.

The detailed modeling and solution methodologies of the problem will be discussed in later chapter. To put it simply, the crew recovery problem can be described in the following manner: when faced with disruptions, how do airlines get the crew back to planned assignments in a timely manner? The goal of the crew recovery problem is to minimize the recovery cost to cover all flights remaining in the schedule with the required and qualified crew, while keeping the crew on their original assignments as much as possible. The crew recovery problem is proven to be NP-hard, a term to describe the intractability of the problem due to its exponential growth in required computational time when the problem size increases. Usually, the number of variables is huge due to the combinatorial number of possible pairings each crew member can take. In Continental's situation, there are millions of discrete variables.

Dr. Yu formed a team consisting of operations research analysts and information technology specialists to tackle the problem. They had breakthroughs in modeling and solution techniques, and multiple patents were generated from their work. Some of their research findings are included in this book.

The next challenge is acquiring massive and accurate information in real time. The CALEB and EDS team designed the system such that the CrewSolver optimization server contains an in-memory data store that represents the current airline operations. The optimization model is always maintained up-to-date in the data store. This way, when a request is received, all processing is dedicated to solution generation, and no time is wasted on external database transactions. It runs continuously, 24/7. Upon receiving a request from the crew graphical user interface, the server launches a new process to set up a problem scenario based on the data input by the user and the data store. Real-time data update is done through messaging. Optimization model update is triggered whenever data is updated.

From a business perspective, the following is the process CrewSolver goes through to solve a disruption problem. CrewSolver takes up to the minute operational data, looks at real time disruptions, applies current crew constraints, and develops optimal and legal crew solutions. It then provides those details to the users, quickly implements and updates all crew records, and pushes that information to other operational systems, which in turn updates the reservations centers and airports. It also pushes the crew changes to the web, so that crew members can review and acknowledge changes to their schedule. Using CrewSolver, this process takes anywhere from 3 to 30 minutes, depending on the recovery window and the size of the problem. What is amazing here is that if the same situation were handled manually, it would take anywhere from an hour to a day, and it would not be an optimal solution. Continental also uses CrewSolver for what-if scenarios, so as the SOCC develops flight delay and cancellation strategies, they can take those proposed changes and determine the crew impact. That is incredible and something Continental could not do in the past. The problem was just too large and the possibilities far too time consuming.

With all the optimization and information technology developments, CrewSolver is put to the ultimate test. Will it work? And will Continental get the value back?

1.1.6 The payback and the testimonials

While CrewSolver can be used for all types of crew disruptions, there were a few events in 2001, which highlight the variety of disruptions handled by CrewSolver.

The first event is New Year's Eve 2000, the East Coast's worst storm in five years. Since Newark is one of Continental's hubs and a major focus of its operations, Continental looked at the weather projections, and that Friday night reduced Saturday's schedule by 35%. Unfortunately, the weather was much more unforgiving, and the storm dumped 18" of snow overnight. This completely closed the Newark airport for a number of hours. Continental regrouped and cancelled an additional 30% of the EWR operation that morning. They were able to very quickly put a plan into place, implement it, and advise the crew members of their changes. The point here is that Continental recovered faster than its competitors, and had confidence that they could fly the reduced flight schedule. They got the passengers where they needed to go as quickly as possible and, in the process, picked up other passengers because Continental was flying again and in record time.

The next is the "reluctant storm" in March 2001. It went from being the East Coast Storm of the Century to a massive storm for the area, to a moderate storm impacting certain areas, and finally to a moderate snowfall. It still had a large impact on the system, but nowhere near the original forecasts. The point of mentioning this storm is to show how Continental reacted. In the past, given this forecast, Continental would have begun canceling flights early, given the magnitude of the crew updates. With CrewSolver, Continental delayed canceling flights until they had a good picture of the actual weather impact, and eventually cancelled only 141 flights. CrewSolver allowed Continental to develop the best information possible, before determining what to do. This was a major win-win situation, since they were able to minimize irregular operations from a series of days to only one day.

Tropical Storm Allison in June 2001 was another big opportunity for CrewSolver. The storm hit Houston for three days, poured over 30 inches of rain, and resulted in Houston being declared a national disaster area. It was not good for Continental, since Houston is one of their three domestic flight hubs and accounts for 30% of their total flight operations. Plus it is a major crew hub, so this storm had the potential to cripple Continental's entire operation due to lack of crews. Unfortunately, in this case there was no master recovery plan. Continental just had to take it a day at a time as the flooding continued. Continental was able to maximize the use of flight crews in EWR and CLE, and minimize the impact of stranded Houston crews on flights operating outside of Houston. That was another big win for Continental.

The most important test of the CrewSolver system's abilities came on and after Tuesday, September 11, 2001, when the FAA closed the airspace over the United States and diverted all planes to the nearest airport following the attacks by terrorists using four aircraft from major US carriers. Suffice it to say that, from a crew perspective, airlines had never before faced a disruption of this magnitude. The first significant challenge was to bring the airline back up after a 3-day period shut down. In one CrewSolver solution alone, Continental repaired over 1,600 pairings on the 737 fleet, which was by far our largest solution ever. Then Continental reduced its flight schedule for the balance of September by 20%, and they needed to reschedule all flight crews for a 14-day period. That is over 13,000 crew events. Although CrewSolver was designed to handle a 3-day operational window, CALEB was able to quickly modify the software to look at this 14-day extended window. Fortunately, when CALEB built CrewSolver, they did it right. When it was finally finished, a total of 14 days of disruption was repaired, and basically all crews for the balance of September were re-planned. Without CrewSolver, Continental would have spent the better part of those two weeks manually recovering the operation one day at a time, which would have resulted in a much larger percentage of overall delays and cancellations.

Here is how Continental fared as compared to other airlines, in terms of start-up delays for those first few days. Continental did cancel 20% of its operations, but they were confident that they could fly the remaining 80% with their aircraft and crews, and do it from day one. Figure 1.1 shows Continental's performance. The delays encountered were due to security, and not operational reasons. This helped to minimize the revenue losses, as well as reduce crew costs. Other airlines were not as fortunate, and incurred 30 to 50% delays in the first few days of flight schedule start-up.

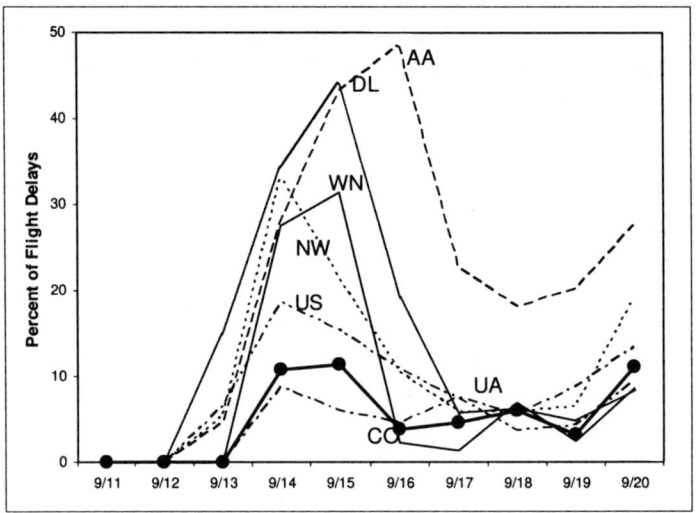

Fig. 1.1 Comparison between Continental and other major airlines after 911 Event

As these events evidence, applying operations research (OR) to the crew recovery problem at Continental, and integrating CrewSolver into daily operations, has resulted in a number of qualitative and quantitative benefits. The OR methods used in CrewSolver allow one to search through millions of possibilities for the best overall crew solution in a matter of minutes. We cannot emphasize enough the time criticality associated with irregular operations, or the positive impact that a good, quick crew plan can have on the entire recovery process. Every hour is money to an airline.

In looking at the 2001 statistics, it can be concluded that using CrewSolver saved Continental anywhere from 1 to 5 million dollars per major disruption. This does not take into account the dollars saved during daily minor disruptions.

Just looking at the four major events from 2001, CrewSolver benefited Continental Airlines to the tune of approximately $40 million dollars. Far and away, the biggest benefit was during September, where Continental sustained major irregular operations for 18 days. To put that $40 million into perspective, in 2000 Continental's net revenues were $341 million, while in 2001 Continental's net losses were $95 million.

Figure 1.2 illustrates Continental's load factor premium compared to the rest of the industry. In part, this is due to Continental's operational consistency. CrewSolver has a significant impact on that consistency.

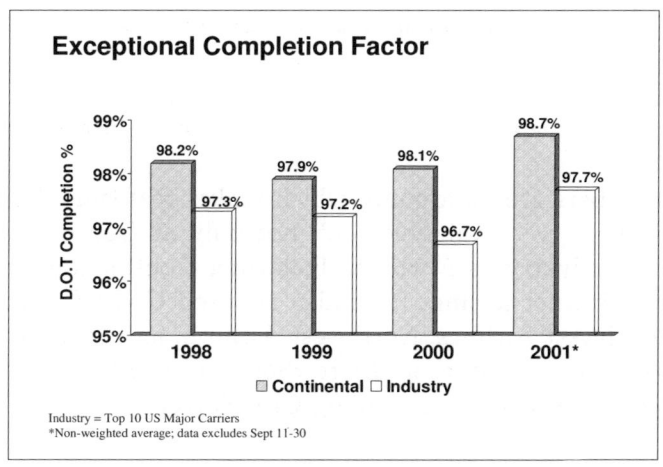

Fig. 1.2 Comparison on the completion factor between Continental and other major airlines

Figure 1.3 shows Continental's Department of Transportation (D.O.T.) arrival statistics. One can see that Continental is an industry leader in on-time performance and it keeps improving over the years especially after adopting CrewSolver. That again makes a difference to the bottom line. So being an on-time airline, and completing the flights promised to fly, makes a large difference in profitability.

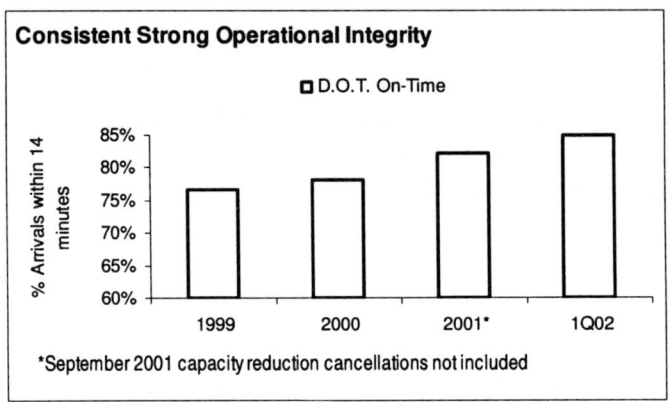

Fig. 1.3 Continental's Department of Transportation on-time performance

Big numbers are all around, which makes real time decision support systems a very valuable tool, not only at Continental, but in the airline industry as a whole. Following Continental's great success, several other airlines have also adopted CALEB recovery systems. Southwest Airlines, Northwest Airlines, and JetBlue had their customized implementation of CrewSolver in production. Delta Air Lines is in the process of installing CrewSolver.

1.1.7 *The vision, the Franz Edelman Award, and the bright future*

On May 6, 2002, Wejman, White, and Dr. Yu presented Continental's remarkable "recovery" story – "A New Era for Crew Recovery at Continental Airlines" – before a panel of judges at the INFORMS Practice Meeting in Montreal. As one of six finalists for the annual Franz Edelman Award for Achievement in Operations Research and the Management Sciences, the Continental and CALEB team was competing in the "Super Bowl" of OR/MS against a worthy field that ranged from French automaker PSA Peugeot Citroen to U.S. candy maker Mars, Inc. A day later, the team presented an encore performance, this time for the world to see as the 2002 winners of the coveted Edelman Award.

"When we started all of these seven years ago, we had a vision," White said. "We thought we could make a contribution to the company, but I had no idea it would be such a major contribution – and so timely. It's especially rewarding winning the Edelman because it demonstrates that a group outside the airline industry has recognized the fact that this product brings real value to Continental."

Wejman reflected upper management's enthusiasm for operations research solutions to complex operational problems at Continental, an enthusiasm that extends all the way up to Chairman and CEO Gordon Bethune and President Larry Kellner. "The airline industry has long understood the value and impact of operations research, and we're proud to be leading the way," says Wejman, noting that Continental was the first airline to adopt the cutting-edge recovery tools. "Larry Kellner and Gordon Bethune understand the value of technology at the airline, and they have been great supporters of our efforts throughout my tenure." She further affirmed, "As CIO, I can tell you that no other single application in my tenure at Continental has saved the company more money than CrewSolver."

Dr. Yu added, "Operations research is at the core of CrewSolver; it's what creates real value. If you just build an information system with databases and a pretty interface, you can only achieve a fraction of what you can do with operations research. With OR, we can really help airlines manage their manpower and save tens of millions of dollars. That's the value of OR. That's the future of OR."

Bethune and Kellner both appeared via videotape providing testimonials. Bethune told the judges that CrewSolver gives Continental "a competitive edge" by helping the airline get the right crews with the right planes back in the air during abnormal operations. "It optimizes not only our performance, but it makes sure we provide the highest levels of customer satisfaction. Technology is wonderful when it gives you an edge. CrewSolver really hit a home run."

Added Kellner: "From a technology perspective, CrewSolver was a key advancement for our company. By applying advanced optimization techniques to real-time business problems, we achieved our objective. The flexibility of the tool could not have been tested more than it was by the event of September 11th. Yet, we had a new schedule in place by October 1 and CrewSolver passed the test with flying colors. From a financial perspective, the project was a homerun: It reduces irregular operations recovery costs from a crew perspective and it reduces passenger re-accommodation costs, and it also reduces cancellations and delays due to crew constraints. We save anywhere from 1 to 5 million dollars on each major disruption. And with several of these disruptions in 2001 including the tropical storm Allison here in Houston and the tragic event of September 11th, the benefits go far beyond dollars. The improvement of our operations from passenger and crew perspectives is the most important benefit. In addition, it fits seamlessly into our operations and our overall strategy for dealing with disruptions. As we look into the future and an ever-changing environment, we always remember how important it is to remain competitive. Thanks to these technological advances which take full advantage of operations research, the future for crews and passengers is brighter than ever before."

1.2 General Description of Disruption Management

The case study in the previous section introduces the concept and philosophy of disruption management in the airline industry, demonstrates its remarkable value, and gives a brief account of the methodology and technology that are applied to put it into practice. We now formally lay out the framework, provide definitions to various terms, and present a general description for disruption management.

Disruptions caused by internal and external factors often cause a system to significantly deviate from its original plan, and severely affect its performance. Changes to the plan may originate from the various sources categorized below.

Changes in system environment
   The environment in which the system is operating has changed unexpectedly. Such a change will affect the sys-

tem's performance. For example, snowstorms may affect air and ground transportations; typhoons will severely impact logistics especially near harbor areas.

Unpredictable events

Spontaneous events unanticipated in the planning stage may severely impact the system. Examples include terrorist attacks, union strikes, power outages, etc.

Changes in system parameters

The parameters characterizing the system may have an unexpected change. For example, the market price in a supply chain may change for raw materials; the delivery time is changed from vendors.

Changes in availability of resources

The resources used in the system may become unavailable due to failure, quality reasons, and sicknesses. Examples include machine failures, resign of key personnel, etc.

New restrictions

New restrictions added to the system may make the original plan inferior or even infeasible. Examples include new government laws, new union contracts, new industry regulations, etc.

Uncertainties in system performance

Very often due to limited understanding of the system, its realized performance may fall below of our expectations. For example, the time for completing a task in a new project may be far from the estimated and thus may cause the delay of the entire project.

New considerations

New considerations that were not present in the planning phase must be handled properly and in a timely manner, or the system will bear cost and penalties. For example, in case of new customer orders or changed customer priorities if the system does not respond promptly and properly, it will lose its share of market.

In general, we denote the plan change as a "disruption" regardless of its cause and nature. Though some of the above issues can be described by certain probabilities and considered in an operational plan, due to the reasons we are to discuss later, the execution of the plan is still subject to real-time revision. In addition, disruptions also include situations that are very difficult or even impossible to anticipate such as a severe typhoon, the September 11th terrorist attack, and the massive blackouts in North America in August of 2003.

Disruption management can be formally stated as follows: At the beginning of a business cycle, an optimal or near-optimal operational plan is obtained by using certain optimization models and solution schemes. When such an operational plan is executed, disruptions may occur from time to time caused by internal and external uncertain factors. As a result, the original operational plan may not remain optimal, or even feasible. Consequently, we need to dynamically revise the original plan and obtain a new one that reflects the constraints and objectives of the evolved environment while minimizing the negative impact of the disruption. This process is referred to as disruption management.

1.3   Approaches to Uncertainties

In the past several decades, people have made great efforts to cope with uncertainties via different approaches. From the highest level, these approaches can be classified into two different stages: in-advance planning and real-time re-planning. The purpose of in-advance planning is to generate an optimal operational plan based on the estimate to future uncertainties. In real-time re-planning, the task is to revise the original plan in its execution period whenever needed.

Contingency Planning

Contingency planning is completely scenario-based. It uses a pre-allocated set of resources and a well-documented recipe to cope with disruptions. For example, to deal with SARS, the government may designate a select group of hospitals for accommodating SARS patients. Each time a suspect emerges, a pre-defined course of actions is taken for isolation, decontamination, examination, and treatment of the person and possibly everyone in contact. Thus, typical contingency planning consists of the following steps:

Step 1. During the planning stage, identify the critical scenarios. Here the criticality can be defined as probability of occurrence, the severity of potential impact, or combination of both.

Step 2. For each scenario, identify the options and associated effectiveness and costs.

Step 3. Based on available resources, choose the best option associated with the potential scenario.

Step 4. Acquire needed resources decided in the last step and place them in reserves. Clearly document the formula for dealing with each scenario. The formula will be closely followed upon occurrence of disruptions.

We immediately realize that such contingency planning can only handle a very limited set of well-understood disruptions, possibly localized, and evolving regularly based on certain rules. In a large system, the number of the possible future scenarios is vast, so it is very difficult to make a contingency plan for each scenario. When an unprepared scenario occurs, the performance of the system may worsen.

Stochastic Models

A typical method of generating an operational plan within an uncertain environment is to use models based on stochastic process. In this way, a contingency plan or policy can be constructed that is optimal in terms of the average outcome. Ideally, a perfect contingency plan can be made that allows for all future possibilities. In other words, it has been perfectly planned for every future possibility. No real-time re-planning is needed. To do this with any measure of success, however, the precise probability distribution of future uncertainty must be known in advance, which is virtually impossible except in very simple cases. Moreover, even if the probability distribution is known, the form it takes may be too complicated to deal with, and thus some compromise would be needed, which could undermine the analysis. In any case, it is unavoidable that any operational plan generated based on the estimate to future uncertainty will have to be revised in its execution period when the uncertainties are resolved.

A typical operational plan or policy based on stochastic models contains the following steps.

Step 1. Build stochastic models to describe future uncertainty.
Step 2. Analyze the stochastic model and find the optimal policy so that the future output is optimized in terms of the average output.
Step 3. Execute the plan by taking the obtained policy for each scenario that occurs.

Robust Optimization

Robust optimization is another approach to handling uncertainty in the planning stage. In robust optimization, future uncertainties are modeled by a set of scenarios. The philosophy of robust optimization is to generate an operational plan that is "good" for most scenarios and acceptable for the worst scenario. The characteristic of robust optimization is that accurate probability distributions are not required; however, all possible scenarios must be specified. A decision can then be made so that it is optimal with respect to some criterion related to the worst-case outcome.

The purpose of robust optimization with regard to uncertainty is to keep the original plan intact no matter what happens. If a solution is chosen accordingly, the original plan will not cause an extremely inferior result. However, the solution may be too conservative if the worst-case scenario is associated with a very small probability. Moreover, it may still be difficult to state all possible scenarios when generating the original plan, even though the probability is not required. Therefore, in practice a robust solution may still be subject to change in its execution stage.

To illustrate robust planning in airline scheduling, suppose we know that a city is highly prone to snowstorms in the winter time. Then first of all, we should not choose the city as an airline hub during the network design phase unless it justifies other important criteria. We may also schedule flights with longer connection times passing the airport and allocate more reserve crews in the city during winter. Thus the worst scenario is considered. When a snowstorm hits, it will not affect a large scope of the network. Disruptions are absorbed locally.

A typical robust planning process is as follows:

Step 1. Identify the potential disruptive scenarios.
Step 2. Choose a robustness criterion appropriate for the decision maker. For example, one criterion defined in Kouvelis and Yu (1995) specifies the robustness as minimizing the maximum deviation from optimality under all possible scenarios.
Step 3. Incorporate the above information and measure in planning to generate a robust plan.
Step 4. Carry out the plan without change no matter what may happen in the future.

The advantage of a robust plan is that it can guarantee the performance of the system even when the worst scenario happens. However, the trade off is that a robust plan will sacrifice average performance to gain robustness against disruptions, especially when the probability of some disruptive events may be very small. Moreover, it is virtually impossible to enumerate all possible future disruptions in advance.

In general, an optimized operational plan can be generated based on either stochastic models or robust optimization models. From the viewpoint of practice, however, no perfect plan exists. Moreover, the execution of an operational plan usually involves some related plans made by other departments within an organization, but their interrelationship is usually neglected when the plans are generated. For example, the system for generating production planning may not take into account the difficulty in compiling a corresponding staffing assignment. The systems for generating production schedules and inventory policies tend to disregard the complexity of its consequent distribution issues. The system for manpower planning does not consider training scheduling and training resource use. The systems for planning decisions do not offer robust solutions needed for speedy recovery when there are disruptions. In all, this lack of integration among different related operational plans leads to inferior responsiveness to change and imposes costs throughout the enterprise. A disruption to one plan will also impact other related plans. Therefore, any operational plan would be subject to dynamic revision in its execution stage.

Disruption Management

The concept of disruption management refers to the real time dynamic revision of an operational plan when disruptions occur. This is especially important in situations where an operational plan has to be published in advance, and its execution is subject to severe random disruptions. When a published operational plan is revised, there will be some deviation cost associated with the transition from the original plan to the new plan. The deviation cost can be a real dollar cost caused by raw material waste, or using on-call or reserved personnel; it can also mean the loss of the customers' goodwill for waiting and delay. To reduce such deviation costs, it is essential to take them into account when generating the new plan. In this sense, providing guidance for revising a predetermined plan is at least as important as making the plan itself.

Pure Rescheduling

People have also been working on the research of various dynamic scheduling problems, on-line scheduling problems, and rescheduling models for decades. However, many current rescheduling problems have not been able to take into account the deviation costs in analysis. Thus we use pure rescheduling models to refer to the above research. In situations where there is no need to make and publish an operational schedule in advance, or a published schedule can be revised with little penalty, the pure rescheduling models can provide a solution to dynamically respond to the changing environment. However, when revision of a predetermined schedule is costly, failing to consider the deviation cost cannot provide a practically satisfactory solution.

We briefly compare the pros and cons of the various approaches below.

The contingency planning requires the listing of a finite set of scenarios. It can thus only handle this limited set of disruptions. If the real world event is not included in the set, then it may create havoc to the system. As possible disruptions are so unpredictable and very often cannot even be identified ahead of time, the limitation for the use of this approach is obvious.

Stochastic models are the most prevailing means of handling uncertainties, and have been approved to be effective in many situations. However, a successful application of stochastic models requires the knowledge of probability distribution, which is not always an easy job.

The robust planning approach also requires knowledge of the scenarios and possibly their probabilities of occurrence. The probability information on disruption scenarios is very difficult to acquire and its accuracy is often problematic. Thus a worst-case robustness measure is often used. However, such a measure emphasizes too much worst cases of small probability and thus makes the plan conservative.

Pure rescheduling focuses on reactive response to the changing environment, but it often ignores the possible deviation cost that may be incurred when changing the original plan, and thus only generates suboptimal solutions.

The major advantage of disruption management is its ability to cope with all disruptions without knowing what is going to unravel, and provide feasible and optimal solutions in real time.

1.4 General Guidance of Disruption Management

From our research and practice on disruption management, we have summarized some general guidelines and concepts for disruption management.

Real-time optimization. Disruption management is a real-time practice and often requires a quick solution when a disruption occurs. The original planning problem usually is regarded as a one-time effort, so it is practically acceptable if generating an optimal operational plan takes a dozens of minutes or hours, or even longer. However, when a disruption occurs, it is critical to immediately provide a resolution to the responsible personnel. For a large scale system, this is not always an easy job. Therefore, real-time optimization techniques should be developed.

Deviation costs. In handling disruptions, we need to correctly identify and quantify the deviation costs and take them into account. Without considering deviation costs, the recovery solution may contain too many undesirable changes to the plan and may be difficult or infeasible to implement the changes due to organizational, human, and other issues. As we have pointed out, the deviation costs may or may not be measured by a real dollar value. One of the roles of introducing the deviation costs is to force the revised plan to stay close to the original plan. In a large organization, many sub-systems are running interdependently. The change of one sub-system will impact other sub-systems. Such an impact is not always described by mathematical models. Therefore, we should make a very careful effort of constructing a balance between staying close to the original operational plan and reducing the cost of doing so.

Multicriteria decision making. A disruption management problem usually is modeled as a bi- or multi-criteria decision making problem. On the one hand, we have an original operational plan that has been optimized based on some criteria. Such criteria should still be taken into account when we are about to revise the original plan because they usually represent the goal of the operational plan, such as maximizing the profits. On the other hand, deviation costs should also be considered.

Returning to the original plan. In some circumstances, the revised plan may need to converge to the original plan, especially when the original plan is a long term repetitive plan, such as either a flight schedule in transportation or a contracted fixed reordering cycle in logistics. Usually, these plans are highly optimized. So when deviating from the plans, the system runs in a costly way. One of the goals of disruption management is to return to the original plan in a timely manner to reduce the cost and impact of a disruption.

Disruption management time window. When a disruption occurs, the decision maker may designate a time point by which the system should restore to its normal operation. This is referred to as the disruption management time window. By setting the time window, the impact of a disruption can be contained within a limited time period. This is necessary for the situations where it is important for the new plan to return to the original plan. We should also realize that there is a trade-off between recovery time and recovery cost. The sooner we would like to recover, the higher cost it will potentially incur.

Multiple solutions. In dealing with a disruption, it may be desired to generate multiple different high-quality solutions for the decision maker to review. This is important for several reasons such as having to consider multiple criteria, not being able to include all information in the optimization model, only near optimal solutions being generated in real time, and the coordination with other operational plans in the system.

Partial solutions. A partial solution refers to a solution that does not satisfy all existing constraints. A partial solution is not allowed in conventional optimization models but is an important concept and practice in disruption management. Facing a real time decision, the "buy-time" policy requires to generate a solution that can be put into execution immediately. Such a solution may violate some constraints that are less important or related to future time periods, which are left to be resolved gradually as time goes on.

1.5 An Overview of the Book

In writing this book, we have tried to make each chapter self-contained so that readers interested in some of the topics do not need to review the entire book. Meanwhile, reductant information in different chapters has been condensed as much as possible. In general, after reviewing the first two chapters for an overall description, the readers can read each following individual chapter separately. The contents of each chapter is briefed as follows.

In Chapter 2, we introduce several general models and methodologies for disruption management. A goal programming model is developed to address the concerns of multiple criteria, and the means of handling these multiple criteria. A scenario-based model is used to describe the disruption management as a dynamic process over time. Some local search approaches to solve disruption management problems are discussed.

In Chapters 3 and 4, we focus on disruption management for applications in airline operations. When a disruption occurs, the airline first needs to assess the disruption, then make revision to their flight and aircraft schedule. This will then disrupt their crew assignment and pairings, which, in turn, has to be repaired. We will address the flight and aircraft rescheduling in Chapter 3, and the crew rescheduling in Chapter 4.

Chapter 5 is concerned with disruption management for machine scheduling models. We present a systematic classification scheme for the research of disruption management for machine scheduling problems. We also discuss in detail problems where the original schedule is given by the shortest-processing-time rule, for both single and multiple machines.

Chapter 6 extends the results to logistics scheduling models. Different from traditional machine scheduling that is mainly concerned with sequencing jobs within a firm, logistics scheduling has to consider more issues between different locations such as transportation time and cost. So the disruption management becomes more important and complicated.

In Chapter 7, we consider the disruption management for continuous-time production and inventory management, in particular the EPQ/EOQ models. Both a single stage EPQ model and a two-stage series model are discussed.

In Chapter 8, we concentrate on disruption management for a discrete-time production and inventory model. The most interesting result there shows that under certain conditions, a greedy local search method can solve the problem to optimality with the least number of steps.

Chapter 9 is dedicated to disruption management for supply chain management. Specifically, we start with a two-player supply chain coordination model subject to demand disruptions. Then the results are extended to cases with more complicated demand functions and a one-supplier-two-retailer model.

In Chapter 10, we study disruption management for project scheduling. A project contains multiple activities which are intercorrelated by limited resource and precedence relationship. Mathematical models and solution schemes are proposed and tested.

1.6 Literature Review

The real-time operations control in the airline industry is one of the successful areas where the models and methodologies of disruption management have been applied. A lot of research results and applications are reported, for example, the flight rescheduling area including Teodorovic and Guberinic (1984), Jarrah et al.(1993), Teodorovic and Stojkovic (1995), Argüello et al.(1997), Cao and Kanafani (1997a, 1997b), Luo and Yu (1997), Yan and Lin (1997), Yan and Tu (1997), Thengvall et al.(2000, 2001), Filar et al.(2001), Bard et al.(2001), and crew rescheduling area including Wei et al.(1997), Lettovsky et al.(2000), Yu et al.(2003).

Machine scheduling and rescheduling is another area that people have been studying in order to respond to an unexpected disruptions. We refer to Aytug et al. (2001) for an extensive survey of rescheduling and executing production schedules while facing uncertainties. For work specifically addressing the deviation impact and cost of changing the original schedule, see Bean et al. (1991), Wu et al.(1993), Abumaizar and Svestka (1997), Akturk and Gorgulu (1999), Hall and Potts (2004).

Some efforts in discussing disruption and delays in project scheduling can be found in Howick and Eden (2001), Eden et al.(2002), and Howick (2003). The application of disruption management in other areas can be found in Clausen et al.(2001), and Sheffi (2003).

References

Akturk, M.S. and E. Gorgulu (1999), Match-up scheduling under a machine breakdown, *European Journal of Operational Research*, 112, 81-97.

Argüello, M.F., J.F. Bard, and G. Yu (1997), A GRASP for aircraft routing in response to groundings and delays, *Journal of Combinatorial Optimization*, 5, 211-228.

Aytug, H., M.A. Lawley, K. McKay, S. Mohan and R. Uzsoy (2002), Executing production schedules in the face of uncertainties: A review and some future directions, *European Journal of Operational Research*, in press.

Bard, J.F., G. Yu and M.F. Argüello (2001), Optimizing aircraft routings in response to groundings and delays, *IIE Transactions on Operations Engineering*, 33(10), 931-947.

Bean, J.C., J.R. Birge, J. Mittenthal and C.E. Noon (1991), Matchup scheduling with multiple resources, release dates and disruptions, *Operations Research*, 39, 470-483.

Bethune, G. (1999), *From Worst to First: Behind the Scenes of Continental's Remarkable Comeback*, John Wiley & Sons.

Cao, J. and A. Kanafani (1997a), Real-time decision support for integration of airline flight cancellations and delays, part I: mathematical formulations, *Transportation Planning and Technology*, 20, 183-199.

Cao, J. and A. Kanafani (1997b), Real-time decision support for integration of airline flight cancellations and delays, part II: algorithms and computational experiments, *Transportation Planning and Technology*, 20, 201-217.

Clausen, J., J. Hansen, J. Larson and A. Larsen (2001), Disruption management, *ORMS Today*, 28, 40-43.

Eden, C., T. Williams, F. Ackermann, and S. Howick (2002), On the nature of disruption and delay (D&D) in major projects, *Journal of the Operational Research Society*, 51, 291-300.

Filar, J.A., P. Manyem and K. White (2001), How airlines and airports recover from schedule perturbations: A survey, *Annals of Operations Research*, 108, 315-333.

Hall, N.G. and C. Potts (2004), Rescheduling for new orders, *Operations Research*, in press.

Howick, S. (2003), Using system dynamics to analyse disruption and delay in complex projects for litigation: Can the modelling purposes be met? *Journal of the Operational Research Society*, 54, 222-229.

Howick, S. and C. Eden (2001), The impact of disruption and delay when compressing large projects: Going for incentives? *Journal of the Operational Research Society*, 52, 26-34.

Jarrah, A.I.Z., G. Yu, N. Krishnamurthy and A. Rakshit (1993), A decision support framework for airline flight cancellations and delays, *Transportation Science*, 27, 266-280.

Kouvelis, P. and G. Yu (1996), *Robust Discrete Optimization and Its Applications*, Kluwer Academic Publishers, Boston.

Lettovsky, L., E.L. Johnson and G.L. Nemhauser (2000), Airline crew recovery, *Transportation Science*, 34, 337-348.

Luo, S.J. and G. Yu (1997), On the airline schedule perturbation problem caused by the ground delay program, *Transportation Science*, 31, 298-311.

Sheffi, Y. (2003), Supply chain disruption management, Presentation at the CMI Supply Chains Under Stress conference, Adastral Park, Ipswitch, United Kingdom.

Teodorovic, D. and S. Guberinic (1984), Optimal dispatching strategy on an airline network after a schedule perturbation, *European Journal of Operational Research*, 15, 178-182.

Teodorovic, D. and G. Stojkovic (1995), Model to reduce airline schedule disturbances, *Journal of Transportation Engineering*, 121, 324-331.

Thengvall, B.G., J.F. Bard and G. Yu (2000), Balancing user preferences for aircraft schedule recovery during irregular operations, *IIE Transactions on Operations Engineering*, 32, 181-193.

Thengvall, B.G., G. Yu and J.F. Bard (2001), Multiple fleet aircraft schedule recovery following hub closures, *Transportation Research Part A: Policy and Practice*, 35, 289-308.

Wei, G., G. Yu and M. Song (1997), Optimization model and algorithm for crew management during airline irregular operations, *Journal of Combinatorial Optimization*, 1, 305-321.

Yan, S. and C. Lin (1997), Airline scheduling for the temporary closure of airports, *Transportation Science*, 31, 72-82.

Yan, S. and Y.-P. Tu (1997), Multifleet routing and multistop flight scheduling for schedule perturbation, *European Journal of Operational Research*, 103, 155-169.

Yu, G., M. Argüello, M. Song, S. McCowan and A. White (2003), A new era for crew recovery at Continental Airlines, *Interfaces*, 33(1), 5-22.

Wu, S.-D., R.H. Storeer and P.C. Chang (1993), On machine rescheduling heuristics with efficiency and stability as criteria, *Computers & Operations Research*, 20, 1-14.

Chapter 2

General Models for Disruption Management

2.1 Introduction

In this chapter, we introduce some general modeling approaches and solution schemes in disruption management. These models and schemes address basic concepts and techniques in disruption management from different aspects, such as optimization with multiple criteria, generation of multiple solutions, disruption management time windows, and partial solutions. Furthermore, these models and schemes are discussed by using simple examples in this chapter, and will be used in the ensuing chapters to cope with problems in more complicated situations.

In the first model, we use a goal programming framework to discuss how to evaluate deviation costs caused by switching from the original plan to a new plan, and how to establish an optimization model to handle multiple criteria that have to be considered in disruption management. The general descriptions are illustrated by a concrete example on the shortest path problem.

In the second model, we focus on the perspective of the system evolution over time with the purpose of providing more insights on the occurrence of a disruption and its impact on the system execution. In this regard, we use the concept of scenario to describe future uncertainty under a discrete time model.

We also discuss the idea of using a local search method to solve disruption management problems. Because of the time restriction, disruption management problems have to be solved in real time. So heuristics are often used. One of the promising heuristics is the local search method which starts from the original plan and improves the solution step by step. It is expected that a well-designed local search algorithm can solve the disruption management problem efficiently due to the inclusion of deviation costs.

2.2 Goal Programming Models

In this section, we propose a disruption management model based on the framework of goal programming. Simply speaking, goal programming is a way to handle multiple criteria decision making problems. In a situation with multiple criteria, each decision has to be evaluated by different measurements. In most cases we cannot find a single solution that optimizes all criteria. To use goal programming to handle multiple criteria, we set up a goal for each criterion, i.e., an expected value, and then try to minimize the gap from the goal for each criterion. In other words, each goal is regarded as a soft constraint in the optimization model, and the purpose of goal programming is to minimize the distance to these goals.

The advantage of a goal programming model is that it offers the flexibility to define different objectives as goals so that the problem can be modeled as an optimization problem of minimizing the deviation from these goals. Goal programming also allows us to effectively deal with partial solutions by enabling violation from the original constraints, and generate different multiple good solutions by changing the way of achieving the goals.

2.2.1 Goal programming in general form

We describe our goal programming model by using an example of a mathematical programming problem defined over the n-dimensional real space $\Re^n$

$$\begin{aligned} \min\ & f(x) \\ \text{subject to}\ & x \in X \end{aligned} \qquad (2.1)$$

where $x \in \Re^n$ is the decision variable, and $X \subset \Re^n$ is the feasible set. Assume we have an optimal solution x^0 to problem (2.1).

Disruptions to problem (2.1) can be captured by either parameter changes in the objective function or the feasible set. Suppose after a disruption, the objective function becomes $\hat{f}(x)$, and the feasible set becomes $\hat{X}$. Then we need to find a new solution x that is optimal in the new problem, where the optimality should be able to reflect the requirements from several different criteria, for example, the new objective function $\hat{f}(x)$, the deviation from the original optimal solution x^0, etc. Goal programming can be used in different ways for different purposes.

Goal 1. Minimizing solution deviation.

One of the simplest problems is to find a new feasible solution that is as close as possible to the original solution x^0. The problem can be written as follows.

$$\begin{aligned}
\min \ & g(a^+, a^-) \\
\text{subject to} \ & x \in \hat{X} \\
& x + a^+ - a^- = x^0 \\
& a^+, a^- \geq 0,
\end{aligned} \qquad (2.2)$$

where $a^+, a^- \in \Re^n$ are used to capture the deviation from the original solution x^0 to the new solution x, and $g(a^+, a^-)$ is a function used to evaluate the deviation cost.

In model (2.2), the goal is set to be the original optimal solution x^0, and we aim at finding a new solution x that is as close to x^0 as possible subject to the new feasibility constraint $x \in \hat{X}$.

Goal 2. Minimizing the new objective function.

Another criterion for the new solution is the new objective function.

$$\begin{aligned}
\min \ & \hat{f}(x) \\
\text{subject to} \ & x \in \hat{X}.
\end{aligned} \qquad (2.3)$$

In model (2.3), we are only interested in minimizing the objective function under the original mathematical programming formulation without considering the possible deviation cost between x^0 and x.

Both models (2.2) and (2.3) are single criterion optimization problems. In many situations, we need an integrated model that can cope with these two criteria simultaneously. However, it does not mean to find a solution that can minimize both criteria at the same time.

Instead, we need to seek a way to make a good balance between the two criteria. We can achieve this by goal programming.

In goal programming, we think of each criterion as a goal, and then to minimize the gap to each goal. For example, as one of our goals, we have used a^+ and a^- to measure the gap between x^0 and the new solution x, and used a function $g(a^+, a^-)$ to measure the deviation cost to achieve this goal.

There are different ways to handle multiple goals in a single optimization model, one of which is the lexicographic goal programming structure with different priority levels. Suppose the goal in model (2.2), i.e., minimizing the solution deviation, is with the highest priority and the goal in model (2.3), i.e., minimizing the new objective function, is with the second priority. In other words, we first need to find an optimal solution with respect to minimizing the solution deviation. If there are multiple such optimal solutions, then we need to find one of them that minimizes the new objective function $\hat{f}(x)$. This is denoted by a goal programming as

$$
\begin{aligned}
\min Lex \ & P1 : g(a^+, a^-) \quad P2 : \hat{f}(x) \\
\text{subject to } & x \in \hat{X} \\
& x + a^+ - a^- = x^0 \\
& a^+, a^- \geq 0.
\end{aligned}
\tag{2.4}
$$

Alternatively, we can let the first-priority goal be to optimize the new objective function $\hat{f}(x)$, and the second to minimize the solution deviation. This is modeled as

$$
\begin{aligned}
\min Lex \ & P1 : \hat{f}(x) \quad P2 : g(a^+, a^-) \\
\text{subject to } & x \in \hat{X} \\
& x + a^+ - a^- = x^0 \\
& a^+, a^- \geq 0.
\end{aligned}
\tag{2.5}
$$

The above models assume that a new solution x can be found in the new feasible set $\hat{X}$. This may not always be the case after a disruption occurs. Even if $\hat{X}$ is not an empty set, searching for a feasible solution may be computationally intractable. In either case, we may simply find a solution that can almost meet the new constraint, a case known as a *partial solution*. In order to allow for partial solutions we extend the lexicographic formulation by defining the highest priority goal to satisfy the feasibility constraint. In other words, we first try to find a solution that satisfies the feasibility constraints as much as possible, then try to optimize other goals. This results in the following model:

$$\begin{aligned}
\min Lex \ & P1: h(\beta^+, \beta^-) \quad P2: g(a^+, a^-) \quad P3: \hat{f}(x) \\
\text{subject to } & x + \beta^+ - \beta^- \in \hat{X} \\
& x + a^+ - a^- = x^0 \\
& a^+, a^-, \beta^+, \beta^- \geq 0.
\end{aligned} \quad (2.6)$$

In model (2.6), $\beta^+, \beta^- \in \Re^n$ are used to measure the gap from the goal of satisfying the feasibility constraints, and $h(\beta^+, \beta^-)$ is a function used to measure the infeasibility cost of not satisfying the new constraint.

Besides the above approaches of using lexicographic structures, there are other means of handling multiple criteria. One way, for example, is to transform the multiple criteria to a single-objective optimization problem by minimizing the weighted sum of all gaps. Consider model (2.6), we can assign a weight $K_1 > 0$ for the measurement $h(\beta^+, \beta^-)$, a weight $K_2 > 0$ for $g(a^+, a^-)$, and a weight $K_3 > 0$ for $\hat{f}(x)$. Then we get a mathematical programming formulation with a single objective function.

$$\begin{aligned}
\min \ & K_1 h(\beta^+, \beta^-) + K_2 g(a^+, a^-) + K_3 \hat{f}(x) \\
\text{subject to } & x + \beta^+ - \beta^- \in \hat{X} \\
& x + a^+ - a^- = x^0 \\
& a^+, a^-, \beta^+, \beta^- \geq 0.
\end{aligned} \quad (2.7)$$

The difficulty of model (2.7) lies in that it is not easy for decision makers to justify what the appropriate values are for the weights K_1, K_2, and K_3 unless each criterion has some real dollar values. However, such a model provides the decision makers with an opportunity to generate multiple solutions with different properties by adjusting the weights.

Another way of handling multiple criteria is based on the concept of efficient solutions. For a multiple criteria optimization problem, a solution x^e is efficient if there is no other solution x such that x

is no worse than x^e for every criteria and is strictly better than x^e for at least one criterion. In other words, comparing x^e with any other solution x, x^e is either strictly better than x for at least one criterion, or they are identical for all criteria.

For example, consider the two criteria in model (2.4). Then x^e is an efficient solution if there is no solution x such that $g(a^+, a^-) \leq g(a^{e+}, a^{e-})$, $\hat{f}(x) \leq \hat{f}(x^e)$, and at least one inequality holds strictly, where a^{e+} and a^{e-} are defined as $x^e + a^{e+} - a^{e-} = x^0$ and $a^{e+}, a^{e-} \geq 0$.

An efficient solution is also known as a Pareto optimal solution. Except for some simple cases, the number of all efficient solutions may be very large, and generating all efficient solutions is difficult. The advantage is that if all efficient solutions are given, then the decision maker will have a more direct and intuitive sense to make trade-offs among different criteria.

Comparing the three different ways of handling multiple goals or criteria, the weighted sum model is more often used. This is mainly due to the fact that the weighted sum model results in a single criterion optimization problem which can then be handled by more traditional optimization techniques. Moreover, from the mathematical point of view, the weighted sum approach is of the most general form. First, the lexicographic structure of handling multiple criteria can be equivalently implemented in the weighted sum model when the first priority criteria is set to be a very large weight. Second, the set of efficient solutions can be generated from the weighted sum model by varying all possible values of the weights.

2.2.2 Goal programming models for disruption management of the shortest path problem

Now we use the disruption management for the shortest path problem to illustrate the above modeling approaches. Suppose we are given a network $G = \{N, E\}$ where N is the set of nodes and E is the set of edges each of which is associated with an edge cost. The shortest path problem is to find a path x between two nodes of which the total edge cost, denoted by $f(x)$, is minimized. This is a classical optimization problem that has many applications in various areas.

In past decades, people have developed many efficient algorithms to find a shortest path, but little work has been done with respect to the disruption management for the shortest path. Let us consider the network in Fig. 2.1, where we want to find a shortest path from node S to node D. The cost of each edge is indicated in the figure.

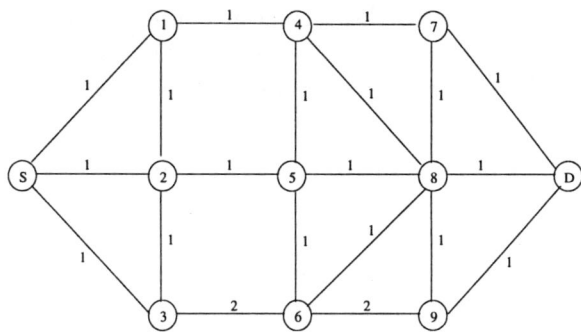

Fig. 2.1 Shortest path problem

It can be seen that the shortest path is not unique in the network. We assume the path $x^0 = \{S, 2, 5, 8, D\}$ is selected as a shortest path. Consider a disruption where edge (2,5) is disconnected. The disruption is known before departure, however, all the arrangements to go through the optimal path x^0 have been made. When such a disruption is detected, a new path from node S to node D should be found, and the criterion for choosing this new path is one of the important issues in disruption management. From the viewpoint of disruption management, the new path should be evaluated under two criteria: the deviation from the original path and the cost of the path.

If we only want to find a path that has the least cost, as suggested by model (2.3), then path $x^1 = \{S, 1, 4, 8, D\}$ or $x^2 = \{S, 1, 4, 7, D\}$ would be selected because they are the shortest paths after edge (2,5) is disconnected. Their costs are $f(x^1) = f(x^2) = 4$. However, in some cases, such solutions may not be practical because they deviate from the original path too much.

Given a new path $x = \{S, a_1, a_2, \ldots, a_n, D\}$, we now see how to analyze the path deviation cost. Suppose when we remove an edge from the original path, a cost of k^+ is incurred, and when we add a new edge, besides its cost indicated in Fig. 2.1, an extra cost of k^- is incurred. Such a measurement of deviation cost can be found in many situations. For example, we need to rent telecommunication cables between two nodes. Then the edge cost in Fig. 2.1 would indicate the rental. When a shortest path is determined, the edges we rent are contracted with the service provider. When we want to change the path, we have to ask to revise the contract, and thus each edge change, either a removal or an addition, will cause a fixed extra cost.

We define α^+ to be the set of edges that are in x^0 but not in x, and α^- be the set of edges that are in x but not in x^0. In other words, set α^+ includes the edges that are removed from the original path, and set α^- includes edges that are new in the new path. Then we can define the criterion of deviation cost as

$$g(\alpha^+, \alpha^-) = k^+|\alpha^+| + k^-|\alpha^-|,$$

where $|x|$ denotes the cardinality of a set x. Thus we can define a problem of finding a path that has the minimum deviation from the original shortest path x^0.

$$\begin{aligned} \min \quad & k^+|\alpha^+| + k^-|\alpha^-| \\ \text{subject to} \quad & x + a^+ - a^- = x^0 \\ & x \text{ is a path from node S to node D.} \end{aligned} \quad (2.8)$$

If $k^+ = k^- = 1$, problem (2.8) can be simply explained as finding a new path that has the smallest number of different edges from the original path. The solution is not unique in this example. It can be verified that both paths $x^3 = \{S, 2, 1, 4, 5, 8, D\}$ and $x^4 = \{S, 2, 3, 6, 5, 8, D\}$ are optimal solutions. In particular, for x^3, $\alpha^- = \{(2,1),(1,4),(4,5)\}$, $\alpha^+ = \emptyset$; for x^4, $\alpha^- = \{(2,3),(3,6),(6,5)\}$, and $\alpha^+ = \emptyset$. Note that arc $(2,5)$, which could have been included in the α^+ for both solutions, is excluded because it is a common term in any feasible solution.

Comparing x^3 and x^4, x^3 seems to be a better solution because it has a less path cost. This is justified by the following goal programming model when we define the goal of minimizing the deviation cost as the primal criterion, and the goal of minimizing the path cost as the second criterion.

$$\min Lex\ P1: k^+|\alpha^+| + k^-|\alpha^-|, \quad P2: f(x)$$
$$\text{subject to } x + a^+ - a^- = x^0 \qquad (2.9)$$
$$x \text{ is a path from node S to node D.}$$

In model (2.9) with $k^+ = k^- = 1$, the unique optimal solution x^3 will be selected, where $f(x^3) = 6$.

Alternatively, we can define the goal of minimizing the path cost as the primal criterion, and the goal of minimizing the deviation cost as the second criterion. We have

$$\min Lex\ P1: f(x), \quad P2: k^+|\alpha^+| + k^-|\alpha^-|$$
$$\text{subject to } x + a^+ - a^- = x^0 \qquad (2.10)$$
$$x \text{ is a path from node S to node D.}$$

For problem (2.10) with $k^+ = k^- = 1$, the unique optimal solution is $x^1 = \{S, 1, 4, 8, D\}$, where $f(x^1) = 4$, the corresponding $\alpha^- = \{(S,1), (1,4), (4,8)\}$, $\alpha^+ = \{(S,2), (5,8)\}$, and $k^+|\alpha^+| + k^-|\alpha^-| = 5$.

Now we demonstrate the other two types of formulation, minimizing the weighted sum of the two criteria, and generating the set of efficient solutions.

The weighted-sum formulation for the disruption management for shortest path problem is

$$\min K_1 f(x) + K_2(k^+|\alpha^+| + k^-|\alpha^-|)$$
$$\text{subject to } x + a^+ - a^- = x^0, \qquad (2.11)$$
$$x \text{ is a path from node S to node D.}$$

For problem (2.11), it can be verified by enumeration that (1) when $K_1 > K_2$, the solution is $x^1 = \{S, 1, 4, 8, D\}$ with the objective function value of $4K_1 + 5K_2$; (2) when $K_1 < K_2$, the solution is $x^3 = \{S, 2, 1, 4, 5, 8, D\}$ with the objective function value of $6K_1 + 3K_2$; and (3) when $K_1 = K_2$, there are three optimal solutions $x^1 = \{S, 1, 4, 8, D\}$, $x^3 = \{S, 2, 1, 4, 5, 8, D\}$, and $x^5 = \{S, 1, 4, 5, 8, D\}$ where $f(x^5) = 5$, $\alpha^- = \{(S,1), (1,4), (4,5)\}$, $\alpha^+ = \{(S,2)\}$, and the objective function value is $5K_1 + 4K_2$.

Regarding the set of efficient solutions in the above problem, it can be verified that there are only three efficient solutions $x^1 = \{S, 1, 4, 8, D\}$, $x^3 = \{S, 2, 1, 4, 5, 8, D\}$, and $x^5 = \{S, 1, 4, 5, 8, D\}$. This set of efficient solutions can also be obtained from the weighted-sum formulation by enumerating the values of all weights K_1 and K_2.

At last we demonstrate the concept of partial solutions. In this regard, we assume a more significant disruption with the disconnection of three edges $(7, D)$, $(8, D)$, and $(9, D)$. Facing such a disruption, no feasible path can be found from node S to node D. We can define a partial solution x^p as a path that will connect nodes S and D after some other edges are added to x^p, and the corresponding infeasibility cost can be measured by the number of edges to be added. For example, any path from mode S to one of the nodes of 7, 8 or 9 is a partial solution that has the infeasibility cost of 1 because it becomes a feasible path after one edge is added.

Using the lexicographic model and letting the first priority goal be searching for a partial path with the minimum infeasibility cost, the second priority goal be either minimizing solution deviation cost or minimizing the path cost, we can see that the optimal solution would be $\{S, 2, 5, 8\}$.

2.3 A Scenario-based Model

In this section, we propose to explain the concepts of disruption and disruption management by a scenario-based model. The purpose of this model is to help understand that the occurrence of a disruption and the corresponding response are a dynamic process over time. Specifically speaking, we try to explain how we can make an operational plan in advance of the uncertainty being resolved, and then dynamically revise the plan during its execution. This differs from the above goal programming model in which only two time periods, making a plan and then revising the plan, are considered.

Future uncertainty can be described by the concept of scenarios, where each scenario is the outcome in which the exogenous system-environmental parameters are within certain ranges over a period of time. Let the set of all scenarios be **S**. In many cases, there is one scenario s_0 whose realization probability is by far the largest. We call this scenario the regular scenario and all the other scenarios in $\mathbf{S}$ the irregular scenarios. When a scenario $\mathbf{s}$ other than s_0 is realized, we say that a disruption has occurred. For different systems operating in different environments, the types of disruptions vary. In general, these types include but are not limited to: uncontrollable events, changes in availability of resources, and new external restrictions.

For example, consider a weekly production plan for a single machine which, in each day, may be with one of the two states: good or failure. Then we can use scenarios to model the weekly state of the machine where each scenario represents a possible combination of daily states such as the machine is good for every day, or the machine fails for Monday and Tuesday. If the machine is reliable enough, then we can say that the regular scenario is that the machine is good for every day, and that any scenario with machine failures is irregular.

Let $\mathbf{X}$ be the set of all possible operational plans. That is, $\mathbf{X}$ is our decision space. Let $c(\mathbf{s}; \mathbf{x})$ be the cost of executing plan $\mathbf{x}$ under scenario $\mathbf{s}$. Note that the case of $\mathbf{x}$ being infeasible under scenario $\mathbf{s}$ can be readily modeled by $c(\mathbf{s}; \mathbf{x}) = +\infty$. That is, at this conceptual level, constraints are reflected in the cost function and differences in scenarios are reflected in differences in costs over the same plan. In the *a priori* planning, the initial plan $\mathbf{x}_I$ should cater to the regular scenario s_0:

$$\mathbf{x}_I = \mathrm{argmin}_{\mathbf{x} \in \mathbf{X}} \{c(s_0; \mathbf{x})\}. \qquad (2.12)$$

Then, when very probably the realized scenario $\mathbf{s}$ is exactly s_0, $\mathbf{x}_I$ should just be the plan to be executed.

Otherwise, when the realized scenario $\mathbf{s}$ is different from s_0, we need a new recovery plan $\mathbf{x}_R$. On the one hand, $\mathbf{x}_R$ should cater to the realized scenario $\mathbf{s}$ as much as possible. On the other hand, the decision over $\mathbf{x}_R$ should take into account the nonnegative deviation cost between plans $\mathbf{x}_I$ and $\mathbf{x}_R$ under the changed environment $\mathbf{s}$, say $\Delta c(\mathbf{s}; \mathbf{x}_I, \mathbf{x}_R)$. Certainly we require that $\Delta c(\mathbf{s}; \mathbf{x}_I, \mathbf{x}_I) = 0$. This cost term reflects the communication and coordination efforts needed to facilitate the change from the initial plan to the new plan among management, labor, and suppliers, the wasted efforts in preparing for the unfolded part of the initial plan, and some peculiar cost in some settings that can only be captured by this cost term. Now, the new plan $\mathbf{x}_R$ should satisfy

$$\mathbf{x}_R = \mathrm{argmin}_{\mathbf{x} \in \mathbf{X}} \Big\{ c(\mathbf{s}; \mathbf{x}) + \Delta c(\mathbf{s}; \mathbf{x}_I, \mathbf{x}) \Big\}. \qquad (2.13)$$

That is, $\mathbf{x}_R$ should arrive at the perfect balance between performing well under the realized scenario and not deviating too much from the initial plan. Note that in such a model we have used the weighted-sum approach to handle two different criteria.

To better grapple with the framework, we need to pay more attention to the time dimension of the planning and re-planning processes. Suppose the planning horizon comprises n discrete periods $1, 2, ..., n$. Then, every scenario $\mathbf{s}$ is a sequence $s[1]s[2] \cdots s[n]$ in which every component $s[i]$ is a certain range for the exogenous system-environmental parameters in period i. For convenience, we use $\mathbf{s}[ij]$ to denote the partial description of scenario $\mathbf{s}$ between periods i and j, $s[i]s[i+1] \cdots s[j]$. Similarly, every operational plan $\mathbf{x}$ is a sequence $x[1]x[2] \cdots x[n]$ in which every component $x[i]$ prescribes the action to be taken in period i. We similarly define partial plan $\mathbf{x}[ij]$ and let $\mathbf{X}[ij]$ be the set of all partial plans for a fixed pair of i and j. The concatenations $\mathbf{s}[ij]\mathbf{s}[j+1,k]$ and $\mathbf{x}[ij]\mathbf{x}[j+1,k]$ are naturally defined.

Still consider the example of a weekly production plan of a single machine. We can use $s[i] = 1$ to denote the case that the machine is good on day i, and $s[i] = 0$ to denote the case that the machine fails on day i. Then $\mathbf{s} = \{1, 1, 1, 1, 1, 1, 1\}$ is the regular scenario, and $\mathbf{s}$ with $s[i] = 0$ for a particular i is an irregular scenario.

We assume the cost is separable over time. Then in period i, we use $c^i_{\mathbf{s}[1,i-1];\mathbf{x}[1,i-1]}(s[i]; x[i])$ to denote the single-period cost of taking action $x[i]$ under system-environmental range $s[i]$ when the history is described by $\mathbf{s}[1, i-1]$ and $\mathbf{x}[1, i-1]$. The total cost $c(\mathbf{s}; \mathbf{x})$ of carrying out plan $\mathbf{x}$ under scenario $\mathbf{s}$ over the entire horizon is therefore defined as in

$$c(\mathbf{s}; \mathbf{x}) = \sum_{i=1}^{n} c^i_{\mathbf{s}[1,i-1];\mathbf{x}[1,i-1]}(s[i]; x[i]).$$

Similarly, the future cost $c_{\mathbf{s}[1,i-1];\mathbf{x}[1,i-1]}(\mathbf{s}[in];\mathbf{x}[in])$ of carrying out the future plan $\mathbf{x}[in]$ under future scenario $\mathbf{s}[in]$ from period i on is defined as in

$$c_{\mathbf{s}[1,i-1];\mathbf{x}[1,i-1]}(\mathbf{s}[in];\mathbf{x}[in]) = \sum_{k=i}^{n} c^{k}_{\mathbf{s}[1,k-1];\mathbf{x}[1,k-1]}(s[k];x[k]).$$

Strictly speaking, the regular scenario $\mathbf{s}_0$ is the most probable scenario conditioned on all the available information right before the beginning of period 1. By the definition of $\mathbf{x}_I$ in (2.12) and the principle of dynamic programming, for every $m = 1, 2, ..., n$, $\mathbf{x}_I$ satisfies

$$\mathbf{x}_I[mn] = \mathrm{argmin}_{\mathbf{x}[mn]\in\mathbf{X}[mn]}\left\{c_{\mathbf{s}_0[1,m-1];\mathbf{x}_I[1,m-1]}(\mathbf{s}_0[mn];\mathbf{x}[mn])\right\}. \quad (2.14)$$

As time goes on, information concerning the system environment is periodically updated in the beginning of each period i. Based on such information, the most probable future scenario from period i on is predicted. Being consistent with the definition of $\mathbf{s}_0[1n]$, we denote this newly updated scenario in the beginning of period i by $\mathbf{s}_i[in]$.

Now, suppose for some m, for $i = 1, 2, ..., m - 1$, $\mathbf{s}_i[in]$ has been equal to $\mathbf{s}_0[in]$, then: if $\mathbf{s}_m[mn]$ is still equal to $\mathbf{s}_0[mn]$, the initial plan $\mathbf{x}_I$ should be carried out for yet another period in period m; while if $\mathbf{s}_m[mn]$ is different from $\mathbf{s}_0[mn]$, i.e., there is at least one period $i = m, m+1, ..., n$ in which $s_m[i] \neq s_0[i]$, a recovery future plan $\mathbf{x}_R[mn]$ must be decided to brace for the most-likely-to-be-changed system environment. When the latter happens, we say that a disruption occurs in the beginning of period m. In most situations, $\mathbf{s}_m[mn]$ differs from $\mathbf{s}_0[mn]$ in the first a few periods $m, m+1, ...$ and this agrees perfectly with our perception about disruptions. However, there can also be situations where $\mathbf{s}_m[mn]$ differs from $\mathbf{s}_0[mn]$ and yet the difference does not occur in the first a few periods.

In a period $i = m, m+1, \ldots, n$, let

$$\Delta c^{i}_{\mathbf{s}_0[1,m-1]\mathbf{s}_m[m,i-1];\mathbf{x}_I[1,m-1]\mathbf{x}[m,i-1]}(s_m[i]; x_I[i], x[i])$$

be the nonnegative single-period deviation cost between the initially-planned action $x_I[i]$ and recovery action $x[i]$ under system-environmental range $s_m[i]$ when the history is described by $\mathbf{s}_0[1, m-1]\mathbf{s}_m[m, i-1]$ and $\mathbf{x}_I[1, m-1]\mathbf{x}[m, i-1]$, with this cost term being equal to 0 when $x_I[i] = x[i]$.

Then, the future deviation cost from period m on, denoted by $\Delta c_{\mathbf{s}_0[1,m-1];\mathbf{x}_I[1,m-1]}(\mathbf{s}_m[mn];\mathbf{x}_I[mn],\mathbf{x}[mn])$ is defined as in

$$\Delta c_{\mathbf{s}_0[1,m-1];\mathbf{x}_I[1,m-1]}(\mathbf{s}_m[mn];\mathbf{x}_I[mn],\mathbf{x}[mn])$$
$$= \sum_{i=m}^{n} \Delta c^i_{\mathbf{s}_0[1,m-1]\mathbf{s}_m[m,i-1];\mathbf{x}_I[1,m-1]\mathbf{x}[m,i-1]}(s_m[i]; x_I[i], x[i]).$$

In more detail, (2.13) is now

$$\mathbf{x}_R[mn] = \mathrm{argmin}_{x[mn] \in X[mn]} \Big\{ c_{\mathbf{s}_0[1,m-1];\mathbf{x}_I[1,m-1]}(\mathbf{s}_m[mn];\mathbf{x}[mn])$$
$$+ \Delta c_{\mathbf{s}_0[1,m-1];\mathbf{x}_I[1,m-1]}(\mathbf{s}_m[mn];\mathbf{x}_I[mn],\mathbf{x}[mn]) \Big\}.$$

In view of (2.14) and the above $\mathbf{x}_R[mn]$, we may from now on always assume that the irregular scenario is discovered in the beginning of period 1 and hence $m = 1$.

The above scenario-based model for disruptions can be used to explain the concept of disruption management time windows and partial solutions.

For an irregular scenario $\mathbf{s}$, it is very common that there is a period $l = 1, 2, ..., n$ such that $\mathbf{s}[1l]$ is different from $\mathbf{s}_0[1l]$ while $\mathbf{s}[l+1, n]$ is equal to $\mathbf{s}_0[l+1, n]$. That is, the effect of the disruption to the system-environmental parameters disappear after period l. We may call l the lingering time of the current disruption.

It is often required in practice that $\mathbf{x}_R$ converges back to $\mathbf{x}_I$ after the first r periods for some $r = l, l+1, ..., n$. This can be enforced by letting $\Delta c^i_{\mathbf{s}[1,i-1];\mathbf{x}[1,i-1]}(s[i]; x_I[i], x[i])$ be $+\infty$ for any $i = r+1, r+2, ..., n$ and $x[i] \neq x_I[i]$. We call the time interval from periods 1 to r the disruption management time window.

When different disruption management time windows need to be compared, the criterion should be the overall cost $F(r)$ resulting from adopting a particular time r. Here is the definition of $F(r)$:

$$F(r) = \min_{\mathbf{x}[1r] \in \mathbf{X}[1r]} \Big\{ c(\mathbf{s}[1l]\mathbf{s}_0[l+1,r]; \mathbf{x}[1r]) +$$

$$\Delta c(\mathbf{s}[1l]\mathbf{s}_0[l+1,r]; \mathbf{x}_I[1r], \mathbf{x}[1r]) \Big\}$$

$$+c_{\mathbf{s}[1l]\mathbf{s}_0[l+1,r]; \mathbf{x}[1r]}(\mathbf{s}_0[r+1,n]; \mathbf{x}_0[r+1,n]).$$

Since the optimal solution for time window r is merely a feasible solution for time window $r+1$, we have $F(r+1) \leq F(r)$. That is, the longer the time window we are given, the better we can recover from the disruption. The question in practice then remains whether the more time spent in solving the $F(r)$ with a larger r reduces cost by a justifiable amount.

We now discuss partial solution. In the goal programming model, a partial solution refers to the case that a feasible solution does not exist or is difficult to be found. Using the scenario-based model over time, a partial solution can be explained as the case that we only need a solution for the limited immediate following p period. This is important when there is still unresolved uncertainty for the future, but we have to make decisions at the time being. To accommodate such cases, a partial solution can be found by solving a problem with smaller scales, i.e., only for the first p periods.

2.4 Local Search Methods

From the perspective of computational complexity, for many optimization problems that are NP-hard, the corresponding disruption management problems are also expected to be computational intractable. The interesting feature of the disruption management problems, however, is that we have some useful information that may help us to solve the problem efficiently. Specifically, the known original optimal solution plays an important role in finding the new optimal solution after a disruption occurs.

One way to use the information of the original optimal solution is the local search method in which we start from the original optimal solution and look for a new, good solution in its neighborhood until no improvement can be made. In this section, we use several examples to illustrate the local search method with emphasis on the efficiency and effectiveness. In particular, we show that under certain circumstance we only need to restrict the search space of a local search algorithm within a limited area.

Using the weighted sum modeling approach, the objective function of a disrupted problem can be generally written as

$$\min F(x) = K_1 F_1(x) + K_2 F_2(x), \qquad (2.15)$$

where function $F_1(x)$ is the measurement in terms of the objective in the original problem, $F_2(x)$ is the measurement of deviation cost from the original solution, K_1 and K_2 are positive weighting coefficients. Let x^0 and x^* be the optimal solutions to the original and the disruption management problems, respectively. By definition, we have $F_1(x^0) \leq F_1(x)$ for any x.

Given x^0, a local search method will try to look for solutions that are close to x^0, which can be performed within its neighborhood. Thus the efficiency of the local search method depends on the definition of the neighborhood. If we can limit the search area, the problem should be solved quickly. In the following, we discuss how this idea can be implemented.

First, we can estimate an upper bound of the difference between $F(x^*)$ and $K_1 F_1(x^0)$, denoted by F_U, such that $F_U \geq F(x^*) - K_1 F_1(x^0)$. Such an upper bound can be readily obtained, for example, by looking for a feasible solution x' to the disruption management problem, i.e.,

$$F_U = F(x') - K_1 F_1(x^0) \geq F(x^*) - K_1 F_1(x^0).$$

We have the following lemma about the property of F_U.

Lemma 2.1 *Any solution x with $K_2 F_2(x) > F_U$ cannot be optimal to the disruption management problem (2.15).*

Proof. Because $K_2 F_2(x) > F_U$, we have

$$F(x) = K_1 F_1(x) + K_2 F_2(x) > K_1 F_1(x^0) + F_U \geq F(x^*).$$

∎

Therefore, for any solution x, if we can easily quantify the deviation cost $K_2 F_2(x)$, the disruption management problem may become easy because we only need to consider the solutions with the deviation cost limited in a specific range. This is more promising for the cases where K_2 is relatively large, i.e., the deviation is given a large penalty. Meanwhile, a tight upper bound F_U also helps to reduce the search area.

In the local search algorithm, in some cases, the deviation cost is approximately proportional to the number of swaps from the original solution. Consequently, we only need to consider a limited number of swaps of which the deviation cost does not exceed F_U. This is illustrated by the following examples.

Example 1. The two-parallel-machine scheduling problem of minimizing the makespan.

In the original problem, we are given a set of n jobs with processing time of p_j for job j. There are two machines available from time 0. The problem is to allocate each job to one of the machines to minimize the makespan of the schedule. It is known that the problem is NP-hard (Pinedo 2002).

Suppose an optimal schedule of the original problem is known, in which the makespan on the two machines are C_1^0 and C_2^0, respectively, and $C_{\max}^0 = \max\{C_1^0, C_2^0\}$. In the disruption management problem, the disruption considered is that machine 1 is down at time 0 and not recovered until time T. Therefore, we need to reschedule the jobs, i.e., move some of the jobs between the two machines and get a new schedule. The criteria for evaluating the new schedule would be the new makespan as well as the deviation cost. In this context, it is natural to define the deviation cost as the number of job moves between the two machines, denoted by M. So the objective function for the disruption management would be $K_1 C_{\max} + K_2 M$.

The upper bound F_U can be estimated by moving none of the jobs between the machines, of which the deviation cost is 0. So we have

$$F_U = K_1 \max\{C_1^0 + T, C_2^0\} - K_1 \max\{C_1^0, C_2^0\} \\ = K_1 \max\{T - \max\{C_2^0 - C_1^0, 0\}, 0\}.$$

From Lemma 2.1, we only need to consider the new schedules which satisfy $K_2 M \leq F_U$. In other words, the new optimal schedule must have at most $L = F_U/K_2$ jobs that are changed to new machines from their original machines. Thus we can define the neighborhood of the original schedule as the set of schedules that moves at most L jobs between the machines. The number of such schedules is given by

$$\binom{n}{1} + \binom{n}{2} + \cdots + \binom{n}{L}.$$

An alternative way to solve the problem without using the information of the original optimal schedule is a dynamic programming algorithm similar to the one that solves the original problem, of which the time complexity is in $O(nB)$ where B is the sum of all processing times. The local search algorithm may outperform the dynamic programming algorithm for smaller L when the weight of deviation cost K_2 is large, or the machine failure time T is small.

Example 2. Single machine scheduling with release times to minimize the number of tardy jobs.

In the original problem, each job j has a release time r_j, processing time p_j, and due date d_j. In a given schedule for the jobs, each job j has a completion time C_j. Define $U_j = 1$ if $C_j > d_j$, and $U_j = 0$ for otherwise. The problem is to minimize $\sum_{j=1}^{n} U_j$, i.e., the total number of tardy jobs. This is also an NP-hard problem (Pinedo 2002).

Suppose we have an optimal schedule for an instance of the above problem. A disruption to the problem is machine unavailability for a period of time. Regarding the deviation cost, since we are interested in whether a job is tardy or not, it is reasonable to assume that a unit cost will be incurred whenever a job changes from not tardy to tardy, and vice versa. Specifically, let M be the number of jobs that change their status. Then the objective function of the disruption management should be defined as $K_1 \sum_{j=1}^{n} U_j + K_2 M$.

Similar to Example 1, we can find an upper bound F_U from a feasible new schedule, for instance, keeping the original job sequence and postponing all jobs for a fixed delay.

To get the new optimal schedule, any new schedule can be viewed as moving some jobs between a set of tardy jobs and a set of the non-tardy jobs from the original optimal schedule. Thus, we only need to consider the new schedules within $L = F_U/K_2$ job moves.

Example 3. Traveling salesman problem.

In a traveling salesman problem, we are given a graph with n nodes and a cost matrix for the links between the nodes. A tour is a path that traverses each node once and only once. The cost of a tour, denoted by L, is defined as the sum of costs for all links on the tour. The problem is to find a tour with the minimum cost. It is a well-known NP-hard problem (Lawler et al. 1985).

For an instance of the traveling salesman problem, suppose an original optimal solution is given. Then it is detected that a link on the optimal tour is disconnected, so a new tour needs to be found. Similar to the shortest path problem, the deviation cost can be measured by the number of newly added or removed links in the new solution. Let M be the number of links that change their status, then the objective of the disruption management should be $K_1 L + K_2 M$.

An upper bound F_U can be obtained from any heuristic for the conventional traveling salesman problem. When F_U is obtained, we only need to consider the new solutions that have at most $L = F_U/K_2$ number of link status changes.

2.5 Literature Review

Goal programming has been used in multiple criteria optimization for decades, for example, see the comprehensive review by Romero (1991) and Schniederjans (1995). The idea of using goal programming to model disruption management was proposed by Golany et al. (2002) where several other examples are presented for demonstration.

The concept of scenario has been used extensively in robust optimization (see Kouvelis and Yu, 1996).

More interesting applications of the modeling approaches and the local search methods in disruption management problems can be found in the following chapters of this book.

References

Golany, B., Y. Xia, J. Yang and G. Yu (2002), An interactive goal-programming procedure for operational recovery problems, *Optimization and Engineering*, 3, 109-127.

Kouvelis, P. and G. Yu (1996), *Robust Discrete Optimization and Its Applications*, Kluwer Academic Publishers, Boston, MA.

Lawler, E.L., J.K. Lenstra, A.H.G. Rinnooy Kan and D.B. Shmoys (1985), *The Traveling Salesman Problem: A Guided Tour of Combinatorial Optimization*, John Wiley & Sons, NY.

Pinedo, M. (2002), *Scheduling : Theory, Algorithms, and Systems*, Prentice Hall, Upper Saddle River, NJ.

Romero, C. (1991), *Handbook of Critical Issues in Goal Programming*, Pergamon Press, Oxford.

Schniederjans, M.J. (1995), *Goal Programming: Methodology and Applications*, Kluwer Academic Publishers, Boston, MA.

Chapter 3

Disruption Management for Flight Scheduling

3.1 Introduction

In this chapter, we discuss disruption management problems in airlines, in particular, the problem of rescheduling flights and aircraft when a disruption occurs. With respect to terminologies, a flight or flight segment refers to a pair of airports, one being the origin airport which is associated with a departure time, and one being the destination airport which is associated with an arrival time. We may use the terms flight and flight segment interchangeably. An aircraft refers to a physical airplane that is used to fulfill the duty of a flight. An aircraft route means a series of connected flight segments that are flown by an aircraft.

The daily operations of an airline are strictly based on a predetermined flight schedule which includes a set of flights each with an assigned aircraft. Such a schedule has been highly optimized concerning many operational constraints such as aircraft capacity, passenger volume, government regulations, union agreements, crew availability, aircraft maintenance requirement, and the airport runway/gate schedule. As a result, a deviation from the flight schedule, for example, a flight delay, causes not only inconvenience to passengers and crew members, but also a large amount of operational cost because the airline has to make a new flight schedule that should satisfy all the above constraints. Most airlines claim that they can earn profit when flying according to the flight schedule, and will lose money whenever deviating from the flight schedule.

Unfortunately, the daily execution of the designed flight schedule is frequently disturbed by various disruptions, such as severe weather, aircraft mechanical failure, crew unavailability, to name a few. It is unavoidable that an airline has to delay or even cancel some of the scheduled flights. The revision of the flight schedule will further disrupt the crew schedule and passenger itineraries. So it is critical for an airline to efficiently deal with these disruptions, i.e., using the minimum cost to recover the original flight schedule as soon as possible.

When a disruption occurs, both the flights and crew members need to be rescheduled. In practice, rescheduling flights and rescheduling crew members are conducted separately. A new flight schedule is first obtained, followed by a new crew schedule to fulfill the new flight schedule. If a new crew schedule cannot be found for the new flight schedule, or the new crew schedule is too expensive, the flight schedule has to be revised in order for a crew schedule to be feasible. It may take several rounds of iterations to reschedule the flights and crew members. Such a practice requires that (1) both rescheduling problems have to be solved quickly, and (2) the flight rescheduling system should have the ability to generate different high-quality solutions.

In this chapter, we only address the flight rescheduling problem. The crew rescheduling problem will be discussed in the next chapter. This chapter is organized as follows. We first introduce the flight scheduling problem in Section 3.2, i.e., how airlines generate their original flight schedule by optimization models. In Section 3.3, we use several examples to introduce the important issues in the flight rescheduling problem. In Section 3.4, we discuss how to model and solve the problem for flight rescheduling by a time-space network flow model in details. Two alternative models are briefly introduced in Sections 3.5 and 3.6, respectively. Some useful literature review is provided in the last section.

3.2 Flight Scheduling Problems

In this section, we introduce how the daily flight schedule is generated by the airlines. In practice, the schedule is determined by a sequence of decision processes.

The first step for the airline to make flight schedules is to design the flight network comprising the flight segments that it will serve. In designing the flight network, some major factors have to be considered including market demand, the capacities of the airline's aircraft fleets, the competition from other airlines, etc. The main goal is to achieve the maximum profit for the airline.

In the second step, an airline makes the decision of fleet assignment. Usually an airline has different aircraft types, such as Boeing 737, Boeing 747, DC10, etc. The aircraft belonging to the same type forms a fleet. Because different fleets have different passenger capacity and operational cost, and different flight segments have different passenger volumes, each flight segments has to be assigned a fleet so that the flight segment is flown in the most profitable way. Main issues in making the fleet assignment decision include the passenger demand, fleet capacity and cost, available number of aircraft in each fleet, various technical constraints, government regulations, and so on. No specific aircraft schedule is involved in this step.

At last, the airline solves the so-called aircraft routing problem where individual aircraft within a fleet are allocated to the flight segments which are assigned for the fleet in the fleet assignment stage. It is also known as the aircraft maintenance routing problem since the main concern is to construct an aircraft route for each aircraft so that the aircraft is able to pass the maintenance bases at a specified frequency.

Research on fleet assignment and aircraft routing can be classified into two different types of models: network flow and set partitioning or covering. In a minimum cost network flow model, flight schedules are represented by a time-space network, and each fleet or aircraft is modeled as a flow. Side constraints are added to the network flow model to enforce various technical and legal constraints. In a set partitioning or covering model, all flight segments form a base set, and a set of legally connected flight segments is regarded as a subset. The problem then becomes how to use a collection of the subsets to cover all flight segments so that the cost is minimized. In the following, we can see that flight rescheduling also relies on these two types of models. Because of the new requirements in flight rescheduling, both models have to be revised.

3.3 Issues in Flight Rescheduling

To better understand the situation of flight rescheduling, we use several concrete examples to illustrate the flight rescheduling problem and related concepts.

The flight schedule for an airline can be described by a time-space flight network which is constructed as follows. For each airport, there are a set of nodes, each of which represents an event at the airport, i.e., a flight departure or landing. In other words, each node is associated with two coordinates, airport and event time. The nodes associated with the same airport form a column in the network, and they are arranged from up to bottom according to the event time. These nodes are called intermediate nodes. In addition, each airport has a supply node which is used to represent the available aircraft at the airport at the beginning of the planning cycle, and a termination node which is used to represent the aircraft that stay at the airport at the end of the planning cycle.

The nodes are connected by arcs in the network, and flows are assigned on the arcs where a unit flow represents an aircraft. An arc between two nodes of different airports represents a scheduled flight from one airport to another airport and is called a flight arc. A unit flow on a flight arc means an aircraft is assigned to fly the corresponding flight. In addition, ground arcs are used to connect all nodes in the same airport one by one according to the time sequence. A flow on a ground arc represents the aircraft grounding at the airport during the specified time period. All flows start from supply nodes and finally arrive at the termination nodes. Flow conservation is maintained at every node.

Note that each aircraft has a minimum turnover time on the ground between its landing and next departure. This turnover time can be modeled as part of the flying time of the preceding flight. In other words, a flight arc ends at a node of which the associated time is actually the earliest possible departure time of the next flight for the same aircraft instead of the real landing time of the flight. This simplifies the analysis rather than explicitly handling the turnover time.

Table 3.1   Example of a flight schedule

Aircraft	Flight	Origin	Destination	Departure	Arrival
1	11	Airport 1	Airport 2	12:00	13:00
	12	Airport 2	Airport 3	14:00	15:00
	13	Airport 3	Airport 4	16:00	17:30
	14	Airport 4	Airport 3	19:00	20:30
2	21	Airport 2	Airport 1	14:00	15:00
	22	Airport 1	Airport 2	19:00	20:00
3	31	Airport 3	Airport 2	14:00	15:00
	32	Airport 2	Airport 1	16:30	17:30

The above concepts can be demonstrated by a simple example. Suppose there are three aircraft serving four airports. The schedule for each aircraft and its assigned flight segments are listed in Table 3.1, and the corresponding time-space network is in Fig. 3.1. Suppose that the three aircraft are in the same fleet and thus substitutable. Note that we assume the minimum turnover time is one hour. Therefore, each flight arc in Fig. 3.1 ends at a node of which the associated time is one hour later than the real landing time in Table 3.1.

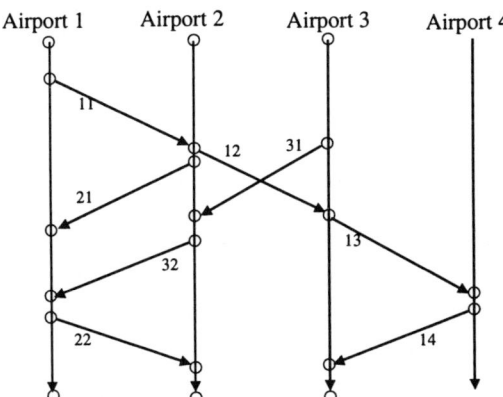

Fig. 3.1   Time-space network for the flight schedule in Table 3.1

The daily execution of the above schedule is subject to various disruptions, causing some flights to be delayed or canceled. The

Table 3.2   Comparison of different rescheduling solutions for a flight cancelation

	Aircraft	Flight	Origin	Destination	Departure	Arrival
Solution 1	-	11	Airport 1	Airport 2	canceled	
		12	Airport 2	Airport 3	canceled	
		13	Airport 3	Airport 4	canceled	
		14	Airport 4	Airport 3	canceled	
	2	21	Airport 2	Airport 1	14:00	15:00
		22	Airport 1	Airport 2	19:00	20:00
	3	31	Airport 3	Airport 2	14:00	15:00
		32	Airport 2	Airport 1	16:30	17:30
Solution 2	-	11	Airport 1	Airport 2	canceled	
	-	21	Airport 2	Airport 1	canceled	
	2	12	Airport 2	Airport 3	14:00	15:00
		13	Airport 3	Airport 4	16:00	17:30
		14	Airport 4	Airport 3	19:00	20:30
	3	31	Airport 3	Airport 2	14:00	15:00
		32	Airport 2	Airport 1	16:30	17:30
		22	Airport 1	Airport 2	19:00	20:00

following two examples illustrate the occurrence of disruptions and possible responses to them.

Example 1: Aircraft 1 is found to have mechanical problems before departing at airport 1, and will not be fixed until the next day. Facing such a disruption, the airline has to decide how to reschedule the other aircraft so that the loss is minimized. One may simply assume that we have to cancel all flight segments that are scheduled to be flown by aircraft 1, i.e., flights 11, 12, 13, and 14 are to be canceled, as shown in Solution 1 in Table 3.2. However, this is only one feasible solution, and we may have other better choices. For example, one option is to cancel flights 11 and 21, assign aircraft 2 to flights 12, 13 and 14, and aircraft 3 to flights 31, 32, and 22, as shown in Solution 2 in Table 3.2. In such a schedule, only two flights are canceled, better than canceling four flights in Solution 1. The detailed cost comparison can be evaluated based on the cancelation cost estimate for each individual flight.

Example 2: Flight 11 is delayed by 30 minutes at airport 1 due to a storm. For such a disruption, a trivial reschedule is to delay the following two flights, flights 12 and 13, that are originally scheduled for aircraft 1, each by 30 minutes, as shown in Solution 1 in Table 3.3. Another better solution can be found by assigning aircraft 2 to flights 12, 13 and 14, and assigning aircraft 1 to flights 21 and 22, i.e., we

Table 3.3 Comparison of different rescheduling solutions for a flight delay

	Aircraft	Flight	Origin	Destination	Departure	Arrival
Solution 1	1	11	Airport 1	Airport 2	**12:30**	**13:30**
		12	Airport 2	Airport 3	**14:30**	**15:30**
		13	Airport 3	Airport 4	**16:30**	**18:00**
		14	Airport 4	Airport 3	19:00	20:30
	2	21	Airport 2	Airport 1	14:00	15:00
		22	Airport 1	Airport 2	19:00	20:00
	3	31	Airport 3	Airport 2	14:00	15:00
		32	Airport 2	Airport 1	16:30	17:30
Solution 2	1	11	Airport 1	Airport 2	**12:30**	**13:30**
		21	Airport 2	Airport 1	**14:30**	**15:30**
		22	Airport 1	Airport 2	19:00	20:00
	2	12	Airport 2	Airport 3	14:00	15:00
		13	Airport 3	Airport 4	16:00	17:30
		14	Airport 4	Airport 3	19:00	20:30
	3	31	Airport 3	Airport 2	14:00	15:00
		32	Airport 2	Airport 1	16:30	17:30

swap aircraft 1 and 2 at airport 2, as shown by Solution 2 in Table 3.3. In such a solution, only one extra flight 21 is delayed. In the table, we have highlighted the delayed flights in bold.

The above examples show that rescheduling flights and aircraft when a disruption occurs is more complicated than simply delaying and canceling all following flights. Exchanging or swapping the aircraft for different flights can provide better solutions. There may be a significant difference between different solutions with respect to operational cost, business profit, and passenger and crew convenience. Therefore, formal mathematical models and optimization techniques have to be applied.

3.4 Time-Space Network Models

In this section, we show how to use the time-space network model to solve the disruption management for flight scheduling.

3.4.1 Disruptions and network formulation

When a disruption occurs, there are two basic options to reschedule flights and aircraft.

- Flight delays.
  A flight can be delayed for a certain period of time. In particular, we assume the cost of delaying a flight is a nondecreasing function of the length of delaying time. The delaying cost also depends on the passenger composition on the flight and the generated illwill.
- Flight cancelation.
  A flight can be canceled with certain penalty if there is no available aircraft or crew member, or if it is to be delayed for a long time. The cost of cancelation is usually large, and can be estimated by the cost of passenger accommodation, passenger recapture rate, as well as illwill.

In making the decisions, the following issues need to be considered.

- Recovery window.
  Disruptions can be minor such as a single flight delay, or major such as the closure of an airport, especially a hub. In either case, the airline will specify a time, referred to as the recovery window, by which all flights should be back to the original schedule. In the following, we assume the recovery window is the end of the day, though in practice it can be set to be an earlier time for a minor disruption or a later time for a major disruption.
- Aircraft balance.
  Given a recovery window, the problem we need to solve can be described as to reschedule all flights during the recovery window so as to minimize total operational costs, and ensure that at the end of the recovery window, the original schedule can be executed without any difficulty. Specifically, we require that all aircraft are at the right airports for the right flights as determined by the original schedule. This is called aircraft balance. Usually, airlines have periodic operations.

Having the right number of aircraft of the right type at the needed airports at the end of each period is critical for properly executing the next period's operations.
- Deviation of aircraft routings.
  The cost assigned to a flight delay or cancelation can only capture the penalty of a single flight deviation. In practice, the deviation of the relationship between a series of connected flights also needs to be considered. For example, two consecutive flights are originally scheduled to one aircraft. After a disruption occurs, we still prefer to use a single aircraft to fly the two flights to keep the original aircraft routing. Advantages of reducing the deviation of aircraft routing include to facilitate crew scheduling, aircraft maintenance scheduling, and passenger connections.

All the above issues can be incorporated in the time-space network with some modification, and mathematical optimization models can then be built. The basic idea of rescheduling flights is to provide a set of options for flight delay and cancelation, evaluate and compare the cost of all possible combinations of the options, and choose the best one.

- Delay arcs.
  To account for flight delays on a particular flight, we first need to determine several delaying options for that flight, for example, 10 minutes, 30 minutes, or 60 minutes. Assume the cost of each delay option can be estimated. Then a series of delay arcs are created to represent the available delaying options, each being assigned with the corresponding cost. In Fig. 3.2, each flight is provided with three delaying options which are denoted by dashed arcs. To make sure that each original flight is only flown once, we have to add a side constraint that requires the sum of flows on all flight arcs (the original flight arc and its delay arcs) representing the same original flight must be no more than 1. Note that when the sum of flows is 0, it represents that the flight is canceled.
- Protection arcs.
  To reduce the deviation from aircraft routing, for the flight segments that are originally flown by one aircraft, we may still

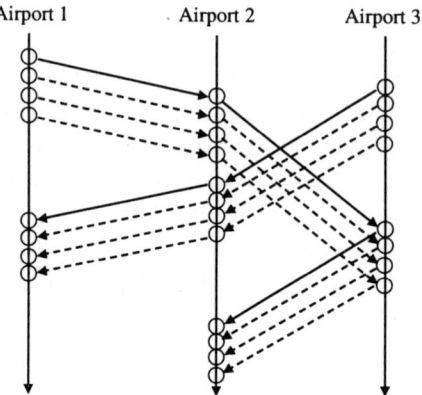

Fig. 3.2 Delay arcs

prefer to use one aircraft after a disruption. To achieve this, a protection arc can be added to provide some incentives for assigning one aircraft to those flight segments. For example, if we want to protect flights 11 and 12 so that they can be still flown by the same aircraft, we can added a protection arc from airport 1 to airport 3, as shown in Fig. 3.3. Moreover, we set the cost of this protection arc as less than the sum of costs of flight arcs 11 and 12. The difference is referred to as the *bonus* awarded to the protection arc. In this way, the optimization will try to take the protection arc whenever possible to decrease total costs. After adding a protection arc, side constraints need to be revised to include the protection arc so that each original flight can actually be flown once at the most.

3.4.2 Mathematical models

Derived from the time-space network model, an integer programming problem can be formulated. In the formulation, we use the following notation.

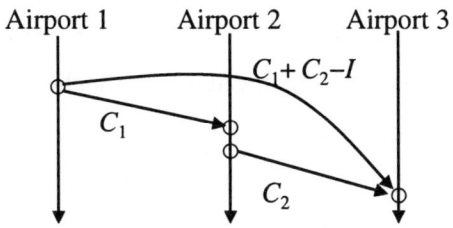

Fig. 3.3 A protection arc and its associated cost

Nodes:

s: index for set of supply nodes S

t: index for set of destination nodes T

i: index for set of intermediate nodes I

η: index for set of scheduled flight segments A

Arcs:

g: index for set of ground arcs $\dot{G}$

f: index for set of flight arcs F

p: index for set of protection arcs P

$O(i)$: set of arcs originating at node i

$T(i)$: set of arcs terminating at node i

$F(\eta)$: set of arcs covering flight η, where $F(\eta) \subset F \cup P$

Parameters:

C_f: cost of a delay arc f

C_p: cost of a protection arc p

C_η: cost of canceling flight η

B_s: initial number of aircraft at supply node s

B_t: number of aircraft required at the destination node t at the end of the recover window

Decision variables:

x_f: binary variable, $=1$ if there is a flow on flight arc f

y_p: binary variable, $=1$ if there is a flow on protection arc p

s_η: binary variable, $=1$ if flight η is canceled

z_g: flow on ground arc g

The mathematical model is as follows:

$$\min \sum_{f \in F} C_f x_f + \sum_{p \in P} C_p y_p + \sum_{\eta \in A} C_\eta s_\eta \tag{3.1}$$

subject to:

$$\sum_{g \in O(s)} z_g = B_s, \quad \forall s \in S \tag{3.2}$$

$$\sum_{g \in T(t)} z_g = B_t, \quad \forall t \in T \tag{3.3}$$

$$\sum_{g \in O(i)} z_g + \sum_{f \in O(i)} x_f + \sum_{p \in O(i)} y_p = \sum_{g \in T(i)} z_g + \sum_{f \in T(i)} x_f + \sum_{p \in T(i)} y_p, \quad \forall i \in I \tag{3.4}$$

$$\sum_{f \in F(\eta)} x_f + \sum_{p \in F(\eta)} y_p + s_\eta = 1, \quad \forall \eta \in A \tag{3.5}$$

$$x_f \in \{0,1\}, \quad \forall f \in F \tag{3.6}$$

$$y_p \in \{0,1\}, \quad \forall p \in P \tag{3.7}$$

$$z_g \geq 0, \quad \forall g \in G \tag{3.8}$$

In the formulation, objective function (3.1) minimizes the total costs in the new schedule, where the first term is the sum of cost for flows on all flight arcs, the second term is the sum of cost for flows on all protection arcs, and the last term is the flight cancelation cost. Constraints (3.2) and (3.3) state flow balance at the supply nodes and destination nodes, respectively. Constraints (3.4) ensure flow balance at intermediate nodes. Constraints (3.5) are side constraints ensuring an originally scheduled flight is either flown once or canceled.

3.4.3 Extensions and discussions

The above model describes the basic requirement for rescheduling flights when a disruption occurs. In reality, there may be some other factors that need to be addressed.

- Ferry flights.
  A ferry flight is a flight without any passengers. The purpose of a ferry flight is to send an empty aircraft from one airport to another airport either to fulfill the following flight duties or to make aircraft balance at the destination airport. The cost of a ferry flight is also very high.
  To make ferry flight an option in rescheduling flights, we have to add ferry arcs in the network. Suppose there is a reserved aircraft at airport 3. As illustrated in Fig. 3.4, a ferry flight (Ferry I) can be used to provide the option of ferrying the reserve aircraft to airport 2 to resume flight duties thereafter. Similarly, arc Ferry II simply ferries the aircraft to airport 2 at the end of the day to achieve aircraft balance if needed.

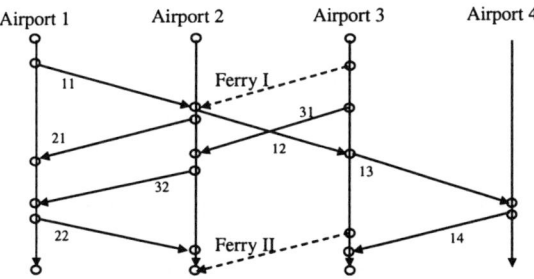

Fig. 3.4 Ferry arcs

- Through-flights.
  Through-flights are mechanisms to serve long-haul markets

with one or more intermediate stops. For instance, Atlanta–Houston–Los Angeles represents a through-flight from Atlanta to Los Angeles via Houston. Passengers traveling from Atlanta to Los Angeles are able to stay on the same plane throughout the trip and often pay a premium to do so. The revenues associated with flight segments that make up through-flights are not independent. If one of the segments is canceled, the through-flight passengers will not make it to their destination as scheduled. To address these special cases another new type of arc, referred to as a through-flight arc, is added to the model as shown in Fig. 3.5, where an additional arc goes from the through-flight's origin airport to its destination airport. A through-flight arc does not represent a new flight option, but rather one aircraft assigned to all of the flight segments in the through-flight. Again, this additional arc must be included in the side constraint in the IP formulation to ensure that flights are not flown by multiple aircraft in the final solution.

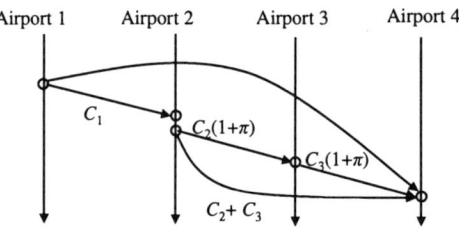

Fig. 3.5 Through-flights

We now show how a through-flight arc can be used so as to try to keep through-flights being serviced by the same aircraft. Assume that the last two of the three flight segments shown in Fig. 3.5 represent a through-flight. Let $0 < \pi < 1$ represent the proportion of passengers that are taking both the second and third flight segments. If either segment is flown individually or if the segments are flown by different aircraft, the revenue gained will be discounted by the factor

$(1-\pi)$. In the context of cost minimization, we can interpret it as the cost of each single flight segment is increased by a percentage penalty of π. If the new arc, shown on the bottom, is taken, then the full revenue will be received for the through-flight. Therefore, the cost of the through-flight arc is the sum of the cost of two individual flight segments. The figure also includes a protection arc to demonstrate how the two constructs are used together.

In practice, it may be difficult to track every individual passenger connection because the model generated would be too unwieldy. However, when a large percentage of passengers are traveling the same set of flight segments, a through-flight can be designated.

- Maintenance requirement.

    In the above model, all aircraft are assumed to be substitutable. This assumption may cause a violation of aircraft maintenance routing. Concretely speaking, an aircraft may be required to stay at a particular airport to do some maintenance checks on some specific days. Therefore, for those aircraft that are scheduled for maintenance at the end of the day, we have to guarantee that they end up flying to the designated airports.

    One possible way to incorporate this constraint is to change the model so that the activity for each individual aircraft is traced, and flow balance in each airport is enforced at the individual aircraft level. This, however, will result in a multicommodity network flow program, and will significantly increase the size of the problem. Another option is to use the protection arc to protect the flight segments that is scheduled for those aircraft that are due for maintenance, and assign very small costs to these protection arcs.

- Multiple fleets.

    Each aircraft belongs to a fleet or equipment type such as Boe737, Boe777, or MD80. Within a fleet type, aircrafts are assumed to be substitutable, and the rescheduling of flights and aircraft is usually constrained within a fleet type. Sometimes, fleet substitution must be included, especially for a major disruption such as a hub closure. To incorporate multi-

ple fleet in rescheduling flights, the time-space network should be revised to a multi-commodity flow model where each commodity represents a fleet type. At the same time, the cost of flying a flight arc depends on which fleet is assigned.
- Multiple solutions.
  Actually the objective function in the formulation may not, more or less, reflect the true dollar operational cost. First, it is difficult to obtain the real cost for each flight delay and cancelation in real time. Second, even the real cost can be estimated with enough accuracy, the addition of protection and through-flight arcs in the model makes the objective function more artificial. Because it is not obvious what the dollar savings to reduce the aircraft routing deviation are, the bonus of a protection arc is an artificial one.
  However, the introduction of protection and through-flight arcs is important in that it allows us to weight these arcs so that the accompanying solution has favorable properties in terms of the number of cancelations, number of flight delays, and the extent of aircraft routing deviation to the original schedule. Through parametric analysis, we are then able to generate a wide range of solutions as a function of the relative importance of these criteria.

3.4.4 LP relaxations and rounding heuristics

The above mathematical programming model is an integer programming problem. As an NP-complete problem, finding an optimal solution is challenging especially in real time. Fortunately, computational experiments show that the LP relaxation of the problem can often generate integer optimal solutions.

In Thengvall *et al.* (2000), some computational experiments are reported. In a situation with a single fleet of 16 aircraft serving 42 flight segments between 13 airports, they test 108 disruptive scenarios. The LP relaxation of all problems can be solved within 1 second, and encouragingly, all optimal solutions of the LP relaxations are integer-valued, implying the optimal IP solutions are found by simply solving the LP relaxations.

In another situation with 27 aircraft serving 162 flight segments between 30 airports, they first test 20 instances with one grounded aircraft and find LP relaxation always returns integer optimal solutions. They then test 192 instances with two grounded aircraft, among which 188 (about 97.9%) instances have integer optimal solutions for the LP relaxation. For the four instances that have to be solved by an IP solver, they find the average percentage difference between the LP and IP solution values is only 0.007%, implying the LP bound is very tight.

When the LP relaxation cannot generate integer optimal solutions, the time used for solving IP problems increases exponentially when the problem size increases. To get an integer solution in real time, heuristic algorithms have to be developed. One heuristic algorithm is to round the fractional solutions of the LP relaxation to integer feasible solutions. The algorithm is described in Fig. 3.6.

Input: Noninteger solution to the LP relaxation of the problem.
Output: A feasible assignment consisting of integer flows for each aircraft.

A. Separate all paths with purely integer flow.
B. For a path with fractional flows
   if no contingencies exist (see below), round flights on the path with the lowest cost to 1 and flights on all other paths to 0. Go to E.
   If contingencies exist, make choice accordingly and go to E.
   If no feasible assignment exists, go to C.
   Contingencies take one of the following three forms:
      1. Aircraft balance must be maintained.
      2. Flight segments may only be flown once.
      3. When paths split or combine one of the options must be chosen.
C. Reverse decisions using contingencies until reaching a feasible assignment.
   If successful go to E, else go to D.
D. Repeated flight segment are causing infeasibility.
   Look for a loop to cancel that will return feasibility. Go to E.
E. If paths with fractional values remain go to B,
   else a feasible integer schedule has been obtained.

Fig. 3.6 Rounding heuristic algorithm

To demonstrate how the heuristic works, consider the solution in Fig. 3.7 consisting of three split paths. Three aircraft begin the day at airports A, B, and C, respectively, and at the end of the day each airport must have one aircraft. In a fractional solution from the LP relaxation, the path for each aircraft splits at some point during the day. In the figure, a solid arc represents a flow of one, and a dashed arc represents a flow of a fractional number. Assume all other integer flows have been removed in the network.

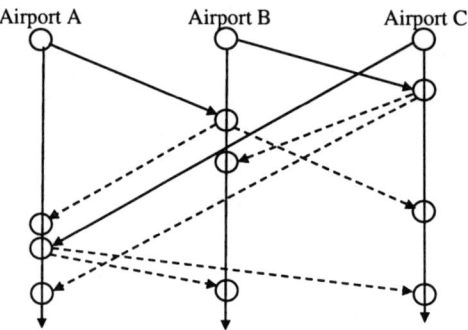

Fig. 3.7   Example for the rounding heuristic algorithm

Look at the aircraft starting from airport A. The flow splits at airport B, one going to airport C, and one going to airport A. Assuming the former flow has a lower cost, we then assign this arc of flow 1 and the aircraft ends at airport C. Consider the aircraft starting at Airport B which splits at airport C. We must choose the arc to airport A to maintain aircraft balance (Step B, contingency 1). Finally, for the third aircraft starting from airport C and splits at airport A, we have to choose the flight ending at airport B to meet the aircraft balance at airport B. Thus a feasible schedule is obtained.

Tests for the rounding heuristic algorithm show that it is very effective. On average, with respective to the objective value, the error of the heuristic solution is around 0.59% from the optimal solution solved by the IP model. When comparing delays, cancellations, swaps and intact flight paths, the solutions obtained using the rounding heuristic have more cancellations and intact flight paths on average, but fewer delays and swaps than the IP solutions. Here a swap refers to the occurrence that a flight is flown by an aircraft that is not originally assigned.

3.4.5 Computational results

In the time-space network for rescheduling flights, two types of arcs are added: delay arcs and protection arcs. Their contribution to the model can be discussed by computational results.

The unique feature in the above model is the usage of protection arcs to state the preference to keep the original routing for each aircraft. By adjusting the value of bonus of a protection arc, the decision maker can obtain different solutions with different number of canceled flight segments, different intact aircraft routings, and different total delay costs. Some results have been reported in Thengvall et al. (2000).

For example, it is observed that the number of delays, total delay minutes, and swaps all decrease near linearly as the bonus value is increased. At the same time, the number of cancelations and intact aircraft routings both increase near linearly as the bonus value is increased. The deviation from the original routing can be mainly measured by the number of intact aircraft routings and the number of swaps. Therefore, by increasing the bonus of protection arcs, we can reduce the deviation of aircraft routings. The price is that more flights may be canceled. The decision maker will have to choose a solution that can better balance the tradeoff.

Another affecting factor in the model is the delay options provided to the model, i.e., the number of delay arcs added for each flight segment. Intuitively, more delay arcs are always better than fewer delay arcs with respect to the solution quality because there are more options to choose. The difficulty is that the problem size increases with the number of delay options and it will take longer time to solve the problem. So there is a trade-off between the solution quality and the computation time. Some experimental results in Thengvall et al. (2000) are as follows.

As expected, the total delay minutes and the average delay cost both decrease as more delay options are included in the model. At the same time, the number of instances that LP relaxation cannot find an integer optimal solution is also increased, implying that it actually takes longer time to solve the problems. Somehow surprisingly, the number of delays, cancelations, swaps, and intact aircraft routes maintain nearly uniform values under different delay options. This observation suggests that the only obvious benefit of providing more delay options is to reduce delay costs. Therefore, it is a reasonable approximation to solve a problem with smaller size which can still generate a solution with very similar performance. Moreover, though the solution found by fewer delay options has a higher delay cost, the real delay may become less after the solution is adjusted according to the real time. For example, a flight may be delayed for 40 minutes in a model that has delay options of delaying 20 minutes and 40 minutes. However, the real delay can only be 30 minutes after an adjustment.

3.5 A Time Band Model

A time band model can be regarded as a simplified version of the above time-space model. In the time band formulation, all airport activities are aggregated into discrete time bands. For example, with a 30-minute time band setting, all arrivals or departures between 9:00 and 9:29 at a particular airport depart from or arrive at a single node. This makes the problem size smaller than the above model.

A time band model also uses a time-space network, in which a node is associated with an airport and a time band. Nodes are classified into station-time nodes and station-sink nodes where the former are used to represent the flight departure and arrival, and the latter are used to represent the aircraft balance at the end of the rescheduling period.

Two types of arcs are defined. Flight arcs are used to represent specific scheduled flights, and termination arcs are used to connect a station-time node to the station-sink node of the same airport to force the aircraft balance.

In a time band model, all flights scheduled to depart from an airport during the recovery period are made available to each node in the corresponding airport, regardless of their scheduled departure time. This allows us to examine all possible permutations of flight connections. The trick of this model is that aircraft available at each airport may be assigned to any of the flights scheduled to depart the node's airport. So all possible flight delay costs may be associated with each connection made at a node in the network.

The time band model will result in the following integer programming formulation.

Indices

i, j: node indices

k: flight index

Sets:

F: set of flights

I: set of station-time nodes

J: set of station-sink nodes

$G(i)$: set of flights departing from station-time node i

$L(i)$: set of flights terminating at station-sink node i

$Q(i)$: set of station-time nodes that have arcs terminating at station-sink node i

$P(k)$: set of station-time nodes from which flight k departs

$H(k, i)$: set of destination nodes for flight k originating at station-time node i

$M(k, i)$: set of originating station-time nodes for flight k terminating at station-sink node i

Parameters

a_i: number of aircraft available at station-time node i at time 0

c_k: cost of canceling flight k

d_{ij}^k: delay cost of flight k from station-time node i to node j

h_i: number of aircraft to terminate at station-sink node i

Variables

x_{ij}^k: binary variable, $=1$ if flight k is flown from station-time node i to node j

y_k: binary variable, $=1$ if flight k is canceled.

z_i: number of aircraft flow from station-time node i to station-sink node at the same airport

Integer programming formulation:

$$\min \sum_{k \in F} \sum_{i \in P(k)} \sum_{j \in H(k,i)} d_{ij}^k x_{ij}^k + \sum_{k \in F} c_k y_k \qquad (3.9)$$

subject to

$$\sum_{i \in P(k)} \sum_{j \in H(k,i)} x_{ij}^k + y_k = 1, \quad \forall k \in F \qquad (3.10)$$

$$\sum_{k \in G(i)} \sum_{j \in H(k,i)} x_{ij}^k + z_i - \sum_{k \in L(i)} \sum_{j \in M(k,i)} x_{ji}^k = a_i, \quad \forall i \in I \qquad (3.11)$$

$$\sum_{k \in L(i)} \sum_{j \in M(k,i)} x_{ji}^k + \sum_{j \in Q(i)} z_j = h_i, \quad \forall i \in J \qquad (3.12)$$

$$x_{ij}^k \in \{0, 1\}, \quad \forall k \in F, i \in I, j \in H(k,i) \qquad (3.13)$$

$$y_k \in \{0, 1\}, \quad \forall k \in F \qquad (3.14)$$

$$z_i \in \{0, 1, 2, \ldots, \}, \quad \forall i \in I \qquad (3.15)$$

In the formulation, the objective function (3.9) minimizes total delay and cancelation costs for all scheduled flights. Constraints (3.10) states a flight is either flown once by an aircraft or canceled. Flow conservation is enforced by constraints (3.11) for station-time nodes and by constraints (3.12) for station-sink nodes, respectively.

The time band solution is still subject to some post processing to transform it to an exact time in the time bands. Because it is an approximation, it is found that the solution quality is worse than the original time-space model. However, computational results show that the integer programming program obtained from a time band model can often be solved quickly, which is more important in the case of multiple fleets. The details of the time band model can be found in Bard et al.(2001).

3.6 Set Packing Model

The flight rescheduling problems can also be modeled as to allocate limited resource (aircraft) to activities (flight segments). This motivates the following set packing model. In general, a set packing problem is defined as one to use a given collection of subsets to cover a base set as much as possible while no two used subsets are allowed to share a common element of the base set. In the set packing model for flight rescheduling, the base set is the set of scheduled flight segments, and each subset is a possible aircraft route. Specifically, an aircraft route is defined as a series of connected flight segments that will be flown by a single aircraft. Note that a route may include the original scheduled flight segments, as well as possible delayed flight segments with specified delay times. Therefore, for each route, we can estimate its cost based on the aircraft assigned, flight delay, and ferrying cost if a ferry flight is included.

In the set packing model, we first define the following notation.

Indices and sets

r: index for an aircraft route

p: index for set of available aircraft P

f: index for set of all flight segments F

R_p: set of feasible routes of aircraft p

Parameters

b_f: cost of canceling flight segment f

c_r: cost of assigning route r to aircraft p

Variables:

y_f: binary variable, $=1$ if flight segment f is canceled

x_r: binary variable, $=1$ if route r is assigned to aircraft p

Then we have the following integer programming in which we are to find a packing with the minimum cost:

$$\min \sum_{p \in P} \sum_{r \in R_p} c_r x_r + \sum_{f \in F} b_f y_f \qquad (3.16)$$

$$\sum_{r \in R_p} x_r = 1, \quad \forall p \in P \qquad (3.17)$$

$$\sum_{r \ni f} x_r + y_f = 1, \quad \forall f \in F \qquad (3.18)$$

$$x_r \in \{0,1\}, \quad \forall r \in R_p, p \in P \qquad (3.19)$$

$$y_f \in \{0,1\}, \quad \forall f \in F \qquad (3.20)$$

In the formulation, the objective function (3.16) is the cost of assigning routes to aircraft and the cost of canceled flight segments. Constraints (3.17) assign one route to an aircraft p, and constraints (3.18) ensure that a flight segment is either canceled or flown by one aircraft at most.

The difficulties of the set packing model lie in the fact that for each aircraft p, all possible routes R_p have to be generated. This would be an extremely large number when the number of aircraft is large and the recovery window is long. As a practical heuristic, the problem size can be reduced by limiting the consideration for only a small number of aircraft, including the directly disrupted aircraft and some other aircraft. Detailed discussions for such an idea can be found in Rosenberger et al.(2003).

Another interesting aspect in Rosenberger et al. is the proposal of defining the objective function as to maintain crew and passenger connections rather than to minimize flight delay costs. This would benefit crew rescheduling and reducing passenger illwill, a similar effort as using protection arcs in the time-space network model.

With regard to this purpose, we can define a trip as a crew pairing or a passenger itinerary, and assign a cost of disruption to a trip that is to be minimized. We further define the following notations to build the new model.

d_{rf}: delay of flight segment f in route r. Note that this is a known parameter from the generation of route r.

q: index for the set of flight connections Q

v: index of the set of trips V

g_v: cost of disrupting trip v

$Q(v)$: set of connection in trip v

$F(v)$: set of flight segments in trip v

f_q^1 and f_q^2: the first and second flight segment for connection q

σ_q: scheduled slack time between the arrival of f_q^1 and the departure of f_q^2

τ: minimum amount of time for a passenger or crew to make a connection

δ_f: maximum delay of a flight segment f

O_q: binary variable, $=1$ if connection q is disrupted

Z_v: binary variable, $=1$ if trip v is disrupted

D_f: delay of flight segment f

Then based on the integer programming (3.16) to (3.20), we can define a new formulation to minimize total disruption cost of all connections by replacing the objective function to

$$\sum_{v \in V} g_v Z_v, \qquad (3.21)$$

and adding the following constraints

$$\sum_{f \in r} d_{rf} x_r = D_f, \quad \forall f \in F \qquad (3.22)$$

$$D_{f_q^2} - D_{f_q^1} + (\delta_{f_q^1} + \tau - \sigma_q) O_q \geq \tau - \sigma_q, \quad \forall q \in Q \qquad (3.23)$$

$$Z_v \geq O_q, \quad \forall q \in Q(v), \forall v \in V \qquad (3.24)$$

$$Z_v \geq y_f, \quad \forall f \in F(v), \forall v \in V \qquad (3.25)$$

In the formulation, constraints (3.22) calculate the delay of a flight segment f, which is used to determine whether a connection q is disrupted in constraints (3.23). Constraints (3.24) and (3.25) state a trip is disrupted if one of its connection q is disrupted or one of its flight segments is canceled. Finally, the new objective function (3.21) is used to minimize the disruption cost over all trips.

3.7 Literature Review

People began to study the disruption management for flight scheduling in 1980's. A review can be found in Filar et al.(2001). Teodorovic and Guberinic (1984) used the network flow model to study the flight-aircraft rescheduling problem, but they only considered the option of delaying flights. Teodorovic and Stojkovic (1990) extended the preceding work to include flight cancelations. Jarrah et al. (1993) presented two special cases based on the network flow model, one considering only flight delays and the other considering only flight cancelations. While delays and cancelations were not addressed simultaneously, this approach was already considered practical enough to be implemented by United Airlines (see Rakshit et al., 1996). Yan and Yang (1996) were the first to incorporate flight delays, cancelations, and ferrying in a single model. Yan and Lin (1997) extended the above model to handle airport closures. Yan and Tu (1997) extended the same model to tackle multiple fleet substitutions. Other related works include Cao and Kanafani (1997a, 1997b).

Thengvall et al.(2000) included the protection arcs to reduce the deviation cost due to passenger unsatisfaction over having to change aircraft in connection airports. Thengvall et al.(2001) considered probably the most complete model so far. They considered flight delays, cancelations, the above peculiar deviation, aircraft ferrying, fleet substitution, and hub closures. Recently, Stojkovic et al. (2002) studied a special case of the problem where the disruption is small enough for the airline to be able to keep the original aircraft itineraries. The problem is interesting in that it can be modeled by a pure network flow model and thus solved in polynomial time.

Details of the time band model can be found in Argüello et al. (1997a) and Bard et al. (2001). The set packing model was proposed by Rosenberger et al.(2003), and computational solution schemes are presented. An earlier similar model was proposed by Argüello et al.(1997a, 1997b), but no efforts on solution schemes were reported.

References

Argüello, M.F., J.F. Bard and G. Yu (1997a), A GRASP for aircraft routing in response to groundings and delays, *Journal of Combinatorial Optimization*, 5, 211-228.

Argüello, M.F., J.F. Bard and G. Yu (1997b), Models and methods for managing airline irregular operations aircraft routing, In *Operations Research in the Airline Industry*, G. Yu Ed., Kluwer Academic Publishers, Boston, 1-45.

Bard, J.F., G. Yu and M.F. Argüello (2001), Optimizing aircraft routings in response to groundings and delays, *IIE Transactions on Operations Engineering*, 33(10), 931-947.

Cao, J. and A. Kanafani (1997a), Real-time decision support for integration of airline flight cancellations and delays, part I: Mathematical formulations, *Transportation Planning and Technology*, 20, 183-199.

Cao, J. and A. Kanafani (1997b), Real-time decision support for integration of airline flight cancellations and delays, part II: Algorithms and computational experiments, *Transportation Planning and Technology*, 20, 201-217.

Filar, J.A., P. Manyem and K. White (2001), How airlines and airports recover from schedule perturbations: A survey, *Annals of Operations Research*, 108, 315-333.

Jarrah, A.I.Z., G. Yu, N. Krishnamurthy and A. Rakshit (1993), A decision support framework for airline flight cancellations and delays, *Transportation Science*, 27, 266-280.

Rakshit, A., N. Krishnamurthy and G. Yu (1996), Systems operations advisor: A real-time decision support system for managing airline operations at United Airlines, *Interfaces*, 26, 50-58.

Rosenberger, J.M., E.L. Johnson and G.L. Nemhauser (2003), Rerouting aircraft for airline recovery, *Transportation Science*, 37, 408-421.

Stojkovic, G., F. Soumis, J. Desrosiers and M.M. Solomon (2002), An optimization model for a real-time flight scheduling problem, *Transportation Research Part A: Policy and Practice*, 36, 779-788.

Teodorovic, D. and S. Guberinic (1984), Optimal dispatching strategy on an airline network after a schedule perturbation, *European Journal of Operational Research*, 15, 178-182.

Teodorovic, D. and G. Stojkovic (1990), Model for operational daily airline scheduling, *Transportation Planning and Technology*, 14, 273-285.

Thengvall, B.G., J.F. Bard and G. Yu (2000), Balancing user preferences for aircraft schedule recovery during irregular operations, *IIE Transactions on Operations Engineering*, 32, 181-193.

Thengvall, B.G., G. Yu and J.F. Bard (2001), Multiple fleet aircraft schedule recovery following hub closures, *Transportation Research Part A: Policy and Practice*, 35, 289-308.

Yan, S. and C. Lin (1997), Airline scheduling for the temporary closure of airports, *Transportation Science*, 31, 72-82.

Yan, S. and Y.-P. Tu (1997), Multifleet routing and multistop flight scheduling for schedule perturbation, *European Journal of Operational Research*, 103, 155-169.

Yan, S. and D. Yang (1996), A decision support framework for handling schedule perturbations, *Transportation Research Part B: Methodology*, 30, 405-419.

Chapter 4

Disruption Management for Airline Crew Scheduling

4.1 Introduction

In this chapter, we discuss another disruption management problem in airlines: how to reschedule crew members when a disruption occurs. Facing a disruption, such as an aircraft mechanical failure or crew sickness, the airline has to respond to the disruption by revising the original flight schedule and crew assignment. Usually, a disruption is handled in two steps: rescheduling flights and aircraft, followed by rescheduling crew to fulfill duties for the new flight schedule. If unfortunately, a feasible crew schedule cannot be found for the new flight schedule, then the flight schedule has to be revised again so that a feasible crew schedule can be found. The entire process may contain several iterations until both new cost-effective and feasible flight and crew schedules are found. Crew rescheduling is important in that it is often the bottleneck in the whole process because of various constraints on constructing feasible crew schedules.

The conventional airline crew scheduling problem has been studied for decades. Crew rescheduling differs from the crew scheduling problem in several aspects. First, while crew scheduling is a long term planning problem covering several months and concerning all crew in all airports, crew rescheduling is a short term problem for at most a few days (known as the disruption recovery time window) and concerns only part of the crew team. Second, solving the crew scheduling problem is not time restrictive usually with the optimal solution being found in several hours or even longer, but crew rescheduling is a real time decision making problem that needs to be solved in a few minutes. Third, while the goal of crew scheduling is the global optimality, crew rescheduling is often only aimed at good feasible solutions. Finally, the solution approach of crew rescheduling should have the capability of generating multiple solutions with different preferences, or even partial solutions, a feature that is not required in the crew scheduling problem. Generating multiple solutions is important in practice because any mathematical model relies on a certain amount of compromise or estimation of parameters such as cost or profit, which usually is only an approximation, especially in real time. Moreover, not every related factors can be effectively handled in a mathematical model such as hotel availability in a city. So it is desirable for the decision maker to have multiple good solutions to choose from. Partial solution is of the same importance in real time decision making where the most urgent crew and flight issues are scheduled first with the given limited time, and some unsolved crew and flight issues are left to be solved later. This is seldom allowed in traditional optimization models.

This chapter is organized as follows. In Section 4.2, we give a simple overview on the conventional airline crew scheduling problem and the related concepts. In Section 4.3, we introduce the network model for crew scheduling and rescheduling with demonstrations by some examples. In Section 4.4, we propose an efficient heuristic algorithm approach. In Section 4.5, we present an integer programming model for crew rescheduling and the solution scheme. A brief literature review is provided in Section 4.6.

4.2 Overview of Crew Scheduling Problem

Before discussing the crew rescheduling problem, we provide a brief overview of the conventional crew scheduling problem. Crew scheduling deals with the problem of assigning individual crew members to pre-scheduled flights. In practice, it is sequentially divided into two separate stages: crew pairing and monthly crew assignment.

In the crew pairing problem, we are given a set of prescheduled flight segments. Among all the airports served by the airline, some of them are called crew bases. Each crew belongs to a specific base, and must start his/her duty from the base and end at the same base. A crew pairing is a sequence of connected flight segments over a period of time, usually 2 to 5 days for domestic flights. In particular, a crew pairing must start and end at the same crew base and satisfy all legality constraints. The crew pairing problem is that of finding the minimum-cost set of legal crew pairings that cover all the given flight segments. At this stage, no individual crew members are involved. The legality constraints for a crew pairing include governmental and contractual restrictions such as maximum daily working hours, minimum overnight rest period, maximum number of flight legs, and maximum time away from a crew base, etc.

Existing models for crew pairing can be classified into two main categories: the set partitioning (covering) type and the network flow type. Using a set partitioning model, a base set is defined as all scheduled flight segments, and each legal pairing is modeled as a subset of flight segments associated with its operational cost. The objective of crew pairing is to minimize the total cost of a collection of selected pairings to cover all flight segments. Most of these algorithms contain primarily two modules, the pairing generation module and the pairing optimization module. The former generates legal pairings that can potentially be included in the final solution, and the latter solves the current problem based on the pairings selected.

In the network flow model, crew pairing is formulated as an integer multi-commodity network flow problem with additional resource variables where a commodity represents a crew, nodes represent airports at different time points, and arcs represent various crew activities such as operational flight segments, connections, and rests. The goal is to find a minimum cost flow.

The second problem in crew scheduling is the monthly crew assignment which is solved after the crew pairings problem. It assigns individual crew members to trips, i.e., sequences of crew pairings over a certain period of time, usually one month. In practice, two approaches have been taken to tackle the problem. The approach relying on the crew rostering problem tries to find an assignment scheme covering all pairings that is "fair" to all crew members, after taking into account their requirements and preferences. In the other approach called bidline system, each crew member has a different seniority, and the person with a higher seniority has a higher priority to satisfy his/her preference. Crew rostering is more frequently used in Europe, and bidline procedures are more common in North America.

An important concept in crew scheduling is deadhead, which refers to the case that a crew is on a flight as a passenger. The purpose of deadhead is to fly a crew to another airport to serve for a flight starting from the airport, or simply send the crew back to his/her base to complete his/her duty. In view of crew pairing, this means that a flight segment is covered by multiple crew pairings, and only one pairing actually works for the flight.

In crew scheduling problems, deadhead is usually avoided as much as possible because a crew, though not working, is paid for deadhead as normal flying hours. In crew rescheduling problems, deadhead appears more often because the originally designed crew pairings have been broken, and it is unavoidable that some crew will be deadheaded.

4.3 Network Flow Formulation

A crew schedule can be modeled by a time-space network as shown in Fig. 4.1. Such a network is also used in modeling and solving the crew rescheduling problem. In the network, each node is associated with two coordinates, the time and the airport. We see that the nodes in the network are classified into different types.

Crew node: The crew nodes represent the availability of crew at the specific airport and time, as either arrival crew or original crew at the airport when the problem occurs, where an original crew means an available crew at the beginning of the problem, and an arrival crew refers to a crew that comes from a flight and becomes available at that node. In the figure, crew nodes are placed in the first column for an airport. The original crews are placed at the time when they are available and the arrival crews are placed at the time of their arrival. In particular, the original crews are indicated by the shaded nodes in the network.

Flight node: The flight nodes represent departure flights at the scheduled time from the associated airport. They are placed at the second column of each airport.

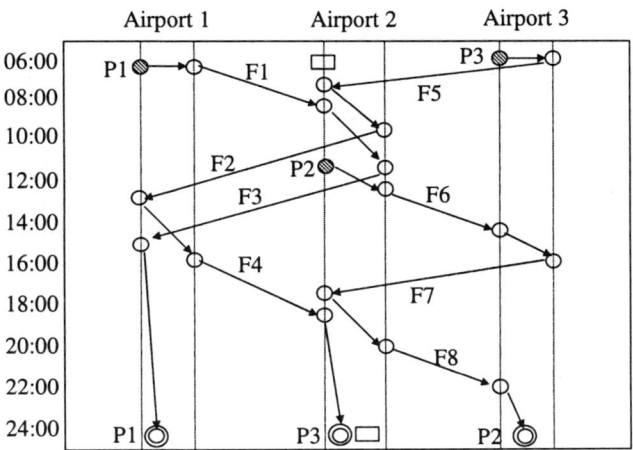

Fig. 4.1 Network for crew schedule

Return node: The return nodes are used to force the crews to return to their scheduled destinations at the end of the scheduling period. Note that only original crews have return nodes. Return nodes are indicated by double rings in the network. The number of original crew nodes must be equal to the number of return nodes in a network for a crew member balance.

Reserve node: The reserve nodes represent the availability of reserve crew. Each reserve crew member is represented by two nodes, one at the time when they are available to serve, and one at the time when they should be back, both with the same airport. Reserve nodes are represented by rectangles in the network.

There are different types of arcs in the network.

Schedule arc: These arcs are used to represent the original crew schedule where each arc emanates from a crew node to the scheduled flight node.

Flight arc: These arcs represent the scheduled flight from one airport to another. They originate from flight nodes at departure airports and end at the corresponding crew nodes at their destination airports.

Return arc: These arcs represent the returning of crew to their corresponding return nodes. Each return arc emanates from a crew node and ends at the return node at the same airport, representing the completion of duty of the crew.

The following two types of arcs will be used in the crew rescheduling problems, which represent different options in rescheduling crew. They are analogous to the delay arcs in the flight rescheduling problem.

Swap arc: These arcs emanate from crew nodes to flight nodes that are not their originally assigned flights to represent the possibility of swapping crew assignment. Obviously, only when the flight node is later in time than the crew node can there be a swap arc between them.

Reserve arc: These arcs emanate from reserve nodes to those flight nodes at the same airport which can be served by the reserve crew, implying the reserve crew will be assigned to the flights.

Using the above network, crew scheduling can be viewed as a multi-commodity network flow problem with side constraints, where each crew is modeled as a commodity. In particular, the schedule of a crew pairing is a path in the network from the original crew node to the corresponding return node. Side constraints are needed to check the legality of a possible pairing.

Now we use some numerical examples to illustrate the above concepts. Consider the crew schedule in Fig. 4.1 for a period of one day. The schedule is described in Table 4.1. It contains three crew pairings serving eight flight segments among three airports. There is also one reserve crew pairing at airport 2.

Note that in Fig. 4.1, no swap and reserve arcs are indicated. The following examples show different scenarios of disruptions and the corresponding solutions.

Example 1. Flight F1 is canceled. In this case, pairing P1 will stay at airport 1, which leaves flight F3 open. To resolve this problem,

Table 4.1 Example of a crew schedule

Crew pairing	Flight	Origin	Destination	Departure	Arrival
P1	F1	Airport 1	Airport 2	6:30	9:30
Available at 6:00	F3	Airport 2	Airport 1	12:00	15:00
P2	F6	Airport 2	Airport 3	13:00	14:30
Available at 12:00	F7	Airport 3	Airport 2	16:30	18:00
	F8	Airport 2	Airport 3	20:00	21:30
P3	F5	Airport 3	Airport 2	6:30	8:00
Available at 6:00	F2	Airport 2	Airport 1	10:00	13:00
	F4	Airport 1	Airport 2	15:40	18:40
Reserve		Airport 2			

we can call reserve crew at airport 2 to serve for flight F3, and send them back to airport 2 on flight F4 by deadhead.

Example 2. Flight F5 is late by 2 hours. Because there is a minimum turnover time between two flights for a crew on the ground, pairing P3 cannot catch the scheduled flight F2. For such a disruption, we can swap crew pairings P1 and P3 at airport 2. In words, pairing P1 will fly on flight F2, and P3 will first fly on flight F3 followed by the originally scheduled flight F4.

Example 3. Flight F5 is late by 4 hours. As in Example 2, we can let P1 fly on fight F2 first. However, P3 cannot catch F3 either. So we have to make another swap between P2 and P3 so that P2 will fly on flights F3 and F4, followed by the original schedule F8, and P3 will fly on flights F6 and F7, and be terminated at airport 2 as originally scheduled.

All the solutions for the above examples can be obtained by adding appropriate swap arcs and reserve arcs. For the aim of simplicity, we only give the network for Example 3 in Fig. 4.2. In the figure, we use bold lines to represent the new crew paths, and dashed lines to represent the original paths that have been revised.

4.4 A Heuristics Algorithm

Based on the above analysis, we introduce a heuristic algorithm to solve the crew rescheduling problem of which the purpose is to repair the crew pairings that are broken due to disruptions. Here a bro-

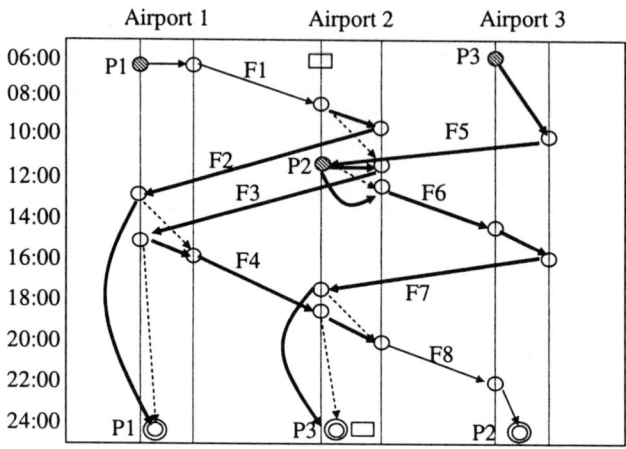

Fig. 4.2 New crew schedule for Example 3

ken pairing refers to the case that a crew pairing cannot resume the original duty because their scheduled flights are canceled or one preceding flight is late so that they cannot catch the following flight. We notice that in the crew rescheduling, most of the crew pairings are still valid even during severe disruptions. So our main focus should be to fix the broken pairings, i.e., to send the crew to the scheduled airports or back to base by the disruption recovery time window.

4.4.1 *Discussion on criteria selection*

We first discuss the criteria used in crew rescheduling. Generally speaking, the objective of handling a disruption is to return the system back to its schedule as soon as possible. This can be concretely specified by two criteria, to find crew for the flights whose original assigned crew are not available due to disruption in schedule, and to fix the broken pairings caused by disruption. If it is not possible to cover all the flights which are disrupted, then it is best to cover as many as possible.

Thus we have two objectives that may conflict with each other. For example, to find crew for a particular flight whose original crew is late because of the lateness of the previous flight, there may be no choice other than to use the crew who are assigned to other flights in the airport with the consequence of disrupting their pairings. If we want to maintain the integrity of crew pairings, some flights may have to be left uncovered. Usually the former criterion is regarded as more important than the latter one. Using the lexicographic modeling, we can set the objective of covering as many flights as possible as the primary criterion, and the objective of maintaining the integrity of maximal number of crew pairings as the second criterion.

Regarding the criterion of maintaining the integrity of crew pairings, more discussions are needed, which provide guidelines in developing the algorithm that will be introduced later. The most important measurement is the number of crew pairings that are affected in a particular solution. Minimizing the number of affected pairings usually dominates other considerations and is thus first used to assess the quality of the solution. As will be seen, this criterion is used to prune branches of a depth-first search tree that are deemed to lead to inferior solutions in the algorithm. Another measurement used is that even if a pairing is modified, it is preferable that the deviation from the original pairing is minimal. The reasons for the above criteria are obvious. Airlines desire to limit the impact of irregular operations. Crews are human; they will complain if their schedules are changed too often or too much. In fact, the deviation from the original schedule may also incur extra cost for the airline. For instance, a crew is scheduled to stay over at a city and it is too late to cancel the hotel room which has been booked. Now, due to a disruption, its pairing is modified, and the crew will have to stay in a different city. Thus, the airline will have to pay for another hotel room in the new city.

4.4.2 Branch and bound algorithm

Based on the above analysis, a branch and bound algorithm can be devised. The algorithm conducts a depth-first search where each node in the search tree represents a partial solution. Specifically, each node includes a set of uncovered flights and a list of pairings that are modified in the search process. We also require that every pairing is repaired, i.e., all crew return to their original scheduled airport by the recovery time window. We will discuss later how to achieve this. In very rare situations when there are pairings which cannot be repaired, i.e., the crews cannot be sent to their scheduled airports, these pairings are saved separately in the current node for later process.

When the set of uncovered flights is empty at a node, we obtain a full solution (called a solution node), which corresponds to a leaf node in the search tree. Otherwise, each non-solution node is branched into several child nodes, each representing a new solution where one more flight is covered. To do this, we select a flight from the uncovered flight set according to some heuristic rules, e.g., the earliest flight. A candidate crew list is then built to cover this flight from available crew at the airport. This crew must be available by the departure time of the flight and qualified for the aircraft type. When there are multiple crews from the candidate list, we have to test the possibility of selecting each crew. Thus each assignment leads to a different child node, a process known as branching in the branch and bound algorithm.

Once the crew is assigned to the flight, either a new pairing must be created for the crew in the case of reserve crew, or the current pairing of the crew must be modified in the case of regular crew. By doing this, we are able to maintain the property of non-broken pairings. There are several requirements with regard to the newly-created or modified pairing: (1) it must be able to send the crew to its designated return airport; (2) the pairing must be legal; and (3) the new pairing should stick to its original pairing as much as possible. If (1) and (2) are not satisfied, the node is fathomed. The consequence of this "pairing generation/modification" step is that either a few more uncovered flights are added to the uncovered flight set, since the chosen crew is likely to skip several flight legs in the original pairing, or the size of the uncovered flight set may be reduced. This process can continue from the newly generated node. The stopping criterion can be a predetermined time limit and/or when the number of solutions required has been achieved.

There are three important components that deserve separate discussions. The first one is the preprocessing which converts the initial problem into a generic one. In particular, we have to repair all broken pairings even in the most inefficient way. For each broken pairing, the preprocessing stage tries to return the crew back to its original pairing schedule as soon as possible. This is done in the program through a negative-cost shortest path algorithm. This negative-cost shortest path algorithm finds a path from the crew's current position in the network to its return node, thus repairing the broken pairing. To solve this shortest path problem, all the arcs in the network are assigned a cost of 0, with the exception of the flight arcs in the crews original pairing, which are assigned negative costs. This tends to encourage the crew to take its original flight legs as much as possible. Still, the crew may have to skip a few of its original legs in order to recover. The negative-cost shortest path algorithm is possible because of the acyclic nature of the underlying space-time network. After each broken pairing is repaired in this way, there are usually still some uncovered flights, which are skipped by the crew in the originally broken pairings. They are collected in the uncovered flight set. The repaired pairings are saved in the list of modified pairings required of the node representation. The output from preprocessing is the start node for the depth-first search tree.

The second component is the pairing generation/modification after the assignment of a crew to an uncovered flight in the search engine. In the program, the same negative-cost shortest path algorithm as in the preprocessing stage is used to find the path which leads the crew to its return node after taking the uncovered flight. So in this way we can maintain every broken crew pairing being repaired, i.e., all crews return to their originally scheduled airports by the recovery time window.

The third component is the legality checking module that is invoked after the pairing generation/modification. The legality checking module is used to check whether or not the just generated or modified pairing is legal. In practice, the legalities rules are numerous and sometimes rather complex. So it is very expensive to do an exhaustive legality checking for every new pairing. To resolve this problem, we can use a classification to separate the legality rules into two categories. One category contains those legalities that are violated more often such as flight time limitations in a duty day or a 24-hour window, duty time limitations and minimum rest requirements. The checking of these rules is done at the pairing generation/modification level, i.e., whenever a pairing is generated or modified, the legality checking is invoked. The other category consists of those legalities that are less frequently violated, such as flight time limitation within a calendar month or a year. These legalities are checked after each solution is obtained.

The flow diagram of the heuristic crew rescheduling approach is given in Fig. 4.3.

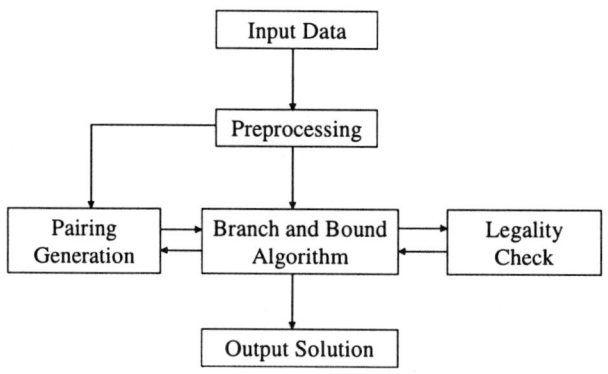

Fig. 4.3 Flow diagram of heuristic crew rescheduling approach

To improve the efficiency of the algorithm, a pruning scheme is necessary to avoid searching for branches that will not lead to better solutions than those already found. We take advantage of the fact that the number of modified pairings are the foremost dominating factor in deciding the quality of a solution, as well as the fact that the number of modified pairings is non-decreasing along any search path, or path from the root node to the current node. The number of modified pairings is the same at the current node as at the parent node when the crew assignment/reassignment leading to this node is for one of the already modified pairings; it is incremented when the assignment/reassignment is for an original pairing. Therefore, if at any node the number of modified pairings is larger than that of the solutions found so far, then there is no need to explore the node. This is known as the bounding scheme in a branch and bound algorithm.

The pseudo code of the algorithm is given in Fig. 4.4. In the algorithm, we maintain a list of feasible solutions to store the required number of feasible solutions. Each time a new feasible solution is found, if it is better than the worst solution in the list, the list is updated so that it always has the set of the required number of best solutions that have been found. The same idea is also used in maintaining a list of partial solutions. Both lists are needed to support the capability of generating multiple solutions and partial solutions.

4.4.3 *Computational results and impacts*

The above heuristic algorithm has been proved to be time efficient and optimality effective. In Wei *et al.* (1997), some interesting observations are reported in their computational experiments.

First, it takes the program only a few nodes and a very short time to obtain the first feasible solution, suggesting that getting a feasible solution is not very difficult. This is important in the sense of real time decision making in that it may not always be necessary or possible given the limited time to find the optimal solution. So it is a practical approach to first have a feasible solution at hand and then gradually improve the solution with the remaining time limit.

Second, the pruning scheme is very effective when there are a large number of solutions. The effectiveness of the algorithm depends on the number of solutions required. Obviously, the more solutions required, the looser the bound will be. When the number of solutions required is set at a very large number, it virtually requires that all solutions be generated. It is found that if only one solution is required, around 50 percent of nodes can be reduced by adopting the bounding scheme, which can hasten the algorithm quite significantly.

Finally, it does not take much additional time or many additional nodes to obtain more solutions after the first solution is obtained. This can be attributed to two reasons. First, it takes considerable

```
Input:
    Current time and disruption management time window
    Flight and crew status as of current time
    Crew destinations at the end of time window
Output:
    A set of required number of feasible or partial solutions
Begin
    Preprocessing
    Construct the start node and put it in the search tree
    Set the upper bound of modified pairings to be infinity
    While (there are unprocessed node) {
        Select an unprocessed node n in the tree by depth-first method
        If (depth of node n is less than the depth bound) {
            Select a flight f in the uncovered flight set of node n
            Build a candidate list L of crew who can be assigned to f
            Generate all child nodes of n by assigning each crew in L to f
            For (each child node s that is a solution node) {
                If (number of solution found < required number of solutions)
                    Save solution s to the feasible solution list
                else {
                    Update the feasible solution list with s
                    Update the upper bound of modified pairings
                }
            }
            For (each child node s that is NOT a solution node)
                Save s in or update the partial solution list
        }
    }
End
```

Fig. 4.4 Pseudo code of the heuristic algorithm

searching to get to the optimal solution as opposed to the first solution, by which time there are a lot of solutions that have already been generated. Second, the difference between solutions in terms of number of modified pairings is not very large, resulting in a lot of solutions with slight variations. This tends to reduce the effectiveness of the bounding/pruning. In fact, many solutions obtained are almost the same, only differing by one or two flight legs. For instance, this can happen when there is a large number of flights between two airports and each of them can be taken by the crew under assignment to fulfill its pairing.

Some extra computational results are reported in Yu *et al.* (2003) on the data of Continental Airlines. In a particular set of examples concerning 11847 crew pairings, 12390 crew members, and 43625 flights, different scenarios of disruptions are tested in terms of the number of disrupted flights.

The computational results show that for a smaller problems with no more than 20 disrupted flights, over a total 1124 instances, the average computation time is below 1 minute and the maximum computation time is 67 seconds on a Sun system with a 300Mhz UltraSPARC processor. Moreover, when compared with the optimal solution obtained by CPLEX, optimal solutions have been found for all instances by the heuristic algorithm.

For large problems with 21 to 30 disrupted flights, over 132 tested instances, the average computation time is about 4 minutes and the maximum time is 287 seconds. It is found that the average gap to the optimal solution is 2.27%. For problems with 31 to 40 disrupted flights, the average computation time is less than 6 minutes and the maximum time is 442 seconds. The average gap to the optimum is less than 5%.

The algorithm has been implemented by CALEB Technologies Corporation in their CrewSolver System which is running in Continental Airlines in their operations control. Continental Airlines estimates that it saved approximately $40 million during 2001 as a direct result of using the CrewSolver system to recover from four major disruptions only. For the first quarter of 2002, Continental estimates that it saved approximately $5 million by using the CrewSolver system to recover from minor disruptions. These savings include fewer en route and predeparture delays, fewer minutes per delay, fewer cancellations, reductions in ferry flights and diversions, fuel savings, crew-penalty savings, and hotel savings. In addition, Continental recognized improved on-time performance, reductions in reaccommodating passengers, and improved passenger goodwill. The CrewSolver system also provided faster and more efficient recovery solutions than Continentals previous system and higher quality of life for crews.

4.5 Integer Programming Model

In this section, we propose an integer programming model to solve the crew rescheduling problem. While we have given an efficient heuristic algorithm to find a good feasible solution, an integer programming model aims at the optimal solution, i.e., to find a set of crew pairings to cover all new flights with the minimum cost.

4.5.1 *Integer programming formulation*

We have the following notation in the formulation.

Indices

   f: index of flight segments

   k: index of crew members

   p: index of crew pairings

Sets

   F: set of flight segments to be covered

   K: set of available crew including normal crew and reserve crew

   P_k: set of pairings that can be flown by crew k, indexed by p

Parameters

   c_p: cost of pairing p

   d_f: deadhead cost for flight segment f

   C_f: cost of canceling flight f

   q_k: cost of not using crew k

   α_{pf}: a binary indicator, $=1$ if flight segment f is included in pairing p.

Variables

   x_p: binary variable, $=1$ if pairing p is used

   y_f: binary variable, $=1$ if flight segment f is canceled

v_k: binary variable, $=1$ if crew k is not used

s_f: number of crew members deadheading on flight segment f

Then we have the integer programming model below.

$$\min \sum_{k \in K} \sum_{p \in P_k} c_p x_p + \sum_{f \in F} C_f y_f + \sum_{f \in F} d_f s_f + \sum_{k \in K} q_k v_k \quad (4.1)$$

subject to

$$\sum_{k \in K} \sum_{p \in P_k} \alpha_{pf} x_p + y_f - s_f = 1, \quad \forall f \in F \quad (4.2)$$

$$\sum_{p \in P_k} x_p + v_k = 1, \quad \forall k \in K \quad (4.3)$$

$$x_p, y_f, v_k \in \{0, 1\}, \ s_f \geq 0. \quad (4.4)$$

In the formulation, the objective function (4.1) is the sum of all costs of assigning crew pairings, canceling flights, deadheading and not using crew members. Constraint (4.2) is the cover constraint for each flight, and constraint (4.3) forces the assignment for each crew member.

In view of reducing the deviation from the original crew schedule, it can be implemented by assigning the cost of each crew pairing. For example, we can discount the cost of an originally scheduled pairing to make it more attractive, add a small penalty for a modification of a scheduled pairing, and a large penalty for a totally new pairing.

4.5.2 LP relaxation

The first step to solve the above integer programming problem is solving the LP relaxation. Here we introduce a primal-dual simplex subproblem method where the dual of the LP relaxation of problem (4.1)-(4.4) is defined as

$$\max \sum_{f \in F} \pi_f + \sum_{k \in K} \theta_k \quad (4.5)$$

subject to

$$\sum_{f \in F} \alpha_{pf} \pi_f + \theta_k \leq c_p, \quad \forall k \in K, \forall p \in P_k \qquad (4.6)$$

$$-d_f \leq \pi_f \leq C_f, \quad \forall f \in F \qquad (4.7)$$

$$\theta_k \leq q_k, \quad \forall k \in K. \qquad (4.8)$$

In the primal-dual simplex method for the subproblem, we define and solve a series of dual subproblems each with a different set of pairings considered. The algorithm starts with a dual feasible solution (π, θ). An initial subproblem is obtained by selecting a certain number of columns with smallest reduced costs. At each iteration, the current subproblem is solved. Its dual solution is either dual optimal to the original problem (the LP relaxation) or is used to improve the current dual feasible solution (π, θ). The details can be found in Hu and Johnson (1999).

4.5.3 Branching strategies

If the LP relaxation is solved with an integral optimal solution, the integer programming problem is also solved. However, in most cases, only a fractional optimal solution can be obtained. Thus branch and bound algorithm should be used to solve the integer programming problem, in which some branching schemes are used to divide the problem into several smaller problems, and the LP relaxation solution scheme is used to obtain a bound of the smaller problem. The problem can be branched in the following schemes.

Branching on cancelation variables

If there is a fractional cancelation variable y_f, then we can branch on this cancelation variable. To do this, let $b'_{\max}$ be the index of the flight segment f such that

$$y_{b'_{\max}} = \max_{f \in F, 0 < y_f < 1} y_f,$$

and $b'_{\min}$ be the index of the flight f such that

$$y_{b'_{\min}} = \min_{f\in F, 0<y_f<1} y_f.$$

If $y_{b'_{\max}} > 0.5$, we choose the branch with $y_{b'_{\max}} = 1$ to force the cancelation of flight $f = b'_{\max}$. Otherwise, we choose the first branch with $y_{b'_{\min}} = 0$ to forbid the cancelation of flight $f = b'_{\min}$.

Branching on deadhead variables

If all cancelation variables are integers, then we branch on a fractional deadhead variable s_f. Similarly, let $b''_{\max}$ be the index of the flight segment f such that

$$s_{b''_{\max}} = \max_{f\in F, s_f-\lfloor s_f\rfloor 0} \{s_f - \lfloor s_f\rfloor\},$$

and $b''_{\min}$ be the index of the flight f such that

$$s_{b''_{\min}} = \min_{f\in F, s_f-\lfloor s_f\rfloor 0} \{s_f - \lfloor s_f\rfloor\}.$$

If $s_{b''_{\max}} - \lfloor s_{b''_{\max}}\rfloor > 0.5$, we choose the branch with $s_{b''_{\max}} = \lceil s_{b''_{\max}}\rceil$, otherwise, we choose the branch with $s_{b''_{\min}} = \lfloor s_{b''_{\min}}\rfloor$.

Branching on follow-ons

If all cancelation and deadhead variables are integers, then we will branch on follow-ons. A follow-on refers to two specific flight segments that appear consecutively in a crew pairing. Branching on follow-ons is to select a follow-on, and either to force the follow-on or to forbid it in the new problems.

4.6 Related Literature

At last, we provide a brief literature review for crew scheduling and rescheduling problems. For crew pairing problems, the work on set partitioning type models include Anbil *et al.* (1991, 1992), Graves *et al.* (1993), and Klabjan *et al.* (2001). The multi-commodity network flow models include Desaulniers *et al.* (1997), Barnhart and Shenoi (1998), and Yan and Tu (2002).

For monthly crew assignment, we refer the crew rostering models to Ryan (1992), Gamache et al. (1999), Lucic and Teodorovic (1999), and Sellmann et al. (2002), and the crew bidline models to Jarrah and Diamond (1997), Christou et al. (1999), and Gamache et al. (1998).

A review for general airline rescheduling problems can be found in Filar et al.(2001). The literature on crew rescheduling is relatively less. Teodorovic and Stojkovic (1995) used a FIFO rule to assign crew members to new flight-aircraft schedules. The heuristic algorithm introduced in this book is from Wei et al. (1997). The integer programming model and the solution schemes are from Lettovsky et al. (2000). Yu et al. (2003) introduced the successful application of crew rescheduling in Continental Airlines, a work that won the 2002 Franz Edelman Award by The Institute for Operations Research and Management Science (INFORMS).

In most models, people have dealt with the flight and aircraft and crew rescheduling problems sequentially. Recently, however, Stojkovic and Soumis (2001) made an attempt to consider the two problems simultaneously under a single framework.

References

Anbil, R., E. Gelman, B. Patty and R. Tanga (1991), Recent advances in crew-pairing optimization at American Airlines, *Interfaces*, 21(1), 62-74.

Anbil, R., R. Tanga and E.L. Johnson (1992), A global approach to crew-pairing optimization, *IBM System Journal*, 31, 71-78.

Barnhart, C. and R.G. Shenoi (1998), An approximate model and solution approach for the long-haul crew pairing problem, *Transportation Science*, 32, 221-231.

Christou, I.T., A. Zakarian, J.-M. Liu and H. Carter (1999), A two-phase genetic algorithm for large-scale bidline-generation problems at Delta Airlines, *Interfaces*, 29(5), 51-65.

Desaulniers, G., J. Desrosiers, Y. Dumas, S. Marc, B. Rioux, M.M. Solomon and F. Soumis (1997), Crew pairing at Air France, *European Journal of Operational Research*, 97, 245-259.

Filar, J.A., P. Manyem and K. White (2001), How airlines and airports recover from schedule perturbations: A survey, *Annals of Operations Research*, 108, 315-333.

Gamache, M., F. Soumis, G. Marquis and J. Desrosiers (1999), A column generation approach for large-scale aircrew rostering problems, *Operations Research*, 47, 247-263.

Gamache, M., F. Soumis and D. Villeneuve (1998), The preferential bidding system at Air Canada, *Transportation Science*, 32, 246-255.

Graves, G.W., R.D. McBride, I. Gershkoff, D. Anderson and D. Mahidhara (1993), Flight crew scheduling, *Management Science*, 39, 736-745.

Hu, J. and E.L. Johnson (1999), Computational results with a primal-dual subproblem simplex method, *Operations Research Letters*, 25, 149-157.

Jarrah, A.I.Z. and J.T. Diamond (1997), The problem of generating crew bidlines, *Interfaces*, 27(4), 49-64.

Klabjan, D., E.L. Johnson and G.L. Nemhauser (2001), Solving large airline crew scheduling problems: Random pairing generation and strong branching, *Computational Optimization and Applications*, 20, 7391.

Lettovsky, L., E.L. Johnson and G.L. Nemhauser (2000), Airline crew recovery, *Transportation Science*, 34, 337-348.

Lucic, P. and D. Teodorovic (1999), Simulated annealing for the multi-objective aircrew rostering problem, *Transportation Research Part A: Policy and Practice*, 33, 19-45.

Ryan, D.M. (1992), The solution of massive generalized set partitioning problems in aircrew rostering, *Journal of the Operational Research Society*, 43, 459-467.

Sellmann, M., K. Zervoudakis, P. Stamatopoulos and T. Fahle (2002), Crew assignment via constraint programming: Integrating column generation and heuristic tree search, *Annals of Operations Research*, 115, 207-225.

Stojkovic, G, and F. Soumis (2001), An optimization model for the simultaneous operational flight and pilot scheduling problem, *Management Science*, 47, 1290-1305.

Teodorovic, D. and G. Stojkovic (1995), Model to reduce airline schedule disturbances, *Journal of Transportation Engineering*, 121, 324-331.

Wei, G., G. Yu and M. Song (1997), Optimization model and algorithm for crew management during airline irregular operations, *Journal of Combinatorial Optimization*, 1, 305-321.

Yan, S. and Y.-P. Tu (2002), A network model for airline cabin crew scheduling, *European Journal of Operational Research*, 140, 531-540.

Yu, G., M. Argüello, M. Song, S. McCowan and A. White (2003), A new era for crew recovery at Continental Airlines, *Interfaces*, 33(1), 5-22.

Chapter 5

Disruption Management for Machine Scheduling

5.1 Introduction

This chapter is dedicated to disruption management in machine scheduling models, which can be categorized under the general framework of machine rescheduling studies. Machine rescheduling refers to the practice of revising a given schedule in its execution period when a disruption occurs. The situation in which rescheduling arises can be described as follows. A fixed set of jobs have to be scheduled on one or more machines subject to various resource and processing constraints to minimize an objective function on job completion times. By using some algorithm, an optimal or near-optimal schedule is obtained. During the execution of this schedule, a machine may become unavailable for a specified period of time. As a result, the original schedule may become infeasible or too far from optimal. Thus we need to seek a new schedule that takes into account the degree and cost of the disruption. For the moment, we use the term disruption to describe the case of machine failure and the term disruption management to describe rescheduling. Later we introduce factors other than a machine failure that can trigger the rescheduling process. Hence, these terms have a broader meaning than implied here.

In the literature, there are two types of rescheduling models. The first is *pure* rescheduling where the objective is to find a new schedule that is optimal in the new environment with respect to the original objective function. The main problems to be addressed include when to trigger a rescheduling process, and how to construct a good initial schedule that can accommodate disruptions. The second considers both the original objective function and a measure of deviation from the original schedule. The reason for considering the deviation is that once the original schedule is established many preparations must be made, such as ordering raw materials, acquiring tools, organizing the workforce, and fixing delivery dates for customers. If any change to the original schedule has a negative impact on these preparations, then it may be desirable to minimize the deviation. Our interest in disruption management concerns the second model.

The chapter is organized as follows. In Section 5.2, we give a formal definition of the problem, discuss the basic issues that arise in the machine scheduling environment due to disruptions, and present a classification scheme that accommodates the proposed models. In Section 5.3, we give a detailed analysis of a single machine problem where the shortest processing time (SPT) rule is optimal for the original problem. These results are extended in Section 5.4 where models with min-max-type objective functions are studied, and in Section 5.5 where parallel machines are considered. A brief literature review is given in the last section.

5.2 Problem Statement and Definitions

In this section, we discuss some general issues in disruption management for machine scheduling, including the source of disruptions, types of policies in disruption management, and the criterion used in evaluating the new schedule.

Disruptions.

The original schedule has to be revised under two types of disruptions, a machine disruption and a job disruption. We make an assumption that only one disruption may occur at any time.

A machine disruption, denoted by Δ_m, is said to occur when a machine becomes unavailable for some period of time. As a result, the jobs originally scheduled to be processed during the disruption period cannot be processed, and thus a new schedule is needed. A machine disruption may be due to a component failure or a worker shortage. It may also be caused by a need to process a high-priority order. In any case, the machine becomes unavailable. In this research, we assume jobs are non-resumable, i.e., if a machine disruption occurs in the middle of processing a job, then the job must be totally reprocessed after the disruption ends.

A job disruption occurs when one or more of the parameters of a specific job changes, such as the processing time or due date. Although the original schedule may still be feasible, it may yield a poor result with respect to the objective function for which it was obtained. Similar to the non-resumability in machine disruption, we assume that if a parameter change occurs during the processing of a job, the schedule cannot be altered until the job is completed.

A job disruption can be described as specifying the parameter change. For example, $p_i + \delta$ denotes the case where the processing time of job i increases from p_i to $p_i + \delta$, while $p_i - \delta$ corresponds to the case where the processing time decreases by δ. A change in either direction may be caused by the introduction of new processing requirements or change in technical capabilities.

Policies in disruption management.

We consider two different types of disruption management policies: post-disruption management and predictive disruption management, denoted respectively by *post-mgt* and *pred-mgt*.

If the disruption is unpredictable, we cannot know it in advance, and can only start to revise the schedule until the disruption actually occurs. This situation is called post-disruption management. In this situation, all jobs scheduled before the disruption have finished processing, so only the remaining jobs need to be considered. Without consequence then, we can always designate the time when the new schedule starts as 0. Consequently, the due dates and release times of the remaining jobs must be revised accordingly. Assuming that there are n uncompleted jobs, we will re-index them from 1 to n.

In other cases, the situation is more informed. As jobs are being processed according to the original schedule, it is possible that we can know a disruption is going to occur at some point in the future. For instance, we know a temporary high-priority order will arrive in 5 hours and thus a machine disruption will occur. When this happens, we revise the schedule in advance to respond a future disruption before it occurs. This is called predictive disruption management.

In such a case, as soon as we learn of the disruption, all uncompleted jobs are re-indexed from 1 to n and the time index is reset to 0.

Objective function.

As with any disruption management problem, we must first discuss the deviation cost incurred in the new schedule.

Let $\overline{C}_i$ be the completion time of job i in the original schedule. If no disruption occurs, job i will finish processing at this time so we can view $\overline{C}_i$ as a special type of due date. We call it the *virtual due date* for job i. If C_i is the real completion time in the new schedule, then the difference between C_i and $\overline{C}_i$ can be used to assess the deviation cost. This idea leads to the definition of several new measures: virtual earliness $\overline{E}_i = \max\{0, \overline{C}_i - C_i\}$, virtual tardiness $\overline{T}_i = \max\{0, C_i - \overline{C}_i\}$, and virtual absolute deviation $\overline{D}_i = |\overline{C}_i - C_i| = \overline{E}_i + \overline{T}_i$, any one of which can be used in the objective.

Virtual earliness can be used to measure the cost incurred when raw material delivery dates are moved up or when finished goods must be stored prior to shipment. For example, if $C_i < \overline{C}_i$, then it may be necessary for a supplier to deliver the raw material for job i earlier than originally scheduled. The supplier then may charge the manufacturer a premium for a rush delivery. If job i is similarly completed earlier than planned but the customer is not willing to take delivery, the manufacturer may incur an inventory holding cost proportional to $\overline{C}_i - C_i$.

Virtual tardiness can be used to measure the penalty cost that must be borne when due dates are violated. When both virtual earliness and virtual tardiness are important, the virtual absolute deviation can be used as the cost measure. When $\overline{E}_i > 0$, job i is called virtually early, or simply early if no due date is specified in the original scheduling problem. When $\overline{T}_i > 0$, job i is called virtually tardy, or simply tardy.

Considering the original objective function, the disruption management is actually a bicriteria optimization problem, where we choose to optimize the weighted sum of the two sub-objectives.

Classification scheme.

Based on the above discussion, we propose that disruption management problems for machine scheduling be classified according to the following three factors: type of disruption, type of disruption management policy, and objective function. This can be done using the well known three-field notation $a|b|c$ to characterize a specific problem, where a indicates the machine environment, b describes constraints, and c defines the objective. We use field b to describe the disruption and the disruption management policy.

To illustrate the use of the classification scheme, $1|\Delta_m, post\text{-}mgt|\alpha \sum C_i + \beta \sum T_i$ would be a post-disruption management problem for machine disruption with the objective of minimizing total completion times and virtual tardiness. When a job disruption occurs, $p_k + \delta$ in field b denotes the change in the processing time of job k, where k is the new index after all uncompleted jobs are re-indexed. If the disruption was not predicted, then a post-disruption policy requires us to wait until the current job is completed. Such a case is denoted by $p_0 + \delta$, where the disrupted job is re-indexed as 0.

5.3 Disruption Management for an SPT Schedule

Suppose that the original problem is to minimize the sum of all completion times on a single machine and that an SPT schedule is an optimal one, where in an SPT schedule all jobs are sequenced in nondecreasing order of their processing times. Let m be the number of original jobs and p_i the processing time of job i. Suppose that the jobs are indexed so that $p_1 \leq p_2 \leq \cdots \leq p_m$. When we re-index the uncompleted jobs after a disruption, we still keep their original order. For example, assume jobs 1 and 2 are completed. Then after re-indexing, job 3 becomes job 1, job 4 becomes job 2, and so on. Recall that we use n to denote the number of uncompleted jobs to be rescheduled.

Given a schedule π, we make use of the following definitions in the analysis.

$f_c(\pi) = \sum_{i=1}^{n} C_i$: total completion times of π

$f_e(\pi) = \sum_{i=1}^{n} \overline{E}_i$: total virtual earliness of π

$f_t(\pi) = \sum_{i=1}^n \overline{T}_i$: total virtual tardiness of π

$f_d(\pi) = \sum_{i=1}^n \overline{D}_i$: total virtual absolute deviation of π

Also, let $f_{ce}(\pi) = \alpha f_c(\pi) + \beta f_e(\pi)$, $f_{ct}(\pi) = \alpha f_c(\pi) + \beta f_t(\pi)$, and $f_{cd}(\pi) = \alpha f_c(\pi) + \beta f_d(\pi)$.

5.3.1 Post-disruption management for machine disruption

As the simplest case, when the SPT schedule is being carried out, the machine is found to be unavailable at certain time. Then our problem is how to reschedule the uncompleted jobs after the machine is recovered. This is referred to as the post-disruption management for machine disruption.

First, we reset the time index to 0 to coincide with the point when the machine becomes available again. In other words, if the machine is unavailable for δ time units, then the disruption actually occurs at time $-\delta$ in the new time index. Then we re-index the uncompleted jobs. When the disruption occurs, job 1 may have been processed for δ_1 time units, $0 \leq \delta_1 < p_1$. Due to our assumption that jobs cannot be resumed when the machine fails but must be re-started, the situation is equivalent to the case where the machine disruption occurs at $-\delta' = -(\delta + \delta_1)$, so $\overline{C}_i = -\delta' + p_1 + \cdots + p_i$.

Consider a new schedule that keeps the uncompleted jobs in the original SPT order but postpones them for δ' units of time. We call the resultant schedule the right shift SPT (RS-SPT) schedule, where we have $C_i = p_1 + \cdots + p_i = \overline{C}_i + \delta'$, $i = 1, \ldots, n$.

Theorem 5.1 *The RS-SPT schedule is optimal for problem* $1|\Delta_m, post\text{-}mgt|\alpha \sum C_i + \beta \sum \overline{T}_i$.

Proof. It is easy to see that the RS-SPT schedule minimizes $\sum_{i=1}^n C_i$ for this case. Moreover, in the RS-SPT schedule, every job is tardy with respect to its virtual due date, and virtual tardiness $\overline{T}_i = C_i - \overline{C}_i = \delta'$. According to Baker (1974), if in an SPT schedule, every job is tardy, then the SPT schedule minimizes total tardiness. Therefore, the RS-SPT schedule minimizes $\sum_{i=1}^n \overline{T}_i$. From these developments, we see that the RS-SPT schedule minimizes $\sum_{i=1}^n \alpha C_i + \beta \sum_{i=1}^n \overline{T}_i$.
∎

Similarly, the RS-SPT schedule is optimal when the total virtual earliness or the total virtual absolute deviation is used as the deviation cost.

Theorem 5.2 *The RS-SPT schedule is optimal for problems* $1|\Delta_m, post\text{-}mgt|\alpha \sum C_i + \beta \sum \overline{E}_i$ *and* $1|\Delta_m, post\text{-}mgt|\alpha \sum C_i + \beta \sum \overline{D}_i$.

Proof. The optimality of the RS-SPT schedule for $1|\Delta_m, post\text{-}mgt|\alpha \sum C_i + \beta \sum \overline{E}_i$ is due to the fact that (i) the RS-SPT schedule minimizes $\sum_{i=1}^{n} C_i$, and (ii) in the RS-SPT schedule, there are no early jobs so it also minimizes $\sum_{i=1}^{n} \overline{E}_i$.

In a similar vein, the optimality of the RS-SPT schedule for $1|\Delta_m, post\text{-}mgt|\alpha \sum C_i + \beta \sum \overline{D}_i$ follows because (i) $\sum_{i=1}^{n} \overline{D}_i = \sum_{i=1}^{n} \overline{E}_i + \sum_{i=1}^{n} \overline{T}_i$, and (ii) the RS-SPT schedule minimizes $\sum_{i=1}^{n} C_i$, $\sum_{i=1}^{n} \overline{T}_i$ and $\sum_{i=1}^{n} \overline{E}_i$ simultaneously. ∎

5.3.2 *Post-disruption management for job disruption*

In this situation, the processing time of a specific job is changed. There are two possibilities, a longer processing time or a shorter processing time. If the processing time becomes longer, because the disrupted job will still be processed until it is completed, the problem can be regarded as the case where the machine is unavailable for some period of time with respect to the following uncompleted jobs. Therefore, we only address the case where the processing time of the disrupted job becomes shorter, denoted by $1|p_0 - \delta, post\text{-}mgt|c$ for a δ reduction and a general objective function.

We reset the time index 0 as the time when the disrupted job finishes and re-index all uncompleted jobs. Then the completion time of job i in the original schedule is $\overline{C}_i = \delta + p_1 + \cdots + p_i$, $i = 1, \ldots, n$. Define the left shift SPT (LS-SPT) schedule to be the schedule in which the jobs are keep in the original SPT order but are started δ time units earlier. In an LS-SPT schedule, the new completion times are $C_i = p_1 + \cdots + p_i$, $i = 1, \ldots, n$.

Because the LS-SPT schedule minimizes $\sum_{i=1}^{n} C_i$ and has no tardy jobs, the LS-SPT schedule is optimal when virtual tardiness is used as the deviation cost. So we have

Theorem 5.3 *The LS-SPT schedule is optimal for problem* $1|p_0 - \delta, post\text{-}mgt|\alpha \sum C_i + \beta \sum \overline{T}_i$.

If virtual earliness or virtual absolute deviation is used as the deviation cost, we discuss the problem by two cases: $\alpha \geq \beta$ and $\alpha < \beta$.

Theorem 5.4 *If* $\alpha \geq \beta$, *LS-SPT schedule is optimal for problems* $1|p_0 - \delta, post\text{-}mgt|\alpha \sum C_i + \beta \sum \overline{E}_i$, $1|p_0 - \delta, post\text{-}mgt|\alpha \sum C_i + \beta \sum \overline{D}_i$.

Proof. First we show that when $\alpha \geq \beta$, there is no idle time before any job. Because moving a job i earlier by a time period x will reduce the weighted completion times by αx and increase either the weighted virtual earliness or the weighted virtual absolute deviation by at most βx, and $\alpha \geq \beta$, the total cost cannot increase when some idle times are eliminated by moving jobs earlier.

Next we show that in an optimal schedule, for any two adjacent jobs i and j, where i is followed by j, we have $i < j$. Suppose $i > j$ which implies that $p_i \geq p_j$ and $\overline{C}_i \geq \overline{C}_j + p_i$. If jobs i and j are now exchanged, the weighted completion time is reduced by $\alpha(p_i - p_j)$. It can also be shown that after the exchange, the total weighted virtual earliness increases at most by $\beta(p_i - p_j)$. When $\alpha \geq \beta$, exchanging jobs i and j cannot increase the total cost. So we can conclude that the LS-SPT schedule is optimal to the problem $1|p_0 - \delta, post\text{-}mgt|\alpha \sum C_i + \beta \sum \overline{E}_i$.

Now consider virtual absolute deviation. Since $p_i \geq p_j$ and $\overline{C}_i > \overline{C}_j$, the exchange cannot increase total virtual tardiness either. Thus the LS-SPT schedule is optimal to the problem $1|p_0 - \delta, post\text{-}mgt|\alpha \sum C_i + \beta \sum \overline{D}_i$. ∎

When $\alpha < \beta$, however, it can be shown that the early completion of the disrupted job, as in the LS-SPT schedule, does not improve the performance of the schedule. To show such a result, we define the ORI-SPT schedule as keeping every uncompleted job starting at its originally scheduled start time, though it has a chance to be started earlier.

Theorem 5.5 *If $\alpha < \beta$, the ORI-SPT schedule is optimal for problems $1|p_0 - \delta, \text{post-mgt}|\alpha \sum C_i + \beta \sum \overline{E}_i$ and $1|p_0 - \delta, \text{post-mgt}|\alpha \sum C_i + \beta \sum \overline{D}_i$.*

Proof. Let C_i be the completion time of job i in the ORI-SPT schedule. Because every job is completed exactly at its virtual due date, we have $f_e(\text{ORI-SPT}) = 0$.

Suppose π^* is the optimal schedule for $1|p_0 - \delta, \text{post-mgt}|\alpha \sum C_i + \beta \sum \overline{E}_i$, and C_i^* is the completion time of job i in π^*. Consider any job i.

If $C_i = C_i^*$, we have $\overline{E}_i = \overline{E}_i^* = 0$ and $\alpha C_i + \beta \overline{E}_i = \alpha C_i^* + \beta \overline{E}_i^*$.

If $C_i < C_i^*$, we have $\overline{E}_i = \overline{E}_i^* = 0$ and $\alpha C_i + \beta \overline{E}_i < \alpha C_i^* + \beta \overline{E}_i^*$.

If $C_i > C_i^*$, we have $\overline{E}_i = 0$ and $\overline{E}_i^* = C_i - C_i^*$, implying $C_i - C_i^* = \overline{E}_i^* - \overline{E}_i$. Because $\alpha < \beta$, we have $\alpha(C_i - C_i^*) < \beta(\overline{E}_i^* - \overline{E}_i)$. Thus $\alpha C_i + \beta \overline{E}_i < \alpha C_i^* + \beta \overline{E}_i^*$.

Summing the weighted completion time and virtual earliness over all jobs, i.e., $\alpha \sum_{i=1}^n C_i + \beta \sum_{i=1}^n \overline{E}_i$, we have $f_{ce}(\text{ORI-SPT}) < f_{ce}(\pi^*)$, implying that the ORI-SPT schedule is optimal to the problem $1|p_0 - \delta, \text{post-mgt}|\alpha \sum C_i + \beta \sum \overline{E}_i$.

Considering the fact that in the ORI-SPT schedule no job is tardy, we can conclude that the ORI-SPT schedule is optimal for problem $1|p_0 - \delta, \text{post-mgt}|\alpha \sum C_i + \beta \sum \overline{D}_i$. ∎

5.3.3 Predictive management for machine disruption

When the machine disruption is predictable, we reset the time index to 0 after the current job is finished and re-index all uncompleted jobs. Suppose that the machine is unavailable during the interval $[t_1, t_2]$. The rescheduling problem involves the n uncompleted jobs, each of which has a virtual due date $\overline{C}_i = p_1 + \cdots + p_i$, $i = 1, \ldots, n$. We assume that $t_1 > p_1$, for otherwise all jobs would have to be processed after the disruption thus reducing the problem to the post-disruption management case.

If we only consider minimizing $\sum_{i=1}^n C_i$, we have the scheduling problem with known future machine unavailability, which is

NP-complete (Lee and Liman 1992). Therefore, all three problems $1|\Delta_m, pred\text{-}mgt|\alpha \sum C_i + \beta \sum \overline{E}_i$, $1|\Delta_m, pred\text{-}mgt|\alpha \sum C_i + \beta \sum \overline{T}_i$ and $1|\Delta_m, pred\text{-}mgt|\alpha \sum C_i + \beta \sum \overline{D}_i$ are NP-complete.

Lemma 5.1 *For the problem* $1|\Delta_m, pred\text{-}mgt|\alpha \sum C_i + \beta \sum \overline{T}_i$, *there exists an optimal schedule in which the jobs before t_1 and the jobs after t_2 form two SPT sequences.*

It can be proven by a pairwise exchange argument and is omitted.

From Lemma 5.1, $1|\Delta_m, pred\text{-}mgt|\alpha \sum C_i + \beta \sum \overline{T}_i$ is reduced to a partitioning-type problem in which the jobs must be divided into two groups and then sequenced in SPT order. The following dynamic programming algorithm can be used to find a solution.

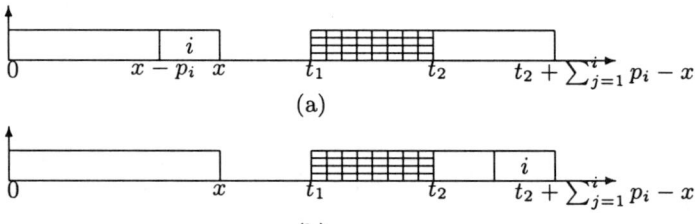

(a) Job i is the last job before t_1
(b) Job i is the last job after t_2

Fig. 5.1   Illustration for the dynamic program

Define a pair (i, x) as a state for jobs 1 to i where the total processing time for the jobs before t_1 is x. Let $f(i, x)$ be the minimum total weighted completion time plus virtual tardiness for state (i, x). Given a state (i, x), from Lemma 5.1 we know that job i must be either the last job before t_1 or the last job after t_2 among all jobs 1 through i. If job i is the last job before t_1, then its completion time is x, as shown in Figure 5.1(a), and we have $f(i, x) = f(i - 1, x - p_i) + \alpha x + \beta \max\{x - \overline{C}_i, 0\}$. Actually, job i cannot be tardy in this case, so we have $f(i, x) = f(i - 1, x - p_i) + \alpha x$. If job i is the last job after t_2, then its completion time is $t_2 + \sum_{j=1}^{i} p_j - x = t_2 + \overline{C}_i - x$, as shown in Figure 5.1(b), and its virtual tardiness is $\max\{t_2 + \overline{C}_i - x - \overline{C}_i, 0\} = t_2 - x$, meaning job i must be tardy in this case. Thus we have $f(i, x) = f(i - 1, x) + \alpha(t_2 + \overline{C}_i - x) + \beta(t_2 - x)$.

This leads to the following dynamic programming recursion.

$$f(i,x) = \min \begin{cases} f(i-1, x-p_i) + \alpha x \\ f(i-1, x) + \alpha(t_2 + \overline{C}_i - x) + \beta(t_2 - x) \end{cases}$$

for $2 \leq i \leq n$ and $0 \leq x \leq t_1$.

The boundary conditions are $f(i,x) = +\infty$ when either $0 < x < p_1$ or $x > \sum_{j=1}^{i} p_j$ for $i = 2, \ldots, n$; the initial conditions for $i = 1$ are $f(1, p_1) = \alpha p_1$, $f(1, 0) = \alpha(t_2 + p_1) + \beta t_2$, and $f(1, x) = +\infty$ for $x \notin \{0, p_1\}$. Finally, the optimal solution is given by the minimum value of $f(n, x)$ for $0 \leq x \leq t_1$.

The computational complexity of the algorithm can be determined as follows. There are a total of $O(nt_1)$ states, and the work associated with each state is $O(1)$ or constant. This gives a total complexity of $O(nt_1)$, which implies that the algorithm is pseudopolynomial. Because the solution contains two SPT sequences, we call the procedure the TWO-SPT algorithm.

Implementation requires that we keep track of the i jobs that yield the minimum cost $f(i,x)$ for state (i,x). One of several bookkeeping schemes for doing this follows. For each state (i,x), define $\Pi(i,x)$ to be a subset of the jobs 1 through i which contains the jobs to be scheduled before t_1 so that the resultant schedule has cost $f(i,x)$. If $f(i,x) = +\infty$, $\Pi(i,x)$ is not defined. Initially, we have $\Pi(1,0) = \emptyset$ and $\Pi(1, p_1) = \{1\}$. In the calculation of $f(i,x)$, when $f(i,x) = f(i-1, x-p_i) + \alpha x$, let $\Pi(i,x) = \Pi(i-1, x-p_i) \cup \{i\}$; otherwise, let $\Pi(i,x) = \Pi(i-1, x)$. In this way, the jobs that should be scheduled before t_1 are recorded. Suppose x^* minimizes $f(n,x)$ for n fixed. Then the optimal schedule can be constructed as follows: sequence the jobs in $\Pi(i, x^*)$ in SPT order before t_1 and the remaining jobs in SPT order after t_2. Note that the computational complexity of this implementation conforms with the derived complexity of the dynamic program.

When virtual earliness or virtual absolute deviation is used as the deviation cost, again two cases have to be considered, $\alpha \geq \beta$ and $\alpha < \beta$. When $\alpha \geq \beta$, we have a result similar to Lemma 5.1.

Lemma 5.2 *For problems* $1|\Delta_m, pred\text{-}mgt|\alpha \sum C_i + \beta \sum \overline{E}_i$ *and* $1|\Delta_m, pred\text{-}mgt|\alpha \sum C_i + \beta \sum \overline{D}_i$, *when* $\alpha \geq \beta$, *there exists an op-*

timal schedule in which there is no idle time immediately before any job, and the jobs before t_1 and the jobs after t_2 form two SPT sequences.

The proof is based on the same arguments used in the proof of Theorem 5.4 and is omitted. The two problems mentioned in Lemma 5.2 can be solved with dynamic programming algorithms similar to the one derived from Lemma 5.1. For the sake of brevity, we only sketch the dynamic program for problem $1|\Delta_m, pred\text{-}mgt|\alpha \sum C_i + \beta \sum \overline{E}_i$.

Let $g(i, x)$ be the minimum total cost for jobs 1 to i where the total processing time for the jobs before t_1 is x. If job i is the last job before t_1, it cannot be tardy; thus we have $g(i, x) = g(i-1, x - p_i) + \alpha x + \beta(\overline{C}_i - x)$. If job i is the last job after t_2, it must be tardy and we have $g(i, x) = g(i-1, x) + \alpha(t_2 + \overline{C}_i - x)$. This leads to the following dynamic programming recursion.

$$g(i, x) = \min \begin{cases} g(i-1, x - p_i) + \alpha x + \beta(\overline{C}_i - x) \\ g(i-1, x) + \alpha(t_2 + \overline{C}_i - x) \end{cases}$$

for $2 \leq i \leq n$ and $0 \leq x \leq t_1$.

The functions $g(i, x)$ and $f(i, x)$ have the same boundary conditions, initial conditions (except $g(1, 0) = \alpha(t_2 + p_1)$), and computational complexity.

When $\alpha < \beta$, Lemma 5.2 does not hold since idle time may exist before a job in an optimal schedule. In this case, we can use the RS-SPT schedule as a heuristic. Here the RS-SPT schedule is defined as follows. All jobs that are completed no later than t_1 remain unchanged while all other jobs are postponed until t_2 and then processed in their original order. To evaluate the effectiveness of the RS-SPT schedule, we cite a theorem from Lee and Liman (1992) as a lemma.

Lemma 5.3 *Considering the problem of minimizing $\sum_{i=1}^{n} C_i$, the worst case bound for the RS-SPT schedule is 2/7, i.e.,*

$$\frac{f_c(\text{RS-SPT}) - f_c(\pi')}{f_c(\pi')} \leq \frac{2}{7},$$

where π' is the optimal schedule to $\sum_{i=1}^{n} C_i$.

Based on Lemma 5.3, we can directly have the following result, which holds true regardless of whether $\alpha \geq \beta$ or $\alpha < \beta$.

Theorem 5.6 *For problem* $1|\Delta_m, pred\text{-}mgt|\alpha \sum C_i + \beta \sum \overline{E}_i$, *the RS-SPT schedule has the worst case bound of 2/7.*

When virtual absolute deviation is used as the deviation cost, we get the problem $1|\Delta_m, pred\text{-}mgt|\alpha \sum C_i + \beta \sum \overline{D}_i$ for which little can be said about the optimal schedule. To find a solution, we propose as a heuristic, running the TWO-SPT and RS-SPT algorithms independently and selecting the better result. We call this the B-SPT algorithm.

5.3.4 Predictive management for job disruption

We now examine the case where the processing time of a specific job, say job k, is anticipated to change from p_k to $p_k \pm \delta$. To begin, let the deviation cost be measured by virtual tardiness. Similar to Lemma 5.1, we have the following result. The proof is based on the fact that for any two jobs i and j $(i, j \neq k)$, $\overline{C}_i \leq \overline{C}_j$ implies $p_i \leq p_j$.

Lemma 5.4 *For problem* $1|p_k \pm \delta, pred\text{-}mgt|\alpha \sum C_i + \beta \sum \overline{T}_i$, *there exists an optimal schedule in which job i will come before job j if $i < j$ and $i, j \neq k$.*

From this lemma, we see that the problem can be solved by finding the best position in the SPT sequence of the jobs $1, 2, \ldots, k-1, k+1, \ldots, n$ in which to insert job k. This can be done in $O(n)$ time by trying all positions, calculating the cost of each, and picking the minimum. For the case where the processing time of job k increases, i.e., problem $1|p_k + \delta, pred\text{-}mgt|\alpha \sum C_i + \beta \sum \overline{T}_i$, we only need to compare the schedule that keeps job k at its original position in the original SPT order with the schedules in which job k is inserted after job $k+1$, job $k+2$, $\ldots$, or job $k+l$, where $p_{k+l} < p_k + \delta$. For the case where the processing time of job k decreases, i.e., problem $1|p_k - \delta, pred\text{-}mgt|\alpha \sum C_i + \beta \sum \overline{T}_i$, we only need to compare the schedule that keeps job k at its original position in the original SPT sequence with the schedules in which job k is inserted before job

$k-1$, job $k-2$, ..., or job $k-l$, where $p_{k-l} > p_k - \delta$. We call the above procedure the insert SPT (INS-SPT) algorithm.

It should be mentioned that the original SPT schedule is not changed if after the disruption for any two jobs i and j (including the case where $i = k$ or $j = k$), $\overline{C}_i \leq \overline{C}_j$ implies $p_i \leq p_j$, which is the case when $p_{k-1} \leq p_k \pm \delta \leq p_{k+1}$. In other words, there is a threshold for the disruption such that there is no need to change the original SPT schedule unless the disruption is beyond the threshold.

When virtual earliness or the virtual absolute deviation is used as the deviation cost, two cases must again be considered: $\alpha \geq \beta$ and $\alpha < \beta$.

Lemma 5.5 *For problems* $1|p_k \pm \delta, pred\text{-}mgt|\alpha \sum C_i + \beta \sum \overline{E}_i$ *and* $1|p_k \pm \delta, pred\text{-}mgt|\alpha \sum C_i + \beta \sum \overline{D}_i$, *when* $\alpha \geq \beta$, *there is no idle time in an optimal schedule. Furthermore, given any two jobs i and j with $p_i \leq p_j$ and $\overline{C}_i < \overline{C}_j$, if they are adjacent in an optimal schedule, then job i must precede job j.*

Proof. The fact that there is no idle time in an optimal schedule for either problem can be seen as follows. When $\alpha \geq \beta$, moving a job earlier decreases the weighted completion time by an amount no greater than the corresponding increase that would result in the weighted virtual earliness or virtual absolute deviation.

Regarding adjacent jobs i and j, for problem $1|p_k \pm \delta, pred\text{-}mgt|\alpha \sum C_i + \beta \sum \overline{E}_i$, the proof that job i must precede job j is based on a pairwise exchange argument which is similar to the proof of Theorem 5.4. The details are omitted.

Now consider $1|p_k \pm \delta, pred\text{-}mgt|\alpha \sum C_i + \beta \sum \overline{D}_i$. From the discussion of $1|p_k \pm \delta, pred\text{-}mgt|\alpha \sum C_i + \beta \sum \overline{E}_i$, we know that when j precedes i, interchanging them can only improve the objective function. Moreover, such an exchange cannot increase the total virtual tardiness of jobs i and j because $p_i \leq p_j$ and $\overline{C}_i < \overline{C}_j$. Given that $\alpha \sum C_i + \beta \sum \overline{D}_i = \alpha \sum C_i + \beta \sum \overline{E}_i + \beta \sum \overline{T}_i$, it follows that i should precede j when minimizing $\alpha \sum C_i + \beta \sum \overline{D}_i$. ∎

Lemma 5.5 holds for all jobs including the disrupted job k; i.e., when i or j equals k. In either of these cases, the processing time of job k should be replaced by $p_k \pm \delta$.

From Lemma 5.5, when $\alpha \geq \beta$ problems $1|p_k \pm \delta, pred\text{-}mgt|\alpha C_i + \beta \sum \overline{E}_i$ and $1|p_k \pm \delta, pred\text{-}mgt|\alpha \sum C_i + \beta \sum \overline{D}_i$ have an optimal schedule that satisfies (i) all jobs that precede k are in SPT order, and (ii) all jobs that follow k are in SPT order. This means that the INS-SPT algorithm can be used to solve either problem if in the optimal schedule, all jobs preceding job k have smaller indices than those jobs following k. This result is now stated formally.

Theorem 5.7 *When $\alpha \geq \beta$, problems $1|p_k \pm \delta, pred\text{-}mgt|\alpha \sum C_i + \beta \sum \overline{E}_i$ and $1|p_k \pm \delta, pred\text{-}mgt|\alpha \sum C_i + \beta \sum \overline{D}_i$ have an optimal schedule where all jobs preceding job k have smaller indices than the jobs following job k.*

Proof. Suppose in an optimal schedule, job j is the job that immediately precedes job k, and job i is the job that immediately follows job k. Based on Lemma 5.5, job j must have the largest index among all jobs preceding job k, and job i must have the smallest index among all jobs following job k. If the theorem does not hold, we should have $j > i$, which implies $\overline{C}_j > \overline{C}_i$ and $p_j \geq p_i$.

Now we need to show that interchanging jobs j and i can reduce the total cost. The details are similar to those given in the proof of Theorem 5.4. Suffice it to say that when the exchange is made (i) the weighted completion time of job k is reduced by $\alpha(p_j - p_i)$, which is no less than its maximum possible weighted earliness increase $\beta(p_j - p_i)$, and (ii) the decrease in the total weighted completion times of jobs j and i is also no less than the increase in their total weighted earliness.

Thus exchanging jobs j and i may reduce $\alpha \sum C_i + \beta \sum \overline{E}_i$. At the same time, such an exchange cannot increase total virtual tardiness so $\alpha \sum C_i + \beta \sum \overline{D}_i$ may also be reduced. As a consequence, we have $j < i$ for both problems, and the theorem follows. ∎

From Theorem 5.7, when $\alpha \geq \beta$ the two problems $1|p_k \pm \delta, pred\text{-}mgt|\alpha \sum C_i + \beta \sum \overline{E}_i$ and $1|p_k \pm \delta, pred\text{-}mgt|\alpha \sum C_i + \beta \sum \overline{D}_i$ can be solved by the INS-SPT algorithm. When $\alpha < \beta$ and the processing time of job k is reduced by δ, we define the ORI-RS-SPT schedule as (1) leaving all jobs except job k unchanged in their original SPT schedule; and (2) right-shift job k by δ so that it still finishes at its original completion time. Similar to Theorem 5.5, we have

Theorem 5.8 *When $\alpha < \beta$, the ORI-RS-SPT schedule is optimal for problems $1|p_k - \delta, pred\text{-}mgt|\alpha \sum C_i + \beta \sum \overline{E}_i$, $1|p_k - \delta, pred\text{-}mgt|\alpha \sum C_i + \beta \sum \overline{D}_i$.*

The proof is similar to that of Theorem 5.5. In essence, in an ORI-RS-SPT schedule, each job is completed exactly at its virtual due date.

When $\alpha < \beta$ and the processing time of job k increases, we have

Theorem 5.9 *When $\alpha < \beta$, problem $1|p_k + \delta, pred\text{-}mgt|\alpha \sum C_i + \beta \sum \overline{E}_i$ can be solved by the INS-SPT algorithm.*

Proof. First, consider jobs 1 to $k-1$. We prove that there exists an optimal schedule in which these jobs remain unchanged. Starting the analysis with job 1, suppose job i immediately precedes job 1 in an optimal schedule. Then $p_i \geq p_1$, which implies that interchanging job i and job 1 cannot increase the sum of the completion times. Also, the virtual earliness of job i can only decrease, while job 1 cannot have any virtual earliness no matter where it is scheduled. Interchanging jobs i and 1, then, can only reduce the total cost. Thus job 1 should be fixed as the first job in an optimal schedule. Repeating the above arguments leads to the general conclusion that job j must be the j-th job in an optimal schedule, $j = 1, \ldots, k-1$. This allows us to fix jobs 1 to $k-1$.

Second, consider jobs $k+1$ to n. We start by proving that all jobs $k+2$ to n must follow job $k+1$. If this is not true, two cases must be considered: (1) there is a job i, $i > k+1$, that immediately precedes job $k+1$, or (2) there is a job i, $i > k+1$, that immediately precedes job k which, in turn, immediately precedes job $k+1$.

Case 1. Suppose job i, $i > k+1$, immediately precedes job $k+1$. Then $p_i \geq p_{k+1}$ and interchanging them cannot increase the total completion time because the two jobs would then be in SPT order. After the exchange, the virtual earliness of job i may be reduced, and the virtual earliness of job $k+1$ may be increased. Note that $\overline{C}_{k+1} = p_1 + \cdots + p_{k-1} + p_k + p_{k+1}$. Because all jobs 1 to $k-1$ are fixed in the first $k-1$ positions, the earliest starting time of job $k+1$ is $p_1 + \cdots + p_{k-1}$ and its virtual earliness, and thus the increase in its virtual earliness, is at most p_k. If after the exchange, job $k+1$ is early, then job i must be early both before and after the exchange, and its virtual earliness is reduced by p_{k+1} because of the exchange. Given that $p_{k+1} \geq p_k$, we conclude that interchanging jobs i and $k+1$ will not increase the total cost.

Case 2. Suppose job i, $i > k+1$, immediately precedes job k which immediately precedes job $k+1$ in an optimal schedule. Using the same arguments, we can show that interchanging jobs i and $k+1$ will not increase the total cost. The details are omitted.

The above analysis can be applied to show that all jobs $k+3, ..., n$ must follow job $k+2$, and so on. Therefore, there must exist an optimal schedule in which all jobs, expect job k, are in the original SPT order. Consequently, the problem can be solved by finding the best position for job k in the SPT schedule formed by the other jobs. This can be done with the INS-SPT algorithm. ■

From Lemma 5.4 and Theorem 5.9, and the fact that $\overline{D}_i = \overline{E}_i + \overline{T}_i$, we have

Corollary 5.1 *When* $\alpha < \beta$, *problem* $1|p_k+\delta, pred$ -$mgt|\alpha \sum C_i + \beta \sum \overline{D}_i$ *can be solved by the INS-SPT algorithm.*

In the above analysis, we find that the RS-SPT schedule and the LS-SPT schedule are optimal for many problems. In practice, these schedules are easy to understand and would probably be applied intuitively. Our work proves the optimality of doing so. It is also worth noting that the construction of either of these schedules is robust with respect to the specific values of the objective function parameters α and β. This property eliminates much of the confusion surrounding the choice of weights for the different sub-criteria, a step that often frustrates practitioners.

5.4 Problems with Min-max Deviation Cost Functions

Up until now, deviation costs have been measured by the sum of the deviations over all jobs. When a disruption leads to a delay, for example, we introduced the concept of total virtual tardiness as an objective function component to be minimized. Models with cost functions such as this might be called min-sum problems. Nevertheless, it might be more appropriate to work with what we call their min-max counterparts. For these problems, the deviation cost is measured by the maximum deviation over all jobs. Examples include maximum virtual tardiness $\overline{T}_{\max} = \max_{1 \leq i \leq n} \{\overline{T}_i\}$, maximum virtual earliness $\overline{E}_{\max} = \max_{1 \leq i \leq n} \{\overline{E}_i\}$, and maximum virtual absolute deviation $\overline{D}_{\max} = \max_{1 \leq i \leq n} \{\overline{D}_i\}$. In this section, we examine three min-max problems with the following objective functions: $\alpha \sum C_i + \beta \overline{T}_{\max}$, $\alpha \sum C_i + \beta \overline{E}_{\max}$ and $\alpha \sum C_i + \beta \overline{D}_{\max}$. Interestingly, many of the results obtained for the min-sum problems can be extended to their min-max counterparts.

5.4.1 Post-disruption management for machine disruption

When the disruption is due to the machine being taken out of service, the RS-SPT schedule is still optimal for all three min-max problems.

Theorem 5.10 *The RS-SPT schedule is optimal for the problems* $1|\Delta_m, post\text{-}mgt|\alpha \sum C_i + \beta \overline{T}_{\max}$, $1|\Delta_m, post\text{-}mgt|\alpha \sum C_i + \beta \overline{E}_{\max}$, *and* $1|\Delta_m, post\text{-}mgt|\alpha \sum C_i + \beta \overline{D}_{\max}$.

Proof. The optimality of the RS-SPT schedule for $1|\Delta_m, post\text{-}mgt|\alpha \sum C_i + \beta \overline{T}_{\max}$ is due to the fact that this schedule (i) minimizes $\sum_{i=1}^n C_i$, and (ii) also minimizes $\overline{T}_{\max}$. The latter claim follows because the RS-SPT schedule is also an EDD (earliest due date) schedule in terms of the virtual due dates.

The optimality of the RS-SPT schedule for $1|\Delta_m, post\text{-}mgt|\alpha \sum C_i + \beta \overline{E}_{\max}$ and $1|\Delta_m, post\text{-}mgt|\alpha \sum C_i + \beta \overline{D}_{\max}$ is due to the fact that it (i) minimizes $\sum_{i=1}^n C_i$, and (ii) has no early jobs. ∎

5.4.2 Post-disruption management for job disruption

Again, we only need to consider the case where the processing time of the disrupted job decreases by δ. Corresponding to Theorem 5.3, we can easily prove the following.

Theorem 5.11 *The LS-SPT schedule is optimal for the problem* $1|p_0 - \delta, post\text{-}mgt|\alpha \sum C_i + \beta \overline{T}_{\max}$, *where job 0 is the disrupted job after re-indexing.*

Now consider the problem $1|p_0 - \delta, post\text{-}mgt|\alpha \sum C_i + \beta \overline{E}_{\max}$. We give the following lemma.

Lemma 5.6 *For problem* $1|p_0 - \delta, post\text{-}mgt|\alpha \sum C_i + \beta \overline{E}_{\max}$, *there is an optimal schedule in which all jobs are in the original SPT sequence and idle time can only exist before job 1.*

Proof. If the original SPT sequence is not optimal, then in an optimal schedule there must exist two adjacent jobs i and j such that $i > j$ and job i precedes job j. There may or may not be idle time between these two jobs. For the given conditions, $C_i < C_j$ because job i precedes job j, and $\overline{C}_i \geq \overline{C}_j + p_i$ because in the original SPT schedule job i follows job j. Now exchange jobs i and j so that j starts at the original start time of i and i immediately follows j. Accordingly, let $C'_j = C_i - p_i + p_j$ and $C'_i = C'_j + p_i$ which indicates that such an exchange can reduce the total weighted completion time. We only need to show that the maximum virtual earliness for jobs i and j cannot increase provided that no other jobs are moved.

Before the exchange $\max\{\overline{E}_i, \overline{E}_j\} = \overline{E}_i$ since $C_i < C_j$ and $\overline{C}_i \geq \overline{C}_j + p_i$. After the exchange, we have

$$\overline{E}'_i = \max\{0, \overline{C}_i - C'_i\} = \max\{0, \overline{C}_i - C'_j - p_i\} \geq \max\{0, \overline{C}_j - C'_j\} = \overline{E}'_j.$$

so $\max\{\overline{E}'_i, \overline{E}'_i\} = \overline{E}'_i$. Because job i finishes later after the exchange, $\overline{E}'_i \leq \overline{E}_i$, which means that the exchange cannot increase the maximum virtual earliness for these two jobs.

The final point to be discussed concerns the existence of idle time in the SPT sequence. Consider any two adjacent jobs i and $i+1$. We know that $\overline{C}_i + p_{i+1} = \overline{C}_{i+1}$. Suppose there is some idle time t between these two jobs. Then we have $C_{i+1} = C_i + t + p_{i+1}$. The virtual earliness of job i is $\overline{E}_i = \max\{0, \overline{C}_i - C_i\}$, and the virtual earliness of job $i+1$ is $\overline{E}_{i+1} = \max\{0, \overline{C}_{i+1} - C_{i+1}\} = \max\{0, \overline{C}_i + p_{i+1} - C_i - t - p_{i+1}\} = \max\{0, \overline{C}_i - C_i - t\}$. Because $t \geq 0$, we have $\overline{E}_i \geq \overline{E}_{i+1}$. Therefore, no matter how much idle time exists before any job, the virtual earliness associated with job 1 is always the maximum. As a consequence, eliminating the idle time before any other job and thereby starting it earlier cannot increase $\overline{E}_{\max}$. Doing this, however, will reduce the total completion time. Thus idle time can only exist before job 1. ∎

Lemma 5.6 implies that $1|p_0 - \delta, post\text{-}mgt|\alpha \sum C_i + \beta \overline{E}_{\max}$ can be solved by using the original SPT sequence and simply deciding the start time of job 1. Specifically, we use the ORI-SPT schedule as the standard. Suppose an SPT sequence starts earlier than the ORI-SPT schedule by t units of time, where $0 \leq t \leq \delta$. Then the weighted total completion time of such a schedule is smaller by $nt\alpha$, and the weighted $\overline{T}_{\max}$ is larger by βt. Therefore, when $n\alpha \geq \beta$, starting earlier can reduce total costs so we should start the schedule as early as possible. This means that the LS-SPT schedule is optimal. When $n\alpha < \beta$, starting earlier is worse than keeping the original schedule. This leads to the following result.

Theorem 5.12 *For the problem* $1|p_0-\delta, post\text{-}mgt|\alpha \sum C_i+\beta \overline{E}_{\max}$, *when* $n\alpha \geq \beta$, *the LS-SPT schedule is optimal; when* $n\alpha < \beta$, *the ORI-SPT schedule is optimal.*

Noting that neither the LS-SPT schedule nor the ORI-SPT schedule has tardy jobs, we have

Corollary 5.2 *For the problem* $1|p_0-\delta, post\text{-}mgt|\alpha \sum C_i+\beta \overline{D}_{\max}$, *when* $n\alpha \geq \beta$, *the LS-SPT schedule is optimal; when* $n\alpha < \beta$, *the ORI-SPT schedule is optimal.*

5.4.3 Predictive management for machine disruption

Analogous to Lemma 5.1, when the disruption time of the machine is known and the objective is to minimize virtual tardiness, two SPT sequences provide the optimal solution. For the min-max objective, we can also identify the critical job.

Lemma 5.7 *For problem* $1|\Delta_m, pred\text{-}mgt|\alpha \sum C_i + \beta \overline{T}_{\max}$, *there exists an optimal schedule in which the jobs before* t_1 *and the jobs after* t_2 *form two SPT sequences. In addition, the maximum virtual tardiness is associated with the first job processed after* t_2.

Proof. The optimality of two SPT sequences follows from the same arguments used to prove Lemma 5.1 and so are omitted. Now consider the maximum virtual tardiness. Suppose job i followed by job j both start after t_2. The SPT sequence implies $i < j$ so $\overline{C}_i + p_j \leq \overline{C}_j$. In the discussion accompanying the TWO-SPT algorithm, we saw that both jobs are tardy, and that $\overline{T}_i = C_i - \overline{C}_i$ and $\overline{T}_j = C_j - \overline{C}_j = C_i + p_j - \overline{C}_j$. Straightforward substitution gives $\overline{T}_i - \overline{T}_j = \overline{C}_j - p_j - \overline{C}_i \geq 0$ so $\overline{T}_i \geq \overline{T}_j$. Similar reasoning for the other jobs is all that is needed to confirm that the first job after t_2 has the largest virtual tardiness. ∎

The dynamic programming algorithm TWO-SPT solves the problem $1|\Delta_m, pred\text{-}mgt|\alpha \sum C_i + \beta \sum \overline{T}_i$. With a slight modification, we can use the same approach to solve $1|\Delta_m, pred\text{-}mgt|\alpha \sum C_i + \beta \overline{T}_{\max}$ giving rise to what we call the M-TWO-SPT algorithm.

Again define (i, x) to be a state of the system for jobs $i = 1, \ldots, n$, where the total processing time for the jobs scheduled before t_1 is x. Let $f(i, x)$ be the minimum total cost with respect to (i, x). We know that job i must be either the last job before t_1 or the last job after t_2 among all jobs 1 to i. If job i is the last job before t_1, then its completion time is x and it is early. In this case we have $f(i, x) = f(i - 1, x - p_i) + \alpha x$. If job i is the last job after t_2, then its completion time is $t_2 + \sum_{j=1}^{i} p_j - x$ and it is tardy with virtual tardiness $\overline{T}_i = t_2 + \sum_{j=1}^{i} p_j - x - \overline{C}_i$. From Lemma 5.7, $\overline{T}_i$ will only contribute to the total cost if job i is the first job after t_2, which is equivalent to having $p_1 + \cdots + p_{i-1} = x$. This situation can be described by defining a function $f'(i, x)$ for $i > 1$ such that

$$f'(i, x) = \begin{cases} \beta(t_2 - x) & \text{if } p_1 + \cdots + p_{i-1} = x \\ 0 & \text{otherwise.} \end{cases}$$

The dynamic programming recursion for the M-TWO-SPT algorithm can be written as

$$f(i, x) = \min \begin{cases} f(i - 1, x - p_i) + \alpha x \\ f(i - 1, x) + \alpha(t_2 + \overline{C}_i - x) + f'(i, x) \end{cases}$$

for $2 \leq i \leq n$, and $0 \leq x \leq t_1$.

The boundary conditions are $f(i, x) = +\infty$ when either $0 < x < p_1$ or $x > \sum_{j=1}^{i} p_j$ for $i = 2, \ldots, n$, and the initial conditions for

$i = 1$ are $f(1,p_1) = \alpha p_1$, $f(1,0) = \alpha(t_2 + p_1) + \beta t_2$, $f(1,x) = +\infty$ for $x \notin \{0, p_1\}$. The optimal solution is given by the minimum value of $f(n,x)$ for $0 \leq x \leq t_1$. The computational complexity of the M-TWO-SPT algorithm is $O(nt_1)$, the same as for the TWO-SPT algorithm.

As in the mim-sum case, we can use the RS-SPT schedule as a heuristic to solve $1|\Delta_m, pred\text{-}mgt|\alpha \sum C_i + \beta \overline{E}_{\max}$. The worst case bound remains unchanged. Similarly, we can use the B-SPT heuristic to solve $1|\Delta_m, pred\text{-}mgt|\alpha \sum C_i + \beta \overline{D}_{\max}$.

5.4.4 Predictive management for job disruption

Consider the problem where maximum virtual tardiness is used in the objective function to measure the deviation cost due to a job disruption. Similar to Lemma 5.4, we have

Lemma 5.8 *For problem* $1|p_k \pm \delta, pred\text{-}mgt|\alpha \sum C_i + \beta \overline{T}_{\max}$, *there exists an optimal schedule in which job i precedes job j if $i < j$ and $i, j \neq k$.*

The implication of this result is that $1|p_k \pm \delta, pred\text{-}mgt|\alpha \sum C_i + \beta \overline{T}_{\max}$ can be solved by the INS-SPT algorithm. Implementation requires that job k be inserted at different positions in the original SPT sequence formed by the other jobs and the corresponding objective value calculated. The insertion position that yields the smallest objective value determines the optimal sequence. The analysis can be refined somewhat as was the case for $.1|p_k \pm \delta, pred\text{-}mgt|\alpha \sum C_i + \beta \sum T_i$ but the details are omitted.

Next consider the problem where the maximum virtual earliness is used as the deviation cost. Assume that job k is disrupted and that its processing time increases by δ. Similar to Theorem 5.9, we have

Theorem 5.13 *The problems* $1|p_k + \delta, pred\text{-}mgt|\alpha \sum C_i + \beta \overline{E}_{\max}$ *and* $1|p_k + \delta, pred\text{-}mgt|\alpha \sum C_i + \beta \overline{D}_{\max}$ *can be solved by the INS-SPT algorithm.*

The proof parallels those given for Theorem 5.9 and Lemma 5.6, and hence is omitted. Now assume that the processing time of job j decreases by δ. When $\alpha \geq \beta$, arguments similar to those used in the proofs of Theorem 5.7 and Lemma 5.6 lead to the following result.

Theorem 5.14 *When $\alpha \geq \beta$, problems $1|p_k - \delta, pred\text{-}mgt|\alpha \sum C_i + \beta \overline{E}_{\max}$ and $1|p_k - \delta, pred\text{-}mgt|\alpha \sum C_i + \beta \overline{D}_{\max}$ can be solved with the INS-SPT algorithm.*

When $n\alpha \leq \beta$, we have

Theorem 5.15 *When $n\alpha \leq \beta$, the ORI-RS-SPT schedule is optimal for the problem $1|p_k - \delta, pred\text{-}mgt|\alpha \sum C_i + \beta \overline{E}_{\max}$.*

Proof. We first prove that an optimal schedule cannot have any virtual earliness. Suppose there is an optimal schedule that has at least one early job. Right shifting this schedule by a small amount t causes the total weighted completion time to increase by $n\alpha t$ and the weighted maximum virtual earliness to decrease by βt. When $n\alpha \leq \beta$, the objective function will decrease as a result of the right shift. Thus an optimal schedule cannot have any virtual earliness.

It is easy to see that among all schedules that have no virtual earliness, the ORI-RS-SPT schedule has the smallest total completion time. Therefore, the ORI-RS-SPT schedule is optimal for $1|p_k - \delta, pred\text{-}mgt|\alpha \sum C_i + \beta \overline{E}_{\max}$. ∎

Because the ORI-RS-SPT schedule has no virtual tardiness, we have

Corollary 5.3 *When $n\alpha \leq \beta$, the ORI-RS-SPT schedule is optimal for the problem $1|p_k - \delta, pred\text{-}mgt|\alpha \sum C_i + \beta \overline{D}_{\max}$.*

It is still an open question whether the two problems $1|p_k - \delta, pred\text{-}mgt|\alpha \sum C_i + \beta \overline{E}_{\max}$ and $1|p_k - \delta, pred\text{-}mgt|\alpha \sum C_i + \beta \overline{D}_{\max}$ are solvable in polynomial time when $\beta < n\alpha < n\beta$.

Comparing the results, it is interesting to see that in most cases, the solution algorithms for the min-sum problems are the same or at least similar to those for the corresponding min-max problems. For the more classical models, a min-sum problem and its min-max counterpart usually have different solutions. For example, minimizing total tardiness on a single machine is NP-hard, while minimizing the maximum tardiness can be solved by the EDD rule in polynomial time. In our scheduling disruption management model, however, the virtual due dates are closely correlated with processing times. As a result, the min-sum problems and the min-max problems often have the same solution. We have not observed such a property in other scheduling problems.

5.5 Extensions to Parallel Machines

In this section, we discuss how the results for a single machine can be extended to multiple parallel machines. For simplicity, we only investigate the 2-machine case but all results can be generalized to m machines without difficulty for any fixed m. In the analysis, it is assumed that only one machine or one job experiences a disruption at a time.

It is known that the problem of minimizing the sum of completion times on two parallel machines, denoted by $P2||\sum C_i$, can be solved by the SPT rule (Baker 1974). In the case of a single machine, the SPT schedule is unique unless there are jobs with identical processing time. In the case of parallel machines, however, there are many optimal SPT schedules even if all processing times differ. To avoid any ambiguity, we specify the original SPT schedule to be the alternate SPT schedule in which the jobs are sequenced alternately on the two machines, i.e., jobs $1, 3, 5, \ldots$, are sequentially processed on machine 1 without any idle time, and jobs $2, 4, 6, \ldots$, are sequentially processed on machine 2 without idle time.

Lemma 5.9 *Consider the original SPT schedule for the problem* $P2||\sum C_i$. *For any two jobs i and j, $i < j$, we have $\overline{C}_j - \overline{C}_i \geq p_j - p_i$.*

Proof. Note that in the SPT schedule, jobs are scheduled sequentially from job 1 to job n. Therefore, when $i < j$, job i should start no later than job j, i.e., $\overline{C}_i - p_i \leq \overline{C}_j - p_j$, thus the lemma follows. ∎

5.5.1 *Post-disruption management for machine disruption*

In the corresponding single machine case, disruption management cannot start until the disruption ends. In the case of multiple machines, however, when one machine goes down the other is still available by assumption. Therefore, we can start the disruption management as soon as the current job on the available machine finishes processing. As a consequence, the problem of how to reset the time index to 0 and re-index uncompleted jobs is now more complex than for the case of a single machine. We show that our disruption management problem can be generally modeled as "parallel machine scheduling with nonsimultaneous machine available time" (Lee 1991). In such a model with $m = 2$, one machine is available at time 0 and the other is not available until some time $\delta \geq 0$.

Without loss of generality, assume that the disruption occurs on machine 2 at time t_1 and ends at time t_2. Suppose job k is being processed on machine 2 when the disruption occurs, i.e., $\overline{C}_k - p_k \leq t_1 < \overline{C}_k$. Note that this includes the case where the disruption occurs exactly at the time when job k starts. From the construction of the original SPT schedule, at time t_1 machine 1 must be processing either job $k-1$ or $k+1$. Similarly, this includes the case where one of them starts exactly at t_1. There are three cases.

Case 1. Job $k-1$ is being processed on machine 1 when the disruption occurs and it is completed no later than the disruption ends, $\overline{C}_{k-1} \leq t_2$. In this case, we reset time $\overline{C}_{k-1}$ to be the new time 0, which means that machine 1 is available at time 0 and machine 2 is not available until $\delta = t_2 - \overline{C}_{k-1}$. We re-index job k to be job 1, job $k+1$ to be job 2, and so on.

Case 2. Job $k+1$ is being processed on machine 1 when the disruption occurs and it is completed no later than the disruption ends, $\overline{C}_{k+1} \leq t_2$. Similarly, we reset time $\overline{C}_{k+1}$ to be the new time 0, which means that machine 1 is available at time 0 and machine 2 is not available until $\delta = t_2 - \overline{C}_{k+1}$. We re-index job k to be job 1, job $k+2$ to be job 2, job $k+3$ to be job 3, and so on.

Case 3. The disruption ends earlier than the current job (either job $k-1$ or $k+1$) on machine 1 is completed. In this case, we reset t_2

to be the new time 0, which means that machine 2 is available at time 0 and machine 1 is not available (for rescheduling) until $\delta = \overline{C}_{k-1} - t_2$ or $\overline{C}_{k+1} - t_2$. We re-index job k to be job 1. If job $k-1$ is being processed on machine 1, we re-index job $k+1$ to be job 2, and so on. If job $k+1$ is being processed on machine 1, we re-index job $k+2$ to be job 2, and so on.

With this re-indexing scheme, post-disruption management for machine disruption can always be modeled as a parallel machine scheduling problem with nonsimultaneous available time. Note that in all three cases, Lemma 5.9 still holds in terms of the new time 0 and the new job indices because the jobs are still indexed in the original SPT order.

We now discuss how to solve the parallel machine problem with nonsimultaneous available time. The problem at issue is denoted by $P2|\Delta_m, post\text{-}mgt|c$ for general objective function c.

Lemma 5.10 *For problem $P2|\Delta_m, post\text{-}mgt|\alpha\sum C_i + \beta\sum \overline{T}_i$, there exists an optimal schedule in which job n has the latest start time.*

Proof. Because job n has the longest processing time and the largest virtual due date, it must be the last job on the machine to which it was assigned. If all jobs are scheduled on the same machine, the lemma is proved. Otherwise, suppose the last job on the other machine is job k, $k < n$. Let t_1 be the start time of job n, and t_2 be the start time of job k. If the lemma does not hold, we should have $t_1 < t_2$. Now we exchange jobs n and k. Such an exchange makes job k starting earlier by $t_2 - t_1$ and job n later by $t_2 - t_1$. The total completion time, however, does not change.

If job k is tardy after the exchange, then it is also tardy before the exchange, so its virtual tardiness is reduced by $t_2 - t_1$. At the same time, the virtual tardiness of job n can increase by at most $t_2 - t_1$. Thus total cost cannot increase due to the exchange.

If job k is early after the exchange, i.e., $t_1 + p_k \leq \overline{C}_k$, then the total virtual tardiness of the two jobs k and n after the exchange depends on job n, i.e.,

$$\overline{T}'_k + \overline{T}'_n = \overline{T}'_n = \max\{0, t_2 + p_n - \overline{C}_n\}.$$

Consider job n. Before the exchange, its virtual tardiness is $\overline{T}_n = \max\{0, t_1 + p_n - \overline{C}_n\}$. Using Lemma 5.9, we have

$$\overline{T}_n = \max\{0, t_1 + p_n - \overline{C}_n\} \leq \max\{0, t_1 + p_k - \overline{C}_k\} = 0,$$

implying that job n was early before the exchange. Therefore, total virtual tardiness of the two jobs k and n before the exchange depends on job k, i.e.,

$$\overline{T}_k + \overline{T}_n = \overline{T}_k = \max\{0, t_2 + p_k - \overline{C}_k\}.$$

From Lemma 5.9, we have $p_n - \overline{C}_n \leq p_k - \overline{C}_k$. Therefore,

$$\overline{T}'_k + \overline{T}'_n \leq \overline{T}_k + \overline{T}_n,$$

which means that the exchange cannot increase total virtual tardiness, and thus total cost. ∎

From Lemma 5.10, problem $P2|\Delta_m, post\text{-}mgt|\alpha \sum C_i + \beta \sum \overline{T}_i$ can be decomposed into a problem of scheduling the first $n-1$ jobs, and then putting job n at the earliest possible time when any one of the machines becomes available. Similarly, the problem with the first $n-1$ jobs can be further decomposed into a problem with the first $n-2$ jobs and scheduling job $n-1$, and so on. Therefore, the overall problem can be solved by scheduling jobs sequentially from 1 to n. In particular, each job is started at the earliest possible time when either of the machines becomes available. As a consequence, the jobs are first scheduled only on the non-disrupted machine; when the other machine becomes available the remaining jobs are scheduled alternately on the two machines. We call this the ALT-SPT algorithm.

Because no job is early when the ALT-SPT algorithm is applied, the resultant schedule must also be optimal when either total virtual earliness or total virtual absolute deviation is used as the deviation cost. Thus we have the following result.

Theorem 5.16 *The ALT-SPT algorithm optimally solves the problems $P2|\Delta_m, post\text{-}mgt|\alpha \sum C_i + \beta \sum \overline{T}_i$, $P2|\Delta_m, post\text{-}mgt|\alpha \sum C_i + \beta \sum \overline{E}_i$ and $P2|\Delta_m, post\text{-}mgt|\alpha \sum C_i + \beta \sum \overline{D}_i$.*

5.5.2 Post-disruption management for job disruption

As in the case of a single machine, we only need to examine what happens when the processing time decreases for a specific job. When the processing time increases, the situation can be viewed as a machine disruption. Suppose job k on machine 1 is disrupted and so finishes at $\overline{C}_k - \delta$ rather than $\overline{C}_k$. Using the same arguments as in Section 5.5.1, it can be shown that the problem here is analogous to the parallel machine scheduling problem with nonsimultaneous available time. We simply reset time 0 to $\overline{C}_k - \delta$ and re-index uncompleted jobs as above. Machine 1 is now available at time 0 and machine 2 is not available until its current job is completed. The problem is denoted by $P2|p_0 - \delta, post\text{-}mgt|c$.

Note that in this case, Lemma 5.10 still holds, which means that $P2|p_0 - \delta, post\text{-}mgt|\alpha \sum C_i + \beta \sum \overline{T}_i$ can be solved by the ALT-SPT algorithm. Interestingly, no job is tardy in the schedule obtained from this algorithm.

Theorem 5.17 *The ALT-SPT algorithm provides an optimal solution to the problem $P2|p_0 - \delta, post\text{-}mgt|\alpha \sum C_i + \beta \sum \overline{T}_i$.*

When virtual earliness is used as the deviation cost, two cases have to be considered, $\alpha \geq \beta$ and $\alpha < \beta$.

Theorem 5.18 *When $\alpha \geq \beta$, problem $P2|p_0 - \delta, post\text{-}mgt|\alpha \sum C_i + \beta \sum \overline{E}_i$ can be solved by the ALT-SPT algorithm.*

We simply outline the main idea of proving this theorem. Using the same argument as in the proof of Theorem 5.4, it can be shown that in an optimal schedule, the jobs on each machine should be sequenced in SPT order without any idle time. To make the ALT-SPT algorithm work, we need to show that in an optimal schedule, job n must have the latest start time among all jobs – the same result as Lemma 5.10, and a similar approach can be used.

Consider the problem where virtual absolute deviation is used as the deviation cost. Because there are no tardy jobs in the scheduled produced by the ALT-SPT algorithm, Theorem 5.18 implies the following.

Corollary 5.4 *When $\alpha \geq \beta$, the problem $P2|p_0 - \delta, post\text{-}mgt|\alpha \sum C_i + \beta \sum \overline{D}_i$ can be solved by the ALT-SPT algorithm.*

When $\alpha < \beta$, we define the ORI-SPT schedule such that all uncompleted jobs start and end at their original time, as we did in the single machine case. Using the same argument, we have

Theorem 5.19 *When $\alpha < \beta$, the ORI-SPT schedule is optimal for the problems $P2|p_0-\delta, post\text{-}mgt|\alpha \sum C_i + \beta \sum \overline{E}_i$ and $P2|p_0-\delta, post\text{-}mgt|\alpha \sum C_i + \beta \sum \overline{D}_i$.*

5.5.3 Predictive management for machine disruption

Suppose that at t_0, it is known that machine 1 will be disrupted at some specific future point in time. When the first of the two current jobs is completed, we can reset the time index to 0 and re-index the remaining jobs. Once again, we get a parallel machine scheduling problem with nonsimultaneous available time. In this case, the problem is denoted by $P2|\Delta_m, pred\text{-}mgt|c$ and can be generally described as follows. Suppose machine 1 is available from δ_1 onward, machine 2 from δ_2 onward, and either δ_1 or δ_2 (or both) is 0. Also assume machine 1 is unavailable between t_1 and t_2, where $\delta_1 < t_1 < t_2$.

First, we have

Lemma 5.11 *For problem $P2|\Delta_m, pred\text{-}mgt|\alpha \sum C_i + \beta \sum \overline{T}_i$, there exists an optimal schedule such that on machine 1, jobs before t_1 and jobs after t_2 form two SPT sequences, and jobs on machine 2 form one SPT sequence.*

Using Lemma 5.11, we can develop a dynamic program to solve the machine disruption problem. Define the triple (i, x, y) as a state associated with jobs 1 to i, where the total processing time for jobs before t_1 is x and the total processing time after t_2 is y. Let $f(i, x, y)$ be the minimum total cost for the state (i, x, y). According to Lemma 5.11, there are three possibilities for job i; namely, it can be the last job before t_1, the last job after t_2, or the last job on machine 2.

If job i is the last job before t_1, its completion time is $\delta_1 + x$ and its virtual tardiness is $\max\{0, \delta_1 + x - \overline{C}_i\}$. We denote this case as $f^1(i, x, y) = f(i-1, x-p_i, y) + \alpha(\delta_1 + x) + \beta \max\{0, \delta_1 + x - \overline{C}_i\}$.

If job i is the last job after t_2, its completion time is $t_2 + y$ and its virtual tardiness is $\max\{0, t_2 + y - \overline{C}_i\}$. This case is denoted as $f^2(i, x, y) = f(i-1, x, y-p_i) + \alpha(t_2 + y) + \beta \max\{0, t_2 + y - \overline{C}_i\}$.

If job i is the last job on machine 2, its completion time is $\delta_2 + \sum_{j=1}^{i} p_j - x - y$, and its virtual tardiness is $\max\{0, \delta_2 + \sum_{j=1}^{i} p_j - x - y - \overline{C}_i\}$. Similarly, we denote it as $f^3(i, x, y) = f(i-1, x, y) + \alpha(\delta_2 + \sum_{j=1}^{i} p_j - x - y) + \beta \max\{0, \delta_2 + \sum_{j=1}^{i} p_j - x - y - \overline{C}_i\}$.

Considering all three possibilities, we have the following dynamic programming recursion.

$$f(i, x, y) = \min\left\{f^1(i, x, y), f^2(i, x, y), f^3(i, x, y)\right\}.$$

for $i \in \{2, \ldots, n\}$, $x \in \{0, \ldots, t_1\}$, $y = \{0, \ldots, \sum_{j=1}^{i} p_j\}$.

The boundary conditions are $f(i, x, y) = +\infty$ when either $0 < x, y < p_1$, or $x + y > \sum_{j=1}^{i} p_j$. The initial conditions for $i = 1$ are $f(1, 0, 0) = \alpha(\delta_2 + p_1) + \beta \max\{0, \delta_2 + p_1 - \overline{C}_1\}$, $f(1, p_1, 0) = \alpha(\delta_1 + p_1) + \beta \max\{0, \delta_1 + p_1 - \overline{C}_1\}$, $f(1, 0, p_1) = \alpha(t_2 + p_1) + \beta \max\{0, t_2 + p_1 - \overline{C}_1\}$, and otherwise $f(1, x, y) = +\infty$. The optimal solution is given by the minimum value of $f(n, x, y)$ for all x and y. Noting that there are n possibilities for i, $O(t_1)$ possibilities for x, and $O(\sum_{j=1}^{n} p_j)$ possibilities of y, the computational complexity of the recursion is $O(nt_1 \sum_{j=1}^{n} p_j)$. We call the overall approach the THREE-SPT algorithm since it contains three SPT sequences.

Parallel to Lemma 5.2, and using the same analysis developed in the proof of Theorem 5.18, we have

Lemma 5.12 *For problems $P2|\Delta_m, pred\text{-}mgt|\alpha \sum C_i + \beta \sum \overline{E}_i$ and $P2|\Delta_m, pred\text{-}mgt|\alpha \sum C_i + \beta \sum \overline{D}_i$, when $\alpha \geq \beta$, there exists an optimal schedule in which there is no idle time immediately before any job, on machine 1 jobs before t_1 and jobs after t_2 form two SPT sequences, and jobs on machine 2 form one SPT sequence.*

As a consequence, when $\alpha \geq \beta$, problems $P2|\Delta_m, pred\text{-}mgt|\alpha \sum C_i + \beta \sum \overline{E}_i$ and $P2|\Delta_m, pred\text{-}mgt|\alpha \sum C_i + \beta \sum \overline{D}_i$ can be solved by a dynamic program similar to the THREE-SPT algorithm. The details are omitted. When $\alpha < \beta$, the ALT-SPT algorithm can be used as a heuristic.

5.5.4 Predictive management for job disruption

When it is possible to predict a job disruption, the same re-indexing scheme and analysis that was used in the preceding subsection for machine disruption can be used here. Generally speaking, suppose that machine 1 is available from δ_1 onward, machine 2 from δ_2 onward, and either δ_1 or δ_2 (or both) is 0. Now assume that the processing time of job k changes from p_k to $p_k \pm \delta$. In the case of a single machine, most problems can be solved by the INS-SPT algorithm. For parallel machines, we again use the idea of exhaustively inserting the disrupted job into the different positions in the SPT sequence associated with the remaining $n - 1$ jobs. The parallel INS-SPT (P-INS-SPT(i)) algorithm takes a parameter i, $i \in \{0, 1, \ldots, k - 1, k + 1, \ldots, n\}$, and is implemented as follows.

Algorithm P-INS-SPT(i): Consider jobs $\{1, \ldots, k - 1, k + 1, \ldots, n\}$. Starting with job 1, sequentially assign each job to the first machine that becomes available. Schedule job k immediately after job i on the same machine. In particular, when $i = 0$, we schedule job k before job 1.

We can run the P-INS-SPT(i) algorithm n times and select the best solution. This may be applied to different deviation measurements as a heuristic algorithm, though the optimality of the solution and the complexity of the problem are open.

5.6 Literature Review

In the literature of machine scheduling, the problem studied in this chapter can be viewed within the category of machine scheduling with availability constraint where the unavailability can be a machine breakdown or maintenance, or lack of available machines due to disruptions. Related literature include Glazebrook (1987), Birge and Glazebrook (1988), Adiri *et al.* (1989), Birge *et al.* (1990), Frostig (1991), Lee (1996,1997,2004), Graves and Lee (1999), Qi *et al.* (1999), Lee and Chen (2000), Schmidt (2000), and Lee and Lin (2001). However, these models only address the scheduling problem subject to machine unavailability, a different situation from disruption management.

Aytug *et al.* (2001) presented an extensive survey for rescheduling and executing production schedules while facing uncertainties. The literature on rescheduling with deviation costs is relatively sparse when compared to the large body of published work on the more traditional forms of machine scheduling. Bean *et al.* (1991) were among the first to recognize the importance of deviation costs by proposing the concept of the match-up schedule where the goal is to develop a new schedule that matches the original after a certain point in time. Building on this idea, Akturk and Gorgulu (1999) studied the match-up problem in a modified flow shop environment.

When the goal is to minimize deviation costs, a common approach is to prescribe an earliness or tardiness penalty based on the difference of job completion times in the original and revised schedules, but the work is rather ad-hoc in the literature, for example, Abumaizar and Svestka (1997) and Wu *et al.*(1993).

More retails of this chapter can be found in Qi *et al.*(2002). In the next chapter of the book, we introduce a closely related model, disruption management for logistics scheduling.

References

Abumaizar, R.J. and J.A. Svestka (1997), Rescheduling job shops under random disruptions, *International Journal of Production Research*, 35, 2065-2082.

Adiri, I., J. Bruno, E. Frostig and A.H.G. Rinnooy Kan (1989), Single machine flow-time scheduling with a single breakdown, *Acta Informatica*, 26, 679-696.

Akturk, M.S. and E. Gorgulu (1999), Match-up scheduling under a machine breakdown, *European Journal of Operational Research*, 112, 81-97.

Aytug, H., M.A. Lawley, K. McKay, S. Mohan and R. Uzsoy (2001), Executing production schedules in the face of uncertainties: A review and some future directions, *European Journal of Operational Research*, in press.

Baker, K.R. (1974), *Introduction to Sequencing and Scheduling*, John Wiley & Sons, New York.

Bean, J., J.R. Birge, J. Mittenthal and C.E. Noon (1991), Matchup scheduling with multiple resources, release dates and disruptions, *Operations Research*, 39, 470-483.

Birge, J. and K.D. Glazebrook (1988), Assessing the effects of machine breakdowns in stochastic scheduling, *Operations Research Letters*, 7, 267-271.

Birge, J., J.B.G. Frenk, J. Mittenthal and A.H.G. Rinnooy Kan (1990), Single-machine scheduling subject to stochastic breakdowns, *Naval Research Logistics*, 37, 661-677.

Frostig, E. (1991), A note on stochastic scheduling on a single machine scheduling subject to breakdown - The preemptive repeat model, *Probability in the Engineering and Informational Sciences*, 5, 349-354.

Glazebrook, K.D. (1987), Evaluating the effects of machine breakdowns in stochastic scheduling problems, *Naval Research Logistics*, 34, 319-335.

Graves, G.H. and C.-Y. Lee (1999), Scheduling maintenance and semiresumable jobs on a single machine, *Naval Research Logistics*, 46, 845-863.

Lee, C.-Y. (1996), Machine scheduling with an availability constraint, *Journal of Global Optimization*, 9, 395-416.

Lee, C.-Y. (1997), Minimizing the makespan in the two-machine flowshop scheduling problem with an availability constraint, *Operations Research letters*, 20, 129-139.

Lee, C.-Y. (2004), Machine scheduling with availability constraints, in *Handbook of Scheduling*, Editor: J. Leung, CRC Press, in press.

Lee, C.-Y. and S.D. Liman (1992), Single-machine flow-time scheduling with scheduled maintenance, *Acta Informatica*, 29, 375-382.

Lee, C.-Y. and Z.L. Chen (2000), Scheduling of jobs and maintenance activities on parallel machines, *Naval Research Logistics*, 47, 145-165.

Lee, C.-Y. and C.-S. Lin (2001), Machine scheduling with maintenance and repair rate-modifying activities, *European Journal of Operational Research*, 135, 491-513.

Qi, X., T. Chen and F. Tu (1999), Scheduling the maintenance on a single machine, *Journal of the Operational Research Society*, 50, 1071-1078.

Qi, X., J.F. Bard and G. Yu (2002), Disruption management for machine scheduling, working paper.

Schmidt, G. (2000), Scheduling with limited machine availability, *European Journal of Operational Research*, 121(1), 1-15.

Wu, S.-D., R.H. Storeer and P.C. Chang (1993), On machine rescheduling heuristics with efficiency and stability as criteria, *Computer & Operations Research*, 20, 1-14.

Chapter 6

Disruption Management for Logistics Scheduling

6.1 Introduction

This chapter studies the problem of logistics scheduling and management under disruptions. Different from conventional machine scheduling models, logistics scheduling not only addresses the problem of job sequencing on a machine or in a facility, but also job transportation and delivery between different machines or facilities. Throughout this chapter, we use the terms of machine and facility in an interchangeable way. In the logistics scheduling problem with disruptions, some jobs assigned to disrupted facilities may have to be transferred to other available facilities and, hence, will involve transportation time and cost. In other words, the deviation costs in the new schedule not only includes the job completion time changes as in the disruption management for machine scheduling, but also the job transportation cost. This brings up research issues on new algorithms and approaches.

Specifically, suppose we have several parallel machines all available from time 0. A set of jobs, each to be processed on one of the machines, have been scheduled according to certain criteria. During the process of carrying out the schedule, a disruption occurs to the machines. This disruption can be a disaster like 9/11, a typhoon where all facilities are unavailable for a period of time in a particular region, or a particular machine breakdown. Our goal is to re-allocate jobs to machines and reschedule jobs on each machine such that the impact of the disruption is minimized in addition to consideration of the original performance criteria.

Like any disruption management models, we have to quantify the impact of a disruption by deviation costs. Deviation costs in logistics scheduling come from two sources. In the first case, referred to as the transportation cost, we need to consider job transportation between different machines. For example, when a job that is originally scheduled on machine 1 has to be moved to machine 2 for processing, a transportation cost may be incurred such as the cost of using a truck. Moreover, if the machines are not in the same place, such a movement may take certain time, which also has to be considered as it affects the earliest available time of the transported job on the new machine. There may be several different transportation modes, such as trucks or containers, ordinary versus expedited delivery, each with a different transportation time and cost, where the trade-off is that a fast transportation mode has a high cost. We may also need to consider the capacity of transportation, for instance, the number of jobs that can be put in a truck, and the number of available trucks.

In the second case, referred to as the job completion deviation, the original schedule has determined a projected completion time for each job, which may have been committed to customers and thus should be observed in the new schedule. Specifically, we need to regard the projected completion time as a virtual due date, and try to minimize the lateness subject to the due date. This is the same concern as in the machine scheduling with disruptions.

The rest of this chapter is organized as follows. We introduce notation and describe the problem in Section 6.2. In Section 6.3, we study problems in which deviation costs are related to job transportation issues. Section 6.4 discusses problems with objective functions containing only job completion time deviation costs. Section 6.5 studies problems with objective functions represented as weighted sum of deviation costs and the original objective. In the last section, a brief literature review is presented.

6.2 Problem Description

As discussed in the disruption management for machine scheduling, we can always assume that a disruption occurs at time 0. We also assume at any time there is only one machine being disrupted and the disrupted machine is machine 1. In addition, we only allow jobs from machine 1 to move to other machines to reduce the impact of the disruption on the whole system. This is consistent with the common practice to handle a disruption locally rather than a whole-system-wide reschedule. We notice that there may exist a better solution if all jobs are free to move among all machines, at least mathematically, but the impact of a complete reschedule on the entire system is often difficult to model and the cost is hard to estimate in practice.

The following notation will be used to describe our problems.

m: number of parallel machines

n_j: number of jobs assigned to machine j in the original schedule

J_{ji}: the i-th job on machine j

J_i: the i-th job if there is only one available machine

p_{ji} or p_i: processing time of job J_{ji} or J_i

w_{ji} or w_i: weight of job J_{ji} or J_i

$S_j = \{J_{ji} | i = 1, \ldots, n_j\}$: set of jobs assigned to machine j in the original schedule

P_j: sum of processing times of jobs in S_j

D: the time that disruption ends. Since we assume that the disruption starts at time 0, D is also referred to as disruption time

q: number of available transportation modes

t_j^k: transportation time of shipping jobs from machine 1 to machine j via transportation mode k

K_j^k: unit transportation cost of shipping jobs from machine 1 to machine j via transportation mode k

TC: total transportation cost

For a problem with only one transportation mode available, we drop the superscript k and simply use t_j to denote the transportation time from machine 1 to machine j. Furthermore, for a two-machine problem, the only possible transshipment is from machine 1 to machine 2 if there is only one transportation mode available. So we drop the subscript j and let t denote the transportation time.

We illustrate the general problem by the following example. Suppose that there is a set of $\{n_1, \ldots, n_m\}$ jobs to be processed by m machines, where n_j jobs are assigned to machine j. The original allocation and schedule of jobs on the machines follows a certain decision criteria, and raw material and required machine tools have been allocated to the specified machines. Hence, for each job J_{ji} on machine j with processing time p_{ji}, there is a corresponding planned completion time C_{ji}.

When the schedule is being executed, suppose a disruption unexpectedly happens. As a result, some machines will not be available for certain time periods. Without loss of generality, we assume the disruption occurs at time 0. Those jobs that are assigned to the disrupted machine, say machine 1, and have not yet been processed can either be processed by other available machines or be processed by the same machine after the end of the disruption. For the former case, certain transportation time and cost are incurred when the jobs are moved to other machines.

Regarding the job transportation, there are q transportation modes available for transporting jobs from one machine to another, each mode with a given corresponding transportation time and cost for transshipping a job. Job transportation may also be subject to vehicle capacity constraints where each time there is a maximum number of jobs that can be transferred as a batch.

Our purpose is to reschedule jobs, and select transportation modes when applicable, so that an objective function, including the original cost function, the possible transportation cost and the disruption cost caused by deviating the completion time from that of the originally planned, is minimized.

The problem can be defined by the standard scheduling three-field conventions. Under this convention, the disruption lasting time, vehicle capacity, and available transportation modes are placed in the middle field. In particular, D indicates the disruption time for the disrupted machine, where $D = \infty$ means the machine becomes unavailable forever; t_j^k represents that there are multiple transportation modes from machine 1 to machine j and each mode has a different transportation time t_j^k, where we use $t_j^k = 0$ to denote the case of negligible transportation time; correspondingly, we use K_j^k to denote the unit transportation cost for moving a single job; when transportation capacity is considered, we used the notation b to denote the capacity for each batch of transportation such as the capacity of a truck.

For example, the notation $P2|D,t^k,K^k|\sum C_i + TC$ describes a problem with two parallel machines where the disruption time is D, the transportation time from machine 1 to machine 2 via transportation mode k is t^k, and it costs K^k for transshipping one job from machine 1 to machine 2 via transportation mode k. Our purpose is to schedule jobs and possible transshipment such that the sum of the total completion time and transportation cost is minimized.

6.3 Minimizing Total Completion Time and Transportation Cost

In this section, we focus on the transportation cost for moving a job from the disrupted machine to other machines. We will discuss two cases, different transportation modes with given limited transportation times, and a zero transportation time.

6.3.1 Problem $P2|D = \infty, t^k, K^k|\sum C_i + TC$

In this problem, there are two machines where machine 1 becomes unavailable forever, so all jobs have to be processed on machine 2. There are different transportation modes for moving jobs from machine 1 to machine 2. We need to determine a particular mode for moving each job that is originally assigned to machine 1, and a new schedule for all jobs on machine 2. The problem is computational intractable as stated by the following theorem.

Theorem 6.1 *The problem $P2|D = \infty, t^k, K^k|\sum C_i + TC$ with only one available transportation mode is NP-hard.*

The following lemma gives a property of an optimal schedule for the problem, and can be used to develop a dynamic programming algorithm.

Lemma 6.1 *For $P2|D = \infty, t^k, K^k| \sum C_i + TC$ with only one available transportation mode, there exists an optimal solution such that for some time epoch r,*
1) before r all jobs are from S_2 and follow SPT order, and
2) after r, those jobs from S_1 are following SPT order and those jobs from S_2 are also following SPT order.

This lemma can be proved by a standard job pairwise exchange.

Now we provide a dynamic programming algorithm in pseudo-polynomial time to solve the general problem $P2|D = \infty, t^k, K^k| \sum C_i + TC$. We assume that there are q available transportation modes to ship jobs from machine 1 to machine 2. Note that we demonstrate the solution procedure by solving the problem for $q = 2$, but it can be easily extended to the problem with more than two transportation modes.

Recall that we let t^k, $k = 1, 2$, to denote the transportation time if the transshipment is via mode k, and let K^k be the transportation cost of using mode k for transporting a job. Without loss of generality, we assume that $t^1 < t^2$ and $K^1 > K^2$. For a group of m jobs moved via mode k, the total cost is mK^k and all these m jobs will arrive at the same time t^k.

Assume that jobs are indexed in non-decreasing order of processing times on each machine. Let $P_{1i} = p_{11} + \cdots + p_{1i}$ for $i = 1, \ldots, n_1$ and $P_{2j} = p_{21} + \ldots + p_{2j}$ for $j = 1, \ldots, n_2$.

Dynamic Program 1:

Define $(i, j, r_1, r_2, s_1, s_2)$ as the state in which (1) we have scheduled i jobs from S_1 and j jobs from S_2; (2) jobs processed before r_1 are all from S_2 with total processing time s_1; (3) jobs processed between r_1 and r_2 are either from S_2 or from S_1 transported via mode 1 and with total processing time s_2; and (4) jobs processed after r_2 are either from S_2 or from S_1 transported via mode 2, where $r_1 \geq t^1$ and $r_2 \geq t^2$. Let $f(i, j, r_1, r_2, s_1, s_2)$ be the minimum total completion time plus transportation cost for the state.

Initial Condition. For $r_1 = t^1, t^1 + 1, \ldots, t^1 + \max\{p_{2j}\}$, $r_2 = \max\{r_1, t^2\}, \ldots, t^2 + \max\{p_{2j}\}$, we have

$$f(1,0,r_1,r_2,s_1,s_2) = \begin{cases} r_1 + p_{11} + K^1 & \text{if } s_1 = 0 \text{ and } s_2 = p_{11} \\ r_2 + p_{11} + K^2 & \text{if } s_1 = 0 \text{ and } s_2 = 0 \\ \infty & \text{otherwise,} \end{cases}$$

and

$$f(0,1,r_1,r_2,s_1,s_2) = \begin{cases} p_{21} & \text{if } s_1 = p_{21} \text{ and } s_2 = 0 \\ r_1 + p_{21} & \text{if } s_1 = 0 \text{ and } s_2 = p_{21} \\ r_2 + p_{21} & \text{if } s_1 = 0 \text{ and } s_2 = 0 \\ \infty & \text{otherwise.} \end{cases}$$

The dynamic programming recursive equation is given by

$$\begin{aligned} & f(i,j,r_1,r_2,s_1,s_2) \\ & = \min \begin{cases} f(i-1,j,r_1,r_2,s_1,s_2-p_{1i}) + (r_1+s_2) + K^1 \\ f(i-1,j,r_1,r_2,s_1,s_2) + (P_{1i}+P_{2j}-s_1-s_2+r_2) + K^2 \\ f(i,j-1,r_1,r_2,s_1-P_{2j}) + s_1 \\ f(i,j-1,r_1,r_2,s_1,s_2-p_{2j}) + r_1 + s_2 \\ f(i,j-1,r_1,r_2,s_1,s_2) + (P_{1i}+P_{2j}-s_1-s_2+r_2). \end{cases} \end{aligned}$$

In the equation, the first two terms correspond to the cases where the last assigned job is J_{1i} via transportation mode 1 and mode 2, respectively. The last three terms correspond to the cases in which the last assigned job is J_{2j} and is scheduled before r_1, between r_1 and r_2, and after r_2, respectively.

The optimal solution can be found from the state corresponding to $\min\{f(n_1,n_2,r_1,r_2,s_1,s_2)\}$ for $r_1 = t_1, t_1+1, \ldots, t_1 + \max\{p_{2j}\}$, $r_2 = \max\{r_1,t_2\}, \ldots, t_2 + \max\{p_{2j}\}$, $s_1 = 0, 1, \ldots, r_1$, and $s_2 = 0, 1, \ldots, r_2 - r_1$.

In the above dynamic program, the number of states is in $O(n^2T^4)$, and it takes a constant time to process each state, where T is the total processing time for all jobs. So the total time complexity of the dynamic program is in $O(n^2T^4)$. The algorithm can be extended to more general cases with q available transportation modes, and runs in $O(n^2T^{2q})$. The time complexity of pseudopolynomial time also shows that Problem $P2|D = \infty, t^k, K^k|\sum C_i$ is NP-hard in the ordinary sense.

6.3.2 Problem $Pm|D, t_j = 0, b| \sum w_i C_i + TC$

Next we consider a problem with m parallel identical machines in which machine 1 becomes unavailable from time 0 to a finite time D. For each job in S_1 we will either keep it on machine 1 or ship and insert it to other machines with the objective of minimizing $\sum w_i C_i + TC$.

Assume that transportation is instantaneous, denoted by $t_j = 0$, i.e., transportation time is negligible compared to job processing times. For example, the facilities are in the same city or even within the same factory. However, we have a transportation capacity b where if we move x_j jobs from machine 1 to machine j, then it will incur a transportation cost of

$$TP(x_j) = \lceil x_j/b \rceil R_j, \quad j = 2, \ldots, m.$$

For instance, the transportation cost may depend on the number of vehicles we need to transport the jobs, and R_j is the cost of using one truck to transporting jobs from machine 1 to machine j. We denote the problem as $Pm|D, t_j = 0, b| \sum w_i C_i + TC$.

Since the objective function is defined as weighted total completion time plus transportation cost, the problem is clearly NP-hard even without considering disruption. However, we can solve the problem by the pseudo-polynomial time algorithm described below. Since our original objective function is $\sum w_i C_i$, assume that the schedule is optimal before disruption, then jobs in each machine must be scheduled in WSPT (weighted SPT) order, i.e., the nondecreasing order of p_i/w_i. Let the total weighted completion time for jobs in machines $2, 3, \ldots, m$ before disruption be denoted by F_w.

For a given machine and a fixed sequence of jobs, if we insert a job, with processing time p and weight w, into the sequence at a specific position, then the total weighted completion time of the new sequence is increased by $p(w + W) + wT$ where W is the total weight of jobs that are sequenced after the inserted job and T is the total processing time of jobs that are sequenced before the inserted job. Due to this observation, we assume that jobs in S_1 are re-indexed in WLPT (weighted longest processing time) order. Namely,

$p_{1i}/w_{1i} \geq p_{1,i+1}/w_{1,i+1}$. We intend to assign jobs from highest p/w ratio in S_1 to machine 1 or ship to other machines to process.

Define $W(k, i)$ as the total weight of jobs in S_k with p/w ratio greater than p_{1i}/w_{1i} and $T(k, i)$ as the total processing time of jobs in S_k with p/w ratio not greater than p_{1i}/w_{1i}. Note that we do not change the job sequence of any machine j ($j > 1$) except that we may insert some jobs from S_1 into that machine.

Dynamic Program 2:

Define $m - 1$ dimensional vectors $\mathbf{J} = (j_2, \ldots, j_m)$, and $\mathbf{W} = (W_2, \ldots, W_m)$. Also define two operators

$$\mathbf{J} - k = (j_2, \ldots, j_{k-1}, j_k - 1, j_{k+1}, \ldots, j_m),$$

$$\mathbf{W} - (k, i) = (W_2, \ldots, W_{k-1}, W_k - w_{1i}, W_{k+1}, \ldots, W_m).$$

Let $f(i, \mathbf{J}, \mathbf{W})$ be the minimum total weighted completion time plus transportation cost, including those jobs in S_k, $k \geq 2$, given that we have assigned for the first i jobs from S_1 such that 1) j_k jobs are inserted into machine k, 2) total weight of jobs of S_1 inserted on machine k is W_k, $k = 2, \ldots, m$.

Initial condition. For $f(1, \mathbf{J}, \mathbf{W})$:

If $\mathbf{J} = \mathbf{W} = \mathbf{0}$, then $f(1, \mathbf{J}, \mathbf{W}) = F_w + w_{11}(D + p_{11})$.

For any k, if $j_k = 1$, $W_k = w_{11}$, and $j_l = W_l = 0, \forall l \neq k$, $f(1, \mathbf{J}, \mathbf{W}) = F_w + p_{11}(w_{11} + W(k, 1)) + TP(1)$.

$f(1, \mathbf{J}, \mathbf{W}) = +\infty$ for all other cases.

The dynamic programming recursive equation is

$$f(i, \mathbf{J}, \mathbf{W})$$
$$= \min \begin{cases} f(i-1, \mathbf{J}, \mathbf{W}) + P_{1i}\left(\sum_{j=i}^{n_1} w_{1j} - \sum_{k=2}^{m} W_k\right) + w_{1i}D \\ \min_{k=2,\ldots,m}\{f(i-1, \mathbf{J} - k, \mathbf{W} - (k, i)) + p_{1i}(W_k + W(k, i)) \\ \qquad + w_{1i}T(k, i) + TP(j_k) - TP(j_k - 1)\}. \end{cases}$$

For each job J_{1i}, there are two possibilities. If it is kept in machine 1, the cost is increased by $P_{1i}\left(\sum_{j=i}^{n_1} w_{1j} - \sum_{j=2}^{m} W_k\right) + w_{1i}D$. This corresponds to the first case. If it is moved to machine k, for $k = 2, \ldots, m$, and inserted into the original job sequence on the machine, the cost is increased by $p_{1i}(w_{1i} + W(k,i)) + w_{1i}T(k,i)$ as well as an extra transportation cost of $TP(j_k) - TP(j_k - 1)$. This corresponds to the second case.

The optimal solution can be found as $\min\{f(n_1, \mathbf{J}, \mathbf{W})\}$ for $j_2 + \ldots + j_m \leq n_1$, and $W_2 + \ldots + W_m \leq \sum_{i=1}^{n_1} w_{1i}$.

The number of states in the dynamic program is in $O(n^m W^{m-1})$, and it takes $O(m)$ time to calculate each state. So the total time complexity is $O(mn^m W^{m-1})$.

Now consider a simpler case where the problem is with the objective function $\sum C_i$. Then $j_k = W_k$ and hence $f(i, \mathbf{J}, \mathbf{W})$ is simplified to $f(n_1, \mathbf{J})$. Moreover, $W(k,i)$ becomes the total number of jobs in S_k with processing time greater than p_{1i}. Thus, the complexity of the algorithm is reduced to $O(mn^m)$.

6.4 Minimizing Only Job Completion Deviation Costs

In this section, our main interest is the deviation cost. In other words, we are to find a new schedule that is close to the original schedule in terms of the completion times of jobs. Note that the transportation issue still plays an important role in constructing the new schedule because of the transportation time, though the transportation cost is ignored. Consequently, we can assume there is only a single transportation mode from machine 1 to other machines. If there are multiple transportation modes, only the fastest one will be used because transportation cost is irrelevant in the analysis.

In these type of problems, we assume that a schedule has been made, and hence the completion time of job j before the disruption is regarded as its due date. Hence, any cost related to this due date can be used to measure the deviation related cost.

6.4.1 Problem $P2|D = \infty, t|L_{\max}$

Re-index the jobs in S_1 and S_2 by increasing order of their due date in each machine, respectively. Assume that the transportation time from machine 1 to machine 2 is t. Our purpose is to reschedule jobs after the disruption, so that $L_{\max}$ is minimized, where $L_{\max}$ is the maximum lateness among all jobs. We first have the following lemma that is easy to be proved.

Lemma 6.2 *For problem $P2|D = \infty, t|L_{\max}$, there exists an optimal solution such that*
1) for some time epoch r, before r all jobs follow Earliest Due Date (EDD) order, and those jobs after r also follow EDD order, and
2) those jobs that are moved from machine 1 to machine 2 follow EDD order.

Based on this lemma, we have

Algorithm 1:

Step 1. If $\max\{P_1, t\} \geq P_2$, then process all jobs of S_1 after S_2 on machine 2, where the sequence within S_1 and S_2 remains unaltered.

Step 2. If $\max\{P_1, t\} < P_2$, then let job J_{2j} be the first job such that $d_{2j} > t$. Let $\Delta_2 = d_{2j} - t$ and $\Delta_1 = p_{2j} - \Delta_2$.

Step 2.1. If $P_1 + \Delta_1 < t + \Delta_2$, then process all jobs of S_1 with the original order immediately after t on machine 2, and process jobs in $S_2 - \{J_{21}, \ldots, J_{2,j-1}\}$ with the original order immediately following jobs in S_1, where jobs in $\{J_{21}, \ldots, J_{2,j-1}\}$ remain the same order and are processed from zero to $t - \Delta_1$.

Step 2.2. If $P_1 + \Delta_1 \geq t + \Delta_2$, then process all jobs of S_1 (with the original order) immediately after $t + \Delta_2$ on machine 2, and process jobs in $S_2 - \{J_{21}, \ldots, J_{2j}\}$ (with the original order) immediately after jobs in S_1, where jobs in $\{J_{21}, \ldots, J_{2j}\}$ remain the same order and are processed from zero to $t + \Delta_2$.

Theorem 6.2 *Algorithm 1 will find an optimal solution for problem $P2|D = \infty, t|L_{\max}$.*

Proof. 1) For the case of $\max\{P_1, t\} \geq P_2$: If $P_1 \geq P_2$, then

$$d_{1,n_1} = \max\{\max_i\{d_{1i}\}, \max_j\{d_{2j}\}\}.$$

For any schedule, we have

$$L_{\max} \geq \max\{P_2, t\} + P_1 - d_{1,n_1} = \max\{P_2, t\} + P_1 - P_1 = \max\{P_2, t\}.$$

If $t \geq P_2 = d_{2,n_2}$, then for any schedule, we have $L_{\max} = t = \max\{P_2, t\}$. Hence, $\max\{P_2, t\}$ is a lower bound for $L_{\max}$. Since $L_{\max} = \max\{P_2, t\}$ can actually be achieved by processing all jobs following Step 1, applying Algorithm 1 will result in an optimal solution.

2) For the case of $\max\{P_1, t\} < P_2$: In such a case, we have

$$d_{2,n_2} = \max\{\max_i\{d_{1i}\}, \max_j\{d_{2j}\}\}.$$

Note that we have $L_{\max} \geq \max\{t, P_1\}$.

2.1) The case of $P_1 + \Delta_1 < t + \Delta_2$.

For a given solution, let the starting time of J_{11} be $t + s$, where $s \geq 0$. If $s \geq \Delta_2$, then for any sequence $L_{\max} \geq t + s \geq t + \Delta_2 > P_1 + \Delta_1$. Now suppose that $s < \Delta_2$. If J_{2j} finishes later than $t + s$, then it must finish after S_1 jobs and hence

$$C_{2j} \geq t + s + P_1 + p_{2j} = t + s + P_1 + \Delta_1 + \Delta_2,$$

and

$$L_{2j} \geq t + s + P_1 + \Delta_1 + \Delta_2 - (t + \Delta_2) = P_1 + s + \Delta_1 \geq P_1 + \Delta_1.$$

If J_{2j} finishes no later than $t + s$, then there is one job in $\{J_{21}, \ldots, J_{2,j-1}\} \cup S_1$ finishing no earlier than $t + \Delta_2 + P_1$ with due date no larger than $\max\{t - \Delta_1, P_1\}$. Hence $L_{\max} = t + \Delta_2 + P_1 - \max\{t - \Delta_1, P_1\} \geq \max\{P_1 + \Delta_1, t\}$ because $P_1 + \Delta_1 < t + \Delta_2$. Combining with the fact $L_{\max} \geq \max\{t, P_1\}$, we conclude that for any schedule $L_{\max} \geq \max\{P1 + \Delta_1, t\}$. Since $L_{\max} = \max\{P_1 + \Delta_1, t\}$ can actually be achieved by processing all jobs following Step 2.1, applying Algorithm 1 will result an optimal solution.

2.2) The case of $P_1 + \Delta_1 \geq t + \Delta_2$.

If $P_1 \geq t + \Delta_2$, then any feasible solution will result $L_{\max} = \max\{t, P_1\} = P_1 = \max\{t + \Delta_2, P_1\}$. Since $L_{\max} = \max\{t + \Delta_2, P1\}$ can actually be achieved by processing all jobs following Step 2.2, applying Algorithm 1 will result an optimal solution.

If $P_1 < t + \Delta_2$, let the starting time of J_{11} be $t + s$, where $s \geq 0$. If $s \geq \Delta_2$, then for any sequence we have $L_{\max} = t + s \geq t + \Delta_2$. Now suppose that $s < \Delta_2$. If J_{2j} finishes later than $t + s$, then it must finish after S_1 jobs and hence

$$C_{2j} \geq t + s + P_1 + p_{2j} = t + s + P_1 + \Delta_1 + \Delta_2$$

and

$$L_{2j} \geq t + s + P_1 + \Delta_1 + \Delta_2 - (t + \Delta_2) = P_1 + s + \Delta_1 \geq t + \Delta_2.$$

If J_{2j} finishes no later than $t + s$, then there is one job in $\{J_{21}, \ldots, J_{2,j-1}\} \cup S_1$ which finishes no earlier than $t + \Delta_2 + P_1$ with due date no larger than $\max\{t - \Delta_1, P_1\}$. Hence

$$L_{\max} \geq t + \Delta_2 + P_1 - \max\{t - \Delta_1, P_1\} \geq t + \Delta_2$$

because $P_1 + \Delta_1 \geq t + \Delta_2$. Combining with the fact $L_{\max} \geq \max\{t, P_1\}$, we conclude that for any schedule $L_{\max} \geq \max\{P_1, t + \Delta_2\}$. Since $L_{\max} = \max\{P_1, t + \Delta_2\}$ can actually be achieved by processing all jobs following Step 2.2, applying Algorithm 1 will result an optimal solution. ∎

6.4.2 Problem $P2|D, t|L_{\max}$

In this case, machine 1 is unavailable from time 0 to a finite time D. Note that J_{11} will not be scheduled earlier than $\max\{D, t\}$. Hence $L_{\max} \geq L_{11} \geq \min\{D, t\}$. If $D \leq t$, then we just schedule all jobs of S_1 to start at time D and $L_{\max} = D$. Thus, we are only interested in the case with $t < D$.

Lemma 6.3 *Problem $P2|D, t|L_{\max}$ has an optimal solution in which there exists an i such that jobs in $S_2 \cup \{J_{11}, J_{12}, \ldots, J_{1i}\}$ are processed on machine 2 and jobs in $\{J_{1,i+1}, \ldots, J_{1n_1}\}$ are processed on machine 1.*

Proof. Let J_{1j} be the smallest-index job to be processed on machine 1 in the schedule. Assume that there is one job J_{1i} with $i > j$ and is scheduled to be processed on machine 2. Clearly, J_{1j} starts at D and $L_{1j} = D + p_{1j} - d_{1j}$ and $L_{1k} \leq L_{1j} - p_{1i}$ for any job J_{1k} that is scheduled on machine 1. In such a case, if we move J_{1i} back to be processed on machine 1, then it will not increase $L_{\max}$. ∎

Let k be the smallest job index such that $d_{1k} \geq D$. Based on Lemma 6.3, the following algorithm will find an optimal solution for $P2|D,t|L_{\max}$.

Algorithm 2:

For $j = 1, \ldots, k$

Schedule jobs in $\{J_{1,j+1}, \ldots, J_{1,n_1}\}$ starting from D and apply Algorithm 1 for scheduling jobs of the set $S_1 = \{J_{11}, \ldots, J_{1j}\}$ and S_2 on machine 2. Find the corresponding $L_{\max}$, and denote it as $L_{\max}(j)$.

Find $\min_{j=1,\ldots,k}\{L_{\max}(j)\}$.

6.4.3 Problem $Pm|D, t_j = 0|\sum w_i U_i$

In this case, machine 1 is disrupted for a limited period of time D, and jobs can be immediately moved to other machines. The objective is to minimize total weighted number of tardy jobs. Note that U_i is defined as a binary variable where $U_i = 1$ if and only if job J_i is tardy. The problem is NP-hard even for $m = 2$ because when D is large enough all jobs are moved to machine 2 and the problem is degenerated to a single machine scheduling problem with the objective function of minimizing total weighted number of tardy jobs.

For the case of $m = 2$, we develop a dynamic programming algorithm in pseudopolynomial time as follows. Although we assume the transportation time is zero, the algorithm can be extended easily to the case with non-zero transportation time. Like most scheduling problems of minimizing the number of tardy jobs, it is easy to see that in an optimal solution, we will process non-tardy jobs first which are followed by tardy jobs on each machine, and the sequence for the tardy jobs is arbitrary.

In the following, we define $g(x, y) = 0$ if $x \leq y$, and ∞ otherwise. We will see that x will be used as the completion time of a job, and y as its due date. Then $g(x, y)$ is used as the feasibility cost for the case where the job is not tardy with respect to completion time x and due date y.

Dynamic Program 3:

Define (i,j,s,t) as the state for the jobs $J_{11},\ldots,J_{1i}, J_{21},\ldots,J_{2j}$ where the last non-tardy job among them finishes on machine 1 at time s and on machine 2 at time t, respectively. Let $f(i,j,s,t)$ be the minimum cost for the state.

Initial condition. For $s = D, D+1, \ldots, D+P_{1,n_1}$, and $t = 0, 1, \ldots, P_{1,n_1} + P_{2,n_2}$, we have

$$f(1,0,s,t) = \begin{cases} w_{11} & \text{if } s = t = 0 \\ g(D+p_{11}, d_{11}) & \text{if } s = D+p_{11}, t = 0 \\ g(p_{11}, d_{11}) & \text{if } s = 0, t = p_{11} \\ \infty & \text{otherwise} \end{cases}$$

and

$$f(0,1,s,t) = \begin{cases} w_{21} & \text{if } s = t = 0 \\ g(p_{21}, d_{21}) & \text{if } s = p_{21}, t = 0 \\ \infty & \text{otherwise} \end{cases}$$

The dynamic programming recursive equation is

$$f(i,j,s,t) = \min \begin{cases} f(i-1,j,s,t) + w_{1i} \\ f(i-1,j,s-p_{1i},t) + g(s, d_{1i}) \\ f(i-1,j,s,t-p_{1i}) + g(t, d_{1i}) \\ f(i,j-1,s,t) + w_{2j} \\ f(i,j-1,s,t-p_{2j}) + g(t, d_{2j}) \end{cases}$$

In the equation, the first three terms correspond to the cases where job J_{1i} is tardy, non-tardy on machine 1, and non-tardy on machine 2, respectively. The last two terms correspond to the cases where job J_{2j} is tardy or non-tardy, respectively.

The optimal solution is given by the state corresponding to $\min\{f(n_1, n_2, s, t)\}$ for $s = D, D+1, \ldots, D+P_1$, and $t = P_2, P_2+1\ldots, P_2+P_1$. The time complexity of the dynamic program is in $O(n^2 P^2)$ where $P = \max\{P_1, P_2\}$.

6.5 Minimizing Weighted Sum of Job Deviation Costs and the Original Objective Function

In this section, we study problems with two criteria: the minimization of total deviation cost of the jobs from the original completion times which are regarded as due dates, and the minimization of the original goal in our objective function. In particular, we use the weighted sum of the two criteria as the new objective function in the scheduling model.

6.5.1 Problem $P2|D = \infty, t = 0|\alpha \sum w_i C_i + \beta \sum w_i T_i$

In this problem, the jobs are originally scheduled optimally with the objective function of minimizing total weighted flow time, $\sum w_i C_i$. Note that this is an NP-hard problem, but our interest is not how to find such an optimal schedule. We simply assume that an optimal schedule has been given. After disruption, all jobs on machine 1 can be moved immediately to machine 2. Our objective function is to minimize $\alpha \sum w_i C_i + \beta \sum w_i T_i$ where the deviation cost is measured by the job tardiness with respect to the due dates equal to those originally scheduled completion times.

Because $D = \infty$, all jobs have to be processed on machine 2. We have

Theorem 6.3 *For problem $P2|D = \infty, t = 0|\alpha \sum w_i C_i + \beta \sum w_i T_i$, after a permanent disruption on machine 1, it is optimal to schedule all jobs in the WSPT order on machine 2.*

Proof. Re-index all jobs in WSPT order, i.e., $p_i/w_i \leq p_{i+1}/w_{i+1}$. Note that in the original schedule, job J_1 is either the first job on machine 1 or machine 2, implying that $d_1 = p_1$.

We first show that job J_1 should still be scheduled first on machine 2 in the new schedule. Suppose there is a job J_i that is immediately scheduled before job J_1. Then we can try to interchange jobs J_1 and J_i so that the objective function is reduced. Let the starting time of job J_i be r, and x and y be the total cost of job J_1 and job J_i before and after the interchange, respectively. We have

$$x = \alpha\bigl(w_i(r+p_i) + w_1(r+p_i+p_1)\bigr)$$
$$+\beta\bigl(w_i(r+p_i-d_i)^+ + w_1(r+p_i+p_1-d_1)^+\bigr)$$
$$y = \alpha\bigl(w_1(r+p_1) + w_i(r+p_1+p_i)\bigr)$$
$$+\beta\bigl(w_1(r+p_1-d_1)^+ + w_i(r+p_1+p_i-d_i)^+\bigr).$$

Hence,

$$x - y$$
$$= \alpha(w_1 p_i - w_i p_1) + \beta\bigl(w_1(r+p_i+p_1-d_1-(r+p_1-d_1))$$
$$+w_i\bigl((r+p_i-d_i)^+ - (r+p_1+p_i-d_i)^+\bigr),$$
$$= \alpha(w_1 p_i - w_i p_1) +$$
$$\beta\Bigl(w_1 p_i + w_i\bigl((r+p_i-d_i)^+ - (r+p_1+p_i-d_i)^+\bigr)\Bigr)$$
$$\geq \alpha(w_1 p_i - w_i p_1) + \beta(w_1 p_i - w_i p_1)$$
$$\geq 0,$$

where we have used the fact that $d_1 = p_1$ and hence $(r+p_1-d_1)^+ = r+p_1-d_1$ and $(r+p_i+p_1-d_1)^+ = r+p_i+p_1-d_1$, and $w_1 p_i - w_i p_1 \geq 0$ by definition.

Thus, we have $x - y \geq 0$. Continuing the interchange scheme, we can show that job J_1 should be sequenced first.

Now we discuss job J_2 of which d_2 is either equal to $p_1 + p_2$ or p_2. We can show that job J_2 should be scheduled at the second position by a similar interchange argument. Suppose that a job J_j is sequenced immediately before job J_2. Let the starting time of job J_j be s, and v and z be the total cost of job J_2 and job J_j before and after the interchange, respectively. We have

$$v = \alpha\bigl(w_j(s+p_j) + w_2(s+p_j+p_2)\bigr)$$
$$+\beta\bigl(w_j(s+p_j-d_j)^+ + w_2(s+p_j+p_2-d_2)^+\bigr),$$
$$z = \alpha\bigl(w_2(s+p_2) + w_j(s+p_2+p_j)\bigr)$$
$$+\beta\bigl(w_2(s+p_2-d_2)^+ + w_j(s+p_2+p_j+d_j)^+\bigr).$$

Note that $s \geq p_1$. Using the fact that $w_2 p_j - w_j p_2 \geq 0$, $(s+p_j+p_2-d_2)^+ = s+p_j+p_2-d_2$ and $(s+p_2-d_2)^+ = s+p_2-d_2$, we can show that $v - z \geq 0$. Continuing the interchange scheme, we can show that job J_2 should be sequenced in the second position.

Repeating the argument, we can show that it is optimal to schedule all jobs in the WSPT order. ∎

Note that this is an interesting demonstration showing how a disruption management problem may become easy even though the original scheduling problem is hard. Though it is NP-hard to find an optimal schedule that minimizes the total weighted completion time on parallel machines, the optimal new schedule after a disruption can be found in polynomial time even if the objective of minimizing the sum of total weighted completion times is still a subcriterion.

6.5.2 Problem $P2|D = \infty, t|\alpha \sum w_i C_i + \beta \sum w_i T_i$

This problem has the same assumption as the previous problem except that it takes a fixed time of t to move jobs from machine 1 to machine 2. Again we can simply assume that there is only one possible transportation for moving jobs from machine 1 to machine 2, and thus all jobs in S_1 will be available to process on machine 2 at time t. We give the following lemma without detailed proof.

Lemma 6.4 *For problem $P2|D = \infty, t|\alpha \sum w_i C_i + \beta \sum w_i T_i$, there exists an optimal solution such that for some time epoch r,*
1) before r all jobs are from S_2 and follow WSPT order, and
2) after r, those jobs from S_1 are following WSPT order and those jobs from S_2 are following WSPT order.

A dynamic programming algorithm is developed as follows.

Dynamic Program 4:

Define (i, j, r, s) as the state describing the case in which we have assigned i jobs from S_1 and j jobs from S_2, jobs processed before r are all from S_2 and with total processing time s, and jobs processed after r are either from S_1 or S_2. Let $f(i, j, r, s)$ be the minimum cost for the state.

Initial Condition. For $r = t, t+1, \ldots, t + \max\{p_{2j}\}$, we have

$$f(1,0,r,s) = \begin{cases} \alpha w_{11}(r + p_{11}) + \beta w_{11}(r + p_{11} - p_{11}) & \text{if } s = 0 \\ \infty & \text{otherwise} \end{cases}$$

$$f(0,1,r,s) = \begin{cases} \alpha w_{21} p_{21} & \text{if } s = p_{21} \\ \alpha w_{21}(r + p_{21}) + \beta w_{21}(r + p_{21} - p_{21}) & \text{if } s = 0 \\ \infty & \text{otherwise} \end{cases}$$

Note that when $s = 0$, job J_{11} (or J_{21}) is completed at time $r + p_{11}$ (or $r + p_{21}$) and its due date is p_{11} (or p_{21}).

Define $Q_{ij} = P_{1i} + P_{2j}$. We have a dynamic programming recursive equation as follows.

$$f(i,j,r,s)$$
$$= \min \begin{cases} f(i-1,j,r,s) + \alpha w_{1i}(r + Q_{ij} - s) + \beta w_{1i}(r + P_{2j} - s) \\ f(i,j-1,r,s) + \alpha w_{2j}(s - P_{2j}) + \beta w_{2j}(s - P_{2j})^+ \\ f(i,j-1,r,s) + \alpha w_{2j}(r + Q_{ij} - s) + \beta w_{2j}(r + P_{1i} - s) \end{cases}$$

In the equation, the first term corresponds to the case in which the last assigned job is J_{1i}. In particular, the job is delayed by $P_{2j} - s$. The last two terms correspond to the cases in which the last assigned job is J_{2j} and it is scheduled before r or after r, respectively.

The optimal solution is given by $\min\{f(n_1, n_2, r, s)\}$ for $r = t, t + 1, \ldots, t + \max\{p_{2j}\}$, and $s = 0, 1, \ldots, r$. The time complexity is in $O(n^2 T^2)$.

6.6 Literature Review

In recent years, more and more research has been conducted in the area of logistics scheduling which is concerned with not only job sequencing but also job transportation consideration. The issues related to job transportation include transportation capacity, time and costs, for example, Lee and Chen (2001), Hall et al.(2001), Chang and Lee (2002), Wang and Lee (2003) and Hall and Potts (2003).

In the literature of machine scheduling, the problem studied in this chapter can be viewed within the category of machine scheduling with availability constraint where the unavailability can be a machine breakdown or maintenance. Related literature include Glazebrook (1987), Birge and Glazebrook (1988), Adiri et al. (1989), Birge et al. (1990), Frostig (1991), Lee (1996,1997,2004), Graves and Lee (1999), Qi et al. (1999), Lee and Chen (2000), Schmidt (2000), and Lee and Lin (2001). However, these models only address the scheduling problem subject to machine unavailability, a different situation from disruption management.

Aytug et al. (2002) presented an extensive survey of rescheduling and executing production schedules while facing uncertainties. The literature on rescheduling with deviation costs is relatively sparse when compared to the large body of published work on the more traditional forms of machine scheduling. Bean et al. (1991) were among the first to recognize the importance of deviation impact by proposing the concept of the matchup schedule where the goal is to develop a new schedule that matches the original after a certain point in time. Building on this idea, Akturk and Gorgulu (1999) studied the matchup problem in a modified flow shop environment.

When the goal is to minimize deviation costs, a common approach is to prescribe an earliness or tardiness penalty based on the difference of job completion times in the original and revised schedules, but the work is rather ad-hoc in the literature, for example, Abumaizar and Svestka (1997) and Wu et al. (1993).

More detailed results on disruption management for logistics scheduling can be found in Lee and Yu (2003).

References

Abumaizar, R.J. and J.A. Svestka (1997), Rescheduling job shops under random disruptions, *International Journal of Production Research*, 35, 2065-2082.

Adiri, I., J. Bruno, E. Frostig and A.H.G. Rinnooy Kan (1989), Single machine flow-time scheduling with a single breakdown, *Acta Informatica*, 26, 679-696.

Akturk, M.S. and E. Gorgulu (1999), Match-up scheduling under a machine breakdown, *European Journal of Operational Research*, 112, 81-97.

Aytug, H., M.A. Lawley, K. McKay, S. Mohan and R. Uzsoy (2002), Executing production schedules in the face of uncertainties: A review and some future directions, *European Journal of Operational Research*, in press.

Bean, J., J.R. Birge, J. Mittenthal and C.E. Noon (1991), Matchup scheduling with multiple resources, release dates and disruptions, *Operations Research*, 39, 470-483.

Birge, J. and K.D. Glazebrook (1988), Assessing the effects of machine breakdowns in stochastic scheduling, *Operations Research Letters*, 7, 267-271.

Birge, J., J.B.G. Frenk, J. Mittenthal and A.H.G. Rinnooy Kan (1990), Single-machine scheduling subject to stochastic breakdowns, *Naval Research Logistics*, 37, 661-677.

Chang, Y.-C. and C.-Y. Lee (2002), Machine scheduling with job delivery coordination, *European Journal of Operational Research*, in press.

Frostig, E. (1991), A note on stochastic scheduling on a single machine scheduling subject to breakdown - The preemptive repeat model, *Probability in the Engineering and Informational Sciences*, 5, 349-354.

Glazebrook, K.D. (1987), Evaluating the effects of machine breakdowns in stochastic scheduling problems, *Naval Research Logistics*, 34, 319-335.

Graves, G.H. and C.-Y. Lee (1999), Scheduling maintenance and semiresumable jobs on a single machine, *Naval Research Logistics*, 46, 845-863.

Hall, N.G., M.A. Lesaoana and C.N. Potts (2001), Scheduling with fixed delivery dates, *Operations Research*, 49, 134-144.

Hall, N.G. and C.N. Potts (2003), Supply chain scheduling: Batching and delivery, *Operations Research*, 51, 566-584.

Lee, C.-Y. (1996), Machine scheduling with an availability constraint, *Journal of Global Optimization*, 9, 395-416.

Lee, C.-Y. (1997), Minimizing the makespan in the two-machine flowshop scheduling problem with an availability constraint, *Operations Research letters*, 20, 129-139.

Lee, C.-Y. (2004), Machine scheduling with availability constraints, in *Handbook of Scheduling*, Editor: J. Leung, CRC Press, in press.

Lee, C.-Y. and Z.L. Chen (2000), Scheduling of jobs and maintenance activities on parallel machines, *Naval Research Logistics*, 47, 145-165.

Lee, C.-Y. and Z.L. Chen (2001), Machine scheduling with transportation considerations, *Journal of Scheduling*, 4, 3-24.

Lee, C.-Y. and C.-S. Lin (2001), Machine scheduling with maintenance and repair rate-modifying activities, *European Journal of Operational Research*, 135, 491-513.

Lee, C.-Y. and G. Yu (2003), Logistics scheduling under disruptions, working paper.

Leon, V.J. and S.D. Wu (1992), On scheduling with ready-times, due-dates and vacations, *Naval Research Logistics*, 39, 53-65.

Qi, X., T. Chen and F. Tu (1999), Scheduling the maintenance on a single machine, *Journal of the Operational Research Society*, 50, 1071-1078.

Schmidt, G. (2000), Scheduling with limited machine availability, *European Journal of Operational Research*, 121(1), 1-15.

Wang, H. and C.-Y. Lee (2003), Two-stage logistics scheduling with multiple mode transportation, working paper.

Wu, S.-D., R.H. Storeer and P.C. Chang (1993), On machine rescheduling heuristics with efficiency and stability as criteria, *Computer & Operations Research*, 20, 1-14.

Chapter 7

Inventory Disruption Management Based on Economic Production Quantity Models

7.1 Introduction

In this chapter, we discuss the disruption management problem for the economic production quantity (EPQ) model which is broadly used in manufacturing systems. Suppose a firm makes a single type of product, the demand of which is relatively stable and assumed to be constant over a long period of time. Then the firm can adopt a periodical batch production policy in order to take the advantage of the economy of scale. Specifically, we assume the production rate is higher than the demand rate. After the firm starts a production batch, the inventory level is gradually accumulated until it reaches a specific level. Then the production stops and the accumulated inventory is used to meet the demand. When the inventory is empty, the next production batch is started. In such a situation, a production plan can be specified by the production quantity in each batch. Assuming such a process is repeatedly executed over a long period of time, it can be shown that the optimal policy is to make the production quantity equal in each batch. Note that the EPQ model is a generalization of the well-known economic ordering quantity (EOQ) model in which the inventory is immediately filled to a specific level at the beginning of each batch.

Due to various disruptions, an EPQ plan may not be executed smoothly. Unexpected disruptions, such as machine breakdowns, supply material cost changes, interest rate fluctuations for the capital loan, and others happen from time to time. Facing the disruptions, it is necessary to adjust the EPQ plan to be better suited for the disrupted environment.

Research has been conducted on how to change the basic EPQ model when disruptions occur. However, two important issues have been neglected in the past research. One is the deviation cost caused by changing the original plan. The EPQ model is a stable periodic production scheme. As a result, certain contracts may have been made with some outside partners. Any change to these contracts may cause a certain penalty that cannot be included in the conventional EPQ model. For example, there may be a contract between a transportation company for shipping a fixed amount of raw materials at certain pre-specified time. To respond to a raw material discount, more materials may be purchased than what is planned. As a result, the transportation company may ask for an extra fee for the modified delivery.

The other neglected issue is to restore the original EPQ plan after a disruption ends. The EPQ model is optimal in a deterministic environment with fixed production rate and constant demand rate at any time. For a temporary disruption, the manufacturer will not want to change the schedule forever due to reasons such as avoiding a contract violation penalty, avoiding sub-optimal solutions and reducing production nervousness. This restriction makes our problem a modified EPQ problem with limited time horizon.

The purpose of this chapter is to address the above two issues by studying the disruption management problem for the EPQ model. We formulate our model in Section 7.2. Two different cases regarding the change of setup times are discussed in Sections 7.3 and 7.4, respectively. In Section 7.5, we extend the results to a two-stage production/inventory model where each stage takes an EPQ/EOQ scheme. Literature review is given in the last section.

7.2 Problem Formulation

In an EPQ configuration, we have a single type of product of which the demand rate, denoted by D, is constant over a long period. The production is also conducted at a constant rate, denoted by R, where $D < R$. The production is executed in the form of batches or cycles.

A fixed setup cost is incurred for each batch, denoted by S. Inventory cost and production cost are linear functions, where the unit inventory cost is H, and the unit production cost is C. The decision variable in an EPQ model is the production quantity in each batch, denoted by Q. For a given Q, the length of a batch is Q/D, the production time in a batch is Q/R, and the maximum inventory level is $Q(R-D)/R$. An EPQ model can be illustrated in Fig. 7.1.

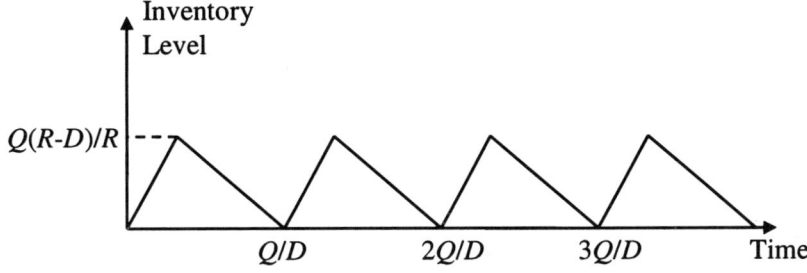

Fig. 7.1   The basic EPQ model

The objective of an EPQ model is to minimize the overall long-term cost:

$$\min TC(Q) = DC + \frac{DS}{Q} + \frac{HQ(R-D)}{2R}, \qquad (7.1)$$

where the first term is the production cost, the second term is the setup cost, and the last term is the inventory cost.

Remark 1. In the classical EPQ model, the optimal solution is independent of the unit production cost C because the production cost is a constant regardless of the decision on production quantity for each batch. However, we have to put the term DC in the formulation when discussing the disruption management problem because one possible disruption we need to consider is the production cost change.

Remark 2. The objective function in (7.1) is the cost for a period of a long time. It is usually interpreted as the annual cost where D is the quantity of annual demand, D/Q is the number of batches annually, $Q(R-D)/(2R)$ is the average inventory level, and H is the annual inventory cost for each unit of the product. For a single batch, the production cost is CQ, the setup cost is S, and the inventory cost is $\frac{HQ(R-D)}{2R}\frac{Q}{D}$, i.e., H multiplied by the area of the triangle formed by the inventory curve during a batch. These results will help us to calculate the cost for limited time periods when disruptions occur.

It is easy to see that the unique optimal solution to (7.1) is

$$Q^* = \sqrt{\frac{2SDR}{H(R-D)}}. \qquad (7.2)$$

7.2.1 Disruptions and disruption management policies

Possible disruptions

Possible disruptions to the EPQ model can be captured by parameter changes. By the nature of disruptions, we also assume they are temporary, which means they only last for a short period of time. For the aim of simplicity, we assume all parameters remain unchanged during a batch, though they may change over different batches. Later we discuss how to handle the general cases where parameters may change any time during a batch.

For batch i, we may have

1) Setup cost change: $S_i = S \pm \delta_S$.
2) Holding cost change: $H_i = H \pm \delta_H$.
3) Demand rate change: $D_i = D \pm \delta_D$.
4) Production rate change: $R_i = R \pm \delta_R$.
5) Production cost change: $C_i = C \pm \delta_C$.

Disruptions can be further classified as major disruptions and minor disruptions. Sometimes there is only one disruption occuring at a time, i.e., a single parameter change. This is referred to as a minor disruption. More complicated cases involve multiple disruptions happening at the same time. This is called a major disruption.

Solution space

Solution space is the set of possible actions in response to the above disruptions. We define our solution space as follows.

- In advance/late production: The start time (setup time) of a batch may be earlier or later than the originally determined setup time.
- Extended production period: We can also keep the original start time for each batch, but extend the production time for some batches. This may happen when we need to produce more product, or produce the same amount in the batch at a lower production rate.
- Batch cancelation and addition: We can cancel the entire production of a scheduled batch, and thus no setup cost and production cost are incurred. We can also add a new batch if necessary, which causes an extra setup cost.

The disruption management model can be further differentiated into two cases, fixed setup times and flexible setup times. In the case of fixed setup times, the start time of any scheduled batch is not allowed to change. As a result, in the above policies, only the extended production period can be applied. In the case of flexible setup times, the start time of a batch can be arbitrarily designated. So any above policy can be used.

Disruption management time window

The procedure of a disruption management process can be illustrated in Fig. 7.2.

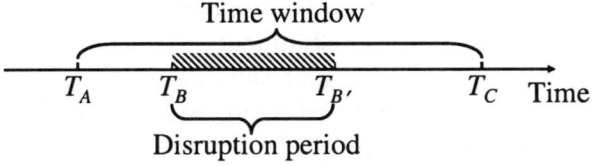

Fig. 7.2 Disruption management time window

In Fig. 7.2, a disruption occurs and lasts during time interval $[T_B, T_{B'}]$. It is possible that the disruption may be detected earlier than its occurrence, say, at time T_A. Then we can start to revise the EPQ plan as early as time T_A. Assume the plan is required to restore to the original EPQ plan by time T_C. Then the time interval $[T_A, T_C]$ is called the disruption management time interval.

In modeling the disruption management for an EPQ model, we only need to consider the plan during the time window $[T_A, T_C]$. Thus the problem has a limited time horizon. Here we assume the time window is given, and try to optimize the new plan within the time window. Another associated problem is how to determine the time window. Simply speaking, the longer the window is, the lower the cost is to handle the disruptions because the optimal solution to the problem with a short time window is essentially a feasible solution to the problem with a longer time window. However, the problem becomes difficult to solve as the time window increases because the problem size also increases.

7.2.2 Deviation cost

We will address the following two types of deviation cost in the model.

Penalty for production quantity change: For a given EPQ model, an optimal quantity Q^* for each batch has been specified, and some penalty will be incurred when it is changed. For example, producing more in one batch may result in over time production, and producing less may cause less effective workforce usage. To address such a deviation cost, we assume that the deviation cost for production quantity change in batch i is described by a function $f(Q_i - Q^*)$ where Q_i is the real production quantity in batch i.

Penalty for setup change: The change of number of setups during the time window is not free. For example, each setup is usually associated with a delivery or shipment. An unplanned setup may call for an expedited delivery and thus be more expensive than an ordinary setup cost. A canceled setup may cause a compensation to the contracted carrier. In modeling, we assume a cost of π^+ is incurred for each new setup, and a cost of π^- for each canceled setup.

7.3 Disruption Management with Fixed Setup Times

In this section, we discuss the case when the setup of each batch is not allowed to change. For example, the firm makes production once a week. If the machines or materials are not available at other times, the start time of each batch cannot be changed.

7.3.1 General models

When the setup times are not allowed to change, the decision boils down to the quantities to produce during each batch. Assume there are total N batches within the disruption management time window. In the new plan, batch i produces Q_i units of the product. We first consider the simplest case where the parameters H_i, S_i, R_i, D_i, C_i are assumed to keep the same within a batch i. We will later show that this assumption can be relaxed.

The optimal production schedule can be described by the following mathematical programming problem $(P1)$,

$$\min \sum_{i=1}^{N} A_i + \sum_{i=1}^{N} f(Q_i - Q^*) + \sum_{i=1}^{N} C_i Q_i$$

Subject to

$$A_i = \frac{H_i}{2}\left(\left(2I_i + \frac{Q_i}{R_i}(R_i - D_i)\right)\frac{Q_i}{R_i} + (I_i + I_{i+1} + \frac{Q_i}{R_i}(R_i - D_i))(\frac{Q^*}{D} - \frac{Q_i}{R_i})\right) \tag{7.3}$$

$$I_i + Q_i - D_i \frac{Q^*}{D} = I_{i+1}, \quad i = 1, \cdots, N \tag{7.4}$$

$$\sum_{i=1}^{l} Q_i \geq \sum_{i=1}^{l} D_i \frac{Q^*}{D}, \quad l = 1, \cdots, N \tag{7.5}$$

$$I_1 = I_{N+1} = 0. \tag{7.6}$$

In the formulation, I_i is the inventory level at the beginning of batch i. The objective function contains three terms, the first one being the holding cost which is calculated from constraint (7.3), the second one being the deviation cost, and the last being the production cost. The setup cost is not included in the model because it is fixed in this case.

Problem ($P1$) involves general nonlinear programming with linear constraints. When the deviation cost function $f(Q - Q^*)$ is a quadratic function, the problem becomes a quadratic programming problem, and thus can be efficiently solved by standard optimization solvers. In the following subsections, we will further simplify the formulation for some special cases.

Note that in this model, we add index i to each of the parameters H, S, R, D, C. In this way, major disruptions can be handled. Now we see how to relax the assumption of constant parameter within a batch. If any parameters change in the middle of a batch, we can divide the batch into several phases so that parameters change only at the beginning of a phase. In this way, the total cost can be calculated by summing all phases.

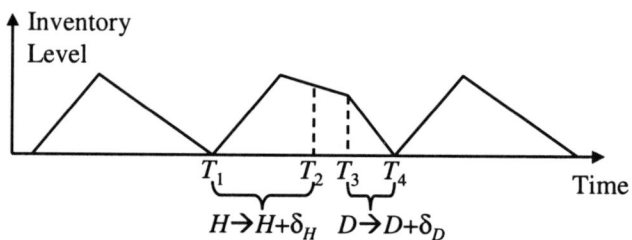

Fig. 7.3 Multiple disruptions during a batch

For example, in Fig. 7.3, two disruptions occur in a batch: from time T_1 to T_2, the holding cost changes to $H + \delta_H$, and from time T_3 to T_4, the demand rate changes to $D + \delta_D$. Then the batch can be divided into three phases, and the cost for each batch can be calculated separately.

7.3.2 Minor disruptions

In the following, we consider special cases for minor disruptions where only one parameter changes once in a batch.

Production rate decrease

Suppose the production rate R becomes $R - \delta_R$ within $[T_B, T_{B'}]$. There are two cases, $R - \delta_R \geq D$ and $R - \delta_R < D$. In the first case, the quantity produced in the disruption period could possibly satisfy the demand in that batch. In the second case, the demand in the disruption batch can only be satisfied by some extra production in the previous batches.

Theorem 7.1 *If $R - \delta_R \geq D$ within $[T_B, T_{B'}]$, it is optimal to keep the same production quantity Q^* for each batch.*

Proof. First, when $R - \delta_R \geq D$, it is feasible to produce Q^* in each batch. Next we will show that in each batch it is optimal to have no inventory left from the previous batch.

Assume in an optimal solution there is some initial inventory I for the last batch, say, batch t, in the time window, and the production quantity for the batch is Q_t. We have $Q_t = Q^* - I$ and $I \leq Q^*$ because no inventory should be moved to later batches beyond the time window. The inventory level of the batch is shown in Fig. 7.4.

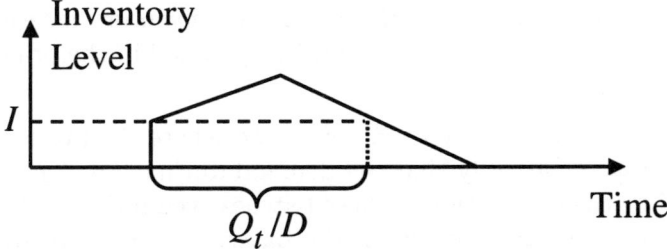

Fig. 7.4 A batch with initial inventory level I

Then what happens in batch t can be interpreted as that demand is first satisfied by the production Q_t, of which the inventory corresponds to the small triangle in the upper area in Fig. 7.4 and its time duration is Q_t/D; then the demand is satisfied by the obtained inventory I of which the inventory cost corresponds to the lower area in Fig. 7.4. The inventory cost for the entire batch can be analyzed as

$$\frac{1}{2}H(\frac{R-D}{R})\frac{Q_t^2}{D} + \frac{1}{2}HI(\frac{Q^*}{D} - \frac{I}{D} + \frac{Q^*}{D}) \quad (7.7)$$

$$= \frac{H}{2D}\left((\frac{R-D}{R})(Q^* - I)^2 + I(2Q^* - I)\right) \quad (7.8)$$

$$= \frac{1}{2}H(\frac{R-D}{R})\frac{Q^{*2}}{D} + \frac{H}{2R}I(2Q^* - I) \quad (7.9)$$

$$> \frac{1}{2}H(\frac{R-D}{R})\frac{Q^{*2}}{D}. \quad (7.10)$$

Note that the term in Eq. (7.10) is the inventory cost for the batch when the production quantity is Q^*, or equivalently $I = 0$. Therefore, when there is no inventory at the beginning, the holding cost will become less. Meanwhile, the production quantity deviation cost in this batch is zero if $I = 0$ and Q^* is produced.

Moreover, if there is some initial inventory I for the last batch, there must be at least one previous batch that produces more than Q^*. Then we can reduce the production quantity for that batch so that both the inventory and deviation costs are reduced. So, the total cost will become less if there is no initial inventory at the beginning of the last batch.

The above argument can be applied to all batches in a backward way so that it is optimal to make no initial inventory for each batch. Thus, each batch should produce Q^* as planned in the original EPQ model. ∎

Now consider the case of $R - \delta_R < D$, where the production rate decreases so remarkably that the demand during $[T_B, T_{B'}]$ cannot be satisfied by the production in these batches even if the machines work all the time. In other words, in the batches in $[T_A, T_B]$, some extra product must be produced to compensate the decreased production rate in $[T_B, T_{B'}]$.

From the proof of Theorem 7.1, the following lemma can be derived.

Lemma 7.1 *If $R - \delta_R < D$ within $[T_B, T_{B'}]$, the production and inventory schedule within $[T_{B'}, T_C]$ will not change.*

Therefore, if the production rate decreases remarkably, the firm only needs to find a plan for the period $[T_A, T_{B'}]$. So the planning cycle of problem $(P1)$ is reduced.

Holding cost change

Similar to Theorem 7.1, regardless whether the holding cost increases or decreases, the production schedule should not be changed since setup cost is the same and the holding cost and deviation cost for production quantity change are the least if a quantity Q^* is produced in all batches.

Production cost increase

When the production cost increases during $[T_B, T_{B'}]$, the manufacturer can keep the original schedule or produce more during previous batches to reduce the production cost during period $[T_B, T_{B'}]$. According to Theorem 7.1, the production and inventory schedules within $[T_{B'}, T_C]$ do not change.

Production cost decrease

When the production cost decreases, the manufacturer can produce more during period $[T_B, T_{B'}]$ and produce less during batches in period $[T_{B'}, T_C]$. Similarly, it can be shown that the production and inventory schedule in $[T_A, T_B]$ does not change. Thus, the optimal plan can be solved by simplifying $(P1)$ which is only about periods $[T_{B'}, T_C]$.

Demand rate increase

When the demand rate increases during $[T_B, T_{B'}]$, the manufacturer can produce more during $[T_B, T_{B'}]$, or in prior batches $[T_A, T_B]$. If the demand rate increases very sharply, the only feasible choice the manufacturer has is to produce more in previous batches. According to Theorem 7.1, the production and inventory schedule within

$[T_{B'}, T_C]$ will not change. Suppose the demand rate is now $D + \delta_D$, then the manufacturer needs $\delta_D \frac{Q^*}{D}$ extra product in $[T_B, T_{B'}]$.

If the production in $[T_B, T_{B'}]$ can satisfy all the demand during this period, we have the following theorem.

Theorem 7.2 *If the manufacturer is able to satisfy all the demand within $[T_B, T_{B'}]$ for the increased demand rate, it is optimal to keep the same quantity Q^* for all the batches in $[T_A, T_B]$ and $[T_{B'}, T_C]$, and produce $Q^* + \frac{Q^*}{D}\delta_D$ in $[T_B, T_{B'}]$.*

The proof is similar to Theorem 7.1.

If the manufacturer cannot satisfy all the demand during $[T_B, T_{B'}]$ when no initial inventory is available, then it is necessary to produce more during $[T_A, T_B]$, and the best schedule can be derived by solving $(P1)$ for the time period $[T_A, T_{B'}]$.

Demand rate decreases

When the demand rate decreases to $D - \delta_D$, the manufacturer can produce less quantity than Q^* in $[T_B, T_{B'}]$ or keep the original production schedule. Similar to the proof of Theorem 7.1, the production and inventory schedule for the manufacturer will not change within $[T_A, T_B]$. The best schedule can be obtained by solving $(P1)$ for the period of $[T_B, T_C]$.

7.4 Disruption Management with Flexible Setup Times

In this section, we discuss the case where the setup time for each batch can be changed. Note that now different batches may have different time durations. Furthermore, we can cancel one batch or add some new batches. Thus, the penalty of setup changes may be incurred.

We start by studying a specific time period where all parameters keep unchanged. In the following theorem, the time interval $[T_a, T_b]$ can be $[T_A, T_B]$, $[T_B, T_{B'}]$, or $[T_{B'}, T_C]$. We assume that the production quantity deviation cost function $f(Q - Q^*)$ is convex.

Theorem 7.3 *For each time interval $[T_a, T_b]$ where all parameters H, S, R, D, and C keep unchanged, in an optimal schedule all batches, except those containing T_a and T_b, have the following properties*
1) a batch starts only when inventory level becomes zero; and
2) the quantity produced in each batch, and thus the batch length, is the same for all batches.

Proof. Assume a batch $[T_1, T_2]$ starts with a non-zero inventory as shown in Fig. 7.5. Then we can always postpone the start of the batch until the inventory becomes zero as shown by the dashed lines in Fig. 7.5 where the batch starts at time T_3. Note that this change does not affect the schedule of any other batches. In the new batch $[T_3, T_2]$, the production quantity keeps the same as that in batch $[T_1, T_2]$, which means the deviation cost does not change. At the same time, the holding cost decreases. Therefore, the new schedule is better than the original one.

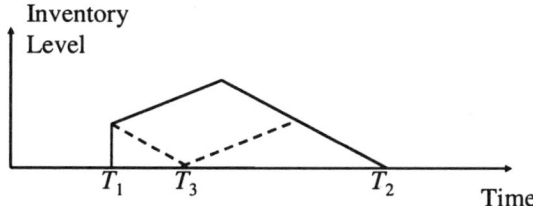

Fig. 7.5 A batch beginning with nonzero inventory

2) Now we prove the property of identical batches. Consider two adjacent batches over a total time period of t, where the length of the first batch is t'. Then the total cost for these two batches can be written as a function of t' as

$$TC(t') = 2S + \frac{1}{2}Dt'^2 H(1 - \frac{D}{R}) + \frac{1}{2}D(t - t')^2 H(1 - \frac{D}{R})$$
$$+ f(Dt' - Q^*) + f(D(t - t') - Q^*)$$
$$= 2S + \Theta + \Gamma,$$

where Θ is the holding cost and Γ is the production deviation cost such as

$$\Theta = \frac{1}{2}H(1-\frac{D}{R})Dt'^2 + \frac{1}{2}H(1-\frac{D}{R})D(t-t')^2,$$

and

$$\Gamma = f(Dt' - Q^*) + f(D(t-t') - Q^*).$$

Consider rescheduling these two batches to make them having equal length, i.e., $t' = \frac{t}{2}$. Then we still have the same setup cost $2S$, but the total holding cost becomes

$$\Theta_1 = 2\left(\frac{1}{2}H(1-\frac{D}{R})D(\frac{t}{2})^2\right). \tag{7.11}$$

We have

$$\Theta - \Theta_1 = \frac{1}{2}H(1-\frac{D}{R})D\left(t'^2 + (t-t')^2 - \frac{t^2}{2}\right)$$

$$= \frac{1}{2}H(1-\frac{D}{R})D\left(2t'^2 - 2tt' + \frac{t^2}{2}\right)$$

$$= \frac{1}{2}H(1-\frac{D}{R})D\left(\sqrt{2}t' - \frac{t}{\sqrt{2}}\right)^2$$

$$\geq 0.$$

Meanwhile, the production quantity deviation cost becomes

$$\Gamma_1 = 2f(D\frac{t}{2} - Dt_0)$$

$$= 2\left(f(\frac{1}{2}(Dt' - Dt_0) + \frac{1}{2}(D(t-t') - Dt_0))\right)$$

$$\leq 2\left(\frac{1}{2}f(Dt' - Dt_0) + \frac{1}{2}f(D(t-t') - Dt_0)\right)$$

$$= \Gamma.$$

The above inequality is due to our assumption that the production quantity deviation cost function is convex.

So both the holding cost and the penalty for deviation from the original production quantity are less when the two batches are equal.

■

Based on the above theorem, an algorithm to solve the problem with flexible setup times is given below.

Without loss of generality, assume the disruption management time window is $[0, T]$, and the disruption occurs in period $[T_1, T_2]$, $0 \leq T_1 < T_2 \leq T$. Let H, S, R, D and C denote the original parameters and H', S', R', D' and C' denote the disrupted parameters. Again, we assume that H', S', R', D' and C' are constant in $[T_1, T_2]$, i.e., the parameters only change once.

We use the following notation in the new schedule.

$k=$ number of batches during period $[0, T_1]$,

$m =$ number of batches during period $[T_1, T_2]$,

$j=$ number of batches during period $[T_2, T]$,

Let x_1, x_2, x_3, x_4, I_1, I_2 be decision variables as shown in Fig. 7.6. Specifically, x_1+x_2 is the batch length where T_1 is located with length x_1 before T_1 and x_2 after T_1; $x_3 + x_4$ is the batch length where T_2 is located with length x_3 before T_2 and x_4 after T_2; and I_1 and I_2 are inventory levels at T_1 and T_2, respectively.

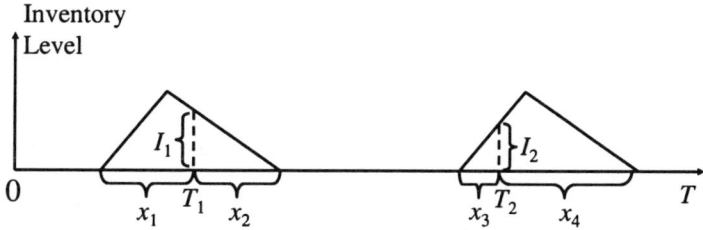

Fig. 7.6 Inventory levels at T_1 and T_2

Based on Theorem 7.3, we can differentiate the inventory levels at T_1 and T_2 into 6 cases. For each case, when k, m, j are fixed, the problem becomes an optimization problem with continuous variables x_1, x_2, x_3, x_4, I_1 and I_2. We can write the cost for each time period as follows.

Let $f_1(k, x_1)$ be the total cost for the batches falling in $[0, T_1]$:

$$f_1(k, x_1) = k\Big(S + \frac{H}{2}(1 - \frac{D}{R})D(\frac{T_1 - x_1}{k})^2 + f(D\frac{T_1 - x_1}{k} - Q^*)\Big).$$

Let $f_2(j, x_4)$ be the total cost for the batches falling in $[T_2, T]$:

$$f_2(j, x_4) = j\Big(S + \frac{H}{2}(1 - \frac{D}{R})D(\frac{T - T_2 - x_4}{j})^2 + f(D\frac{T - T_2 - x_4}{j} - Q^*)\Big).$$

Let $f_3(m, x_2, x_3)$ be the total cost for batches falling in $[T_1, T_2]$:

$$f_3(m, x_2, x_3) = m\Big(S' + \frac{H'}{2}(1 - \frac{D'}{R'})D'(\frac{T_2 - T_1 - x_2 - x_3}{m})^2 \\ + f(D'\frac{T_2 - T_1 - x_2 - x_3}{m} - Q^*)\Big).$$

Define

$$f_0(k, j, m, x_1, x_2, x_3, x_4) = f_1(k, x_1) + f_2(j, x_4) + f_3(m, x_2, x_3),$$

which is the sum of cost for all batches that do not cross times T_1 and T_2. With the above notation, we can see that $f_0(k, j, m, x_1, x_2, x_3, x_4)$ gives the total cost for all the batches in the disruption management time window, except the two possible batches that cross T_1 and T_2, which must be discussed separately.

Consider a batch that crosses time t ($t = T_1$ or T_2). We say the batch has increasing inventory level at t if t is within the production time period, and has decreasing inventory at t if t is within the non-production period. For example, in Figure 7.6, the batch crossing T_1 has decreasing inventory at T_1, and the batch crossing T_2 has increasing inventory at T_2.

Now we can discuss the cost for the two potential batches that cross T_1 and T_2. Let $f_4(x_3, x_4, I_2)$ be the cost for the batch crossing T_2 with the inventory level being I_2 at T_2 and increasing inventory at T_2:

$$f_4(x_3, x_4, I_2) = S + \frac{H'}{2}(R' - D')x_3^2 + f(D'x_3 + Dx_4 - Q^*) \\ + \frac{H}{2}(1 - \frac{D}{R})D\Big((x_4 + \frac{I_2}{R - D})^2 - (\frac{I_2}{R - D})^2\Big).$$

Let $f_5(x_3, x_4, I_2)$ be the cost for the batch which crosses T_2 with the inventory level being I_2 at T_2 and decreasing inventory at T_2:

$$f_5(x_3, x_4, I_2) = S + \frac{1}{2}DHx_4^2 + f(D'x_3 + Dx_4 - Q^*)$$
$$+ \frac{H'}{2}(1 - \frac{D'}{R'})D'\left((x_3 + \frac{I_2}{D'})^2 - \frac{H'D'}{2}(\frac{I_2}{D'})^2\right).$$

Let $g(x_1, x_2, I_1)$ be the cost for the batch which includes time T_1 with the inventory level being I_1 at T_1, which is to be calculated in the following cases.

Case 1. No setup at T_1, and increasing inventory at both T_1 and T_2. In this case, the cost of the batch containing T_1 is

$$g_1(x_1, x_2, I_1) = S + \frac{1}{2}(R - D)Hx_1^2 + f(Dx_1 + D'x_2 - Q^*)$$
$$+ \frac{H'}{2}(1 - \frac{D'}{R'})D'\left((x_2 + \frac{I_1}{R' - D'})^2 - (\frac{I_1}{R' - D'})^2\right),$$

and the cost of the batch containing T_2 is $f_4(x_3, x_4, I_2)$. Therefore, we have the total cost during $[0, T]$ as

$$TC_1(k, j, m) = \pi^+(k + m + j + 2 - n)^+ + \pi^-(n - (k + m + j + 2))^+$$
$$+ \min_{\{x_i, I_l\}} \Big\{ f_0(k, j, m, x_1, x_2, x_3, x_4)$$
$$+ g_1(x_1, x_2, I_1) + f_4(x_3, x_4, I_2) \Big\}.$$

Case 2. No setup at T_1, increasing inventory at T_1, and decreasing inventory at T_2. We have

$$TC_2(k, j, m) = \pi^+(k + m + j + 2 - n)^+ + \pi^-(n - (k + m + j + 2))^+$$
$$+ \min_{\{x_i, I_l\}} \Big\{ f_0(k, j, m, x_1, x_2, x_3, x_4)$$
$$+ g_1(x_1, x_2, I_1) + f_5(x_3, x_4, I_2) \Big\}.$$

Case 3. No setup at T_1, decreasing inventory at T_1, and increasing inventory at T_2. We have

$$g_2(x_1, x_2, I_1) = S + \frac{1}{2}D'H'x_2^2 + f(Dx_1 + D'x_2 - Q^*)$$
$$+ \frac{1}{2}H(1 - \frac{D}{R})D\Big((x_1 + \frac{I_1}{D})^2 - \frac{1}{2}HD(\frac{I_1}{D})^2\Big),$$

and

$$TC_3(k, j, m) = \pi^+(k + m + j + 2 - n)^+ + \pi^-(n - (k + m + j + 2))^+$$
$$+ \min_{\{x_i, I_l\}} \Big\{ f_0(k, j, m, x_1, x_2, x_3, x_4)$$
$$+ g_2(x_1, x_2, I_1) + f_4(x_3, x_4, I_2) \Big\}.$$

Case 4. No setup at T_1, and decreasing inventory at both T_1 and T_2. We have

$$TC_4(k, j, m) = \pi^+(k + m + j + 2 - n)^+ + \pi^-(n - (k + m + j + 2))^+$$
$$+ \min_{\{x_i, I_l\}} \Big\{ f_0(k, j, m, x_1, x_2, x_3, x_4)$$
$$+ g_2(x_1, x_2, I_1) + f_5(x_3, x_4, I_2) \Big\}.$$

Case 5. One setup at T_1, and increasing inventory at T_2. Then,

$$g_3(x_1, x_2, I_1) = S + \frac{1}{2}H(1 - \frac{D}{R})D\Big((x_1 + \frac{I_1}{D})^2 - \frac{1}{2}HD(\frac{I_1}{D})^2\Big) + S'$$
$$+ \frac{H'}{2}(1 - \frac{D'}{R'})D'\Big((x_2 + \frac{I_2}{R' - D'})^2 - \frac{H'D'}{2}(\frac{I_2}{R' - D'})^2\Big)$$
$$+ f(Dx_1 + I_1 - Q^*) + f(D'x_2 + I_1 - Q^*),$$

and

$$TC_5(k, j, m) = \pi^+(k + m + j + 3 - n)^+ + \pi^-(n - (k + m + j + 3))^+$$
$$+ \min_{\{x_i, I_l\}} \Big\{ f_0(k, j, m, x_1, x_2, x_3, x_4)$$
$$+ g_3(x_1, x_2, I_1) + f_4(x_3, x_4, I_2) \Big\}.$$

Case 6. One setup at T_1, and decreasing inventory at T_2. We have

$$TC_6(k,j,m) = \pi^+(k+m+j+3-n)^+ + \pi^-(n-(k+m+j+3))^+$$
$$+ \min_{\{x_i, I_l\}} \Big\{ f_0(k,j,m,x_1,x_2,x_3,x_4)$$
$$+ g_3(x_1,x_2,I_1) + f_5(x_3,x_4,I_2) \Big\}.$$

One point worth mentioning is that there is no setup if the inventory at T_2 is positive since returning to normal production after time T_2 and waiting for all inventory to drop to zero before a new production run will always be the best for the purpose of cost saving.

The optimal production schedule for handling disruptions is given by

$$TC^* = \min_{\{i,k,j,m\}} \{TC_i(k,j,m)\}. \tag{7.12}$$

In the following, we discuss a simple case with only setup cost disruptions.

Theorem 7.4 *Suppose the setup cost changes from S to $S + \delta_S$ during the disruption period $[T_1, T_2]$ which contains only one setup. The optimal schedule is the better one of*
1) keeping the original schedule, or
2) a new schedule which has no setup during the disruption period.

Proof. Let π_0 be the original EPQ plan for the disruption management time window and π^* be an optimal new production plan different from π_0. Now suppose π^* has k, $k \geq 1$, setups during the disruption period.

For any production plan π, define $F_0(\pi)$ to be the cost under the original setup cost and $F(\pi)$ to be the cost evaluated after the setup cost change. Since π_0 is originally optimal, we have $F_0(\pi_0) \leq F_0(\pi^*)$.

If we keep π_0 as the new production plan after the setup cost increase, we have $F(\pi_0) = F_0(\pi_0) + \delta_S$.

Consider π^*. It is easy to see that $F(\pi^*) > F_0(\pi^*) + k\delta_S$ if $\pi^* \neq \pi_0$. This is because the left-hand side has some quantity deviation penalty cost more than the right-hand side. Therefore,

$$F(\pi^*) > F_0(\pi^*) + k\delta_S \geq F_0(\pi_0) + k\delta_S \geq F(\pi_0), \qquad (7.13)$$

which means π^* cannot have any setups during the disruption period. ∎

Based on the above result, we only need to consider a schedule which has no setups in the disruption period $[T_1, T_2]$.

Now assume that the setup cost decreases by δ_S from T_1 to T_2. We have the following conclusion.

Theorem 7.5 *Suppose the setup cost changes from S to $S - \delta_S$ during the disruption period $[T_1, T_2]$ which contains only one setup. Then the optimal schedule is the better one of*
1) keeping the original schedule, or
2) multiple setups in $[T_1, T_2]$.

The proof is similar to the proof of Theorem 7.4, and thus omitted.

7.5 Two-Stage Models

In this section, we extend the above results to a two-stage production inventory system. We will show that similar analysis approaches are still applicable, though the problem becomes more complicate.

In the system, the product is periodically moved from the first stage to the second stage where the external demand is met. The first stage has both production and inventory, and follows an EPQ scheme; while the second stage orders the product from the first stage and follows an EOQ scheme to manage the inventory. In such a system, it can be proved that the optimal production quantity for each batch in the first stage is a multiple integer size of the second stage order quantity. We define the following notation.

D: constant demand rate for the system

R: production rate of the first stage

H_1, H_2: unit holding cost for the first and second stages, respectively.

S_1^p: batch production setup cost for the first stage

S_1^o: the fixed cost for handling an order issued by the second stage

S_2: batch setup cost for the second stage

C: unit production cost at the first stage

For the second stage, an EOQ model is used, and its total operational cost is given by

$$TC_2(Q_2) = \frac{D}{Q_2}S_2 + \frac{H_2 Q_2}{2},$$

where the first term is the setup cost and the second term is the holding cost.

For the first stage, its production quantity for each batch is an integer multiple of the second stage's order quantity, $Q_1 = nQ_2$. The cost can be written as

$$TC_1(Q_2, n) = DC + \frac{DS_1^p}{nQ_2} + \frac{DS_1^o}{Q_2} + \frac{H_1 Q_2}{2}\left((n-1) - (n-2)\frac{D}{R}\right),$$

where the first term is the total production cost, the second term is the production setup cost, the third term is the handling cost associated with the second stage orders, and the fourth term is the inventory holding cost for the first stage.

The total cost for the two-stage system is

$$TC(Q_2, n) = TC_1(Q_2, n) + TC_2(Q_2),$$

which is to be minimized over Q_2 and n. Suppose the optimal solution to such a problem is Q_{20} and n_0.

For the disruption management of the two-stage EPQ model, we have the same definition of disruptions, solution space, and deviation costs. First, we formulate the disruption management problem for the general case.

We assume $[0, T_c]$ is the disruption management time window, and the disruption occurs during $[T_A, T_B]$. We define the following deviation cost functions.

$f_1(Q)$: the penalty function for deviations in the production quantity from the original plan in the first stage.

$f_2(Q)$: the penalty function for deviations in the order quantity of the second stage's handled by the first stage.

$f_3(Q)$: the penalty function for deviations in the order quantity of the second stage from the original plan.

7.5.1 Case for fixed setup times

We start with the case for fixed setup times. Assume there are $N = N_1 + N_2 + N_3$ production batches in the first stage within the given disruption management time window where N_1, N_2 and N_3 correspond to $[0, T_A]$, $[T_A, T_B]$ and $[T_B, T_C]$, respectively. Note that either N_1 or N_3 or both could be zero, which means that there is no pre-disruption period or no post-disruption period or both. In a new production/ordering plan, the production quantity of production cycle i is Q_{1i} in the first stage, $i = 1, \ldots, N$, and the order quantity of ordering cycle j is Q_{2j} in the second stage, $j = 1, \ldots, n_0 N$, where the ordering batches $(i-1)n_0 + 1, \ldots, in_0$ correspond to production batch i.

Assume that during the disruption period $[T_A, T_B]$, the first stage parameters R, H_1, S_1^p, S_1^o, and C change to $R'_i, H'_{1i}, S_{1i}^{p\,\prime}, S_{1i}^{o\,\prime}$, and C' respectively, for $i = 1, \ldots, N_2$. For the second stage, the parameters D, H_2 and S_2 change to D_i, H'_{2j} and S'_{2j}, respectively, for $j = 1, \ldots, n_0 N_2$. Without loss of generality, we consider only the case in which the parameters R'_i, H'_{1i}, $S_{1i}^{p\,\prime}$, $S_{1i}^{o\,\prime}$, C', D_i, H'_{2j} and S'_{2j} do not change within the same production or ordering batch. Also, for notational convenience, we denote the parameters in the pre-disruption period $[0, T_A]$ and post-disruption period $[T_B, T_C]$ as $R'_i = R$, $H'_{1i} = H_1$, $S_{1i}^{p\,\prime} = S_1^p$, $S_{1i}^{o\,\prime} = S_1^o$, $C' = C$ for the first stage, and $D_i = D$, $H'_{2j} = H_2$, $S'_{2j} = S_2$ for the second stage. Let $I_{1,i-1}$ be the inventory level at the beginning of production cycle i in the first stage and $I_{2,j-1}$ be the inventory level at the beginning of order cycle j in the second stage.

Note that setup costs do not play any role here since we assume fixed setup times.

For the second stage, the total relevant cost of the new plan is

$$TC_2(Q_{21},\ldots,Q_{2,n_0N})$$
$$=\sum_{i=1}^{N}\sum_{j=(i-1)n_0+1}^{in_0}\left(\frac{1}{2}H'_{2j}\frac{Q_{20}}{D}(I_{2,j-1}+Q_{2j}+I_{2j})+f_3(Q_{2j}-Q_{20})\right),$$

where

$$I_{2,j-1}+Q_{2j}-\frac{Q_{20}}{D}D_i=I_{2j},\ i=1,\ldots,N,\ j=(i-1)n_0+1,\ldots,in_0 \tag{7.14}$$

$$I_{20}=I_{2,n_0N}=0 \tag{7.15}$$

$$I_{2j}\geq 0,\ j=1,\ldots,n_oN-1. \tag{7.16}$$

For the first stage, the total relevant cost of the new plan is

$$TC_1(Q_{11},\ldots,Q_{1,N})$$
$$=\sum_{i=1}^{N}\left(C'_iQ_{1i}+H'_{1i}\left((I_{1,i-1}+\frac{Q_{1i}}{2})\frac{Q_{1i}}{R'_i}+(I_{1,i-1}+Q_{1i})(\frac{n_0Q_{20}}{D}-\frac{Q_{1i}}{R'_i})\right.\right.$$
$$-\sum_{j=1}^{n_0}Q_{2,(i-1)n_0+j}(\frac{(n_0+1-j)Q_{20}}{D}-\frac{Q_{20}}{R'}))$$
$$\left.+f_1(Q_{1i}-n_0Q_{20})+\sum_{j=1}^{n_0}f_2(Q_{2,(i-1)n_0+j}-Q_{20})\right),$$

where

$$I_{1,i-1}+Q_{1i}-\sum_{j=1}^{n_0}Q_{2,(i-1)n_0+j}=I_{1i},\ i=1,\ldots,N \tag{7.17}$$

$$Q_{1i}\leq R'_i\frac{n_0Q_{20}}{D},\ i=1,\ldots,N \tag{7.18}$$

$$I_{10}=I_{1N}=0 \tag{7.19}$$

$$I_{1,i-1}\geq 0,\ i=1,\ldots,N. \tag{7.20}$$

The optimal new schedule can be obtained by solving the following mathematical programming problem $(P2)$:

$$\min_{Q_{11},\ldots,Q_{1,N},Q_{21},\ldots,Q_{2,n_0 N}} TC_1(Q_{11},\ldots,Q_{1,N}) + TC_2(Q_{21},\ldots,Q_{2,n_0 N})$$

subject to constrains (7.14) to (7.20).

7.5.2 Case for flexible setup times

In this section, we assume that the penalty functions for production/ordering quantity change are convex. Further, we assume that $H_1 < H_2$ as we expect the storage space to be more expensive as material flows downstream in the supply chain. Starting with the second stage, we have the following result.

Theorem 7.6 *Given a disruption interval $[T_A, T_B]$, if all the disrupted parameters are constants, $R' \geq D'$, and if the ordering times are flexible, then all cycles of the optimal new plan in the disruption interval, except those containing T_A and T_B, have the following properties:*
1) an ordering cycle starts only when the inventory level in the second stage becomes zero, and
2) two adjacent ordering cycles corresponding to the same production cycle have the same order quantity, and thus the ordering cycle lengths are identical.

For the two cycles that cross T_A and T_B, we note that they could have different forms. For example, with decreased production cost, the second stage may order a large quantity right before T_B to share the inventory cost with the first stage.

When the setup times are flexible, the first stage may have different production quantities within the disruption period. For example, when facing a raw material discount, the manufacturer might produce large quantities towards the end of the discount period to take advantage of the cheaper material while having less inventory cost compared to the alternative of producing equal quantities for each cycle. However, when the production and ordering stages have a lot-for-lot policy, we have the following result.

Theorem 7.7 *Given a disruption interval $[T_A, T_B]$, if all the disrupted parameters $R'_i, H'_{1i}, S^{p'}_{1i}, S^{o'}_{1i}, C', D_i, H'_{2j}$ and S'_{2j} stay unchanged, $R' \geq D'$, and if the production and ordering times are flexible but adopt a lot-for-lot policy, then all cycles of the optimal new plan in the interval, except those containing T_A and T_B, have the following properties:*
1) *a production cycle starts only at the time when the inventory level in the first stage is zero and the production of the first order can be completed just before its scheduled delivery;*
2) *the ordering cycles corresponding to two adjacent production cycles have identical cycle length, thus, all ordering cycles have identical cycle length; and*
3) *the production quantities for all production cycles are the same.*

Note that if the parameters change several times in the disruption period $[T_A, T_B]$, we could divide $[T_A, T_B]$ into several disjoint periods so that within each period the parameters do not change their values. Then, within each of the periods, Theorem 7.6 still holds, i.e., the order cycles have the same length and quantity. Moreover, if a lot-for-lot production policy is adopted, Theorem 7.7 holds as well. That is, the production quantities for all production cycles will be the same. Theorems 7.6 and 7.7 extend the result in the current literature, which states that ordering cycle lengths are the same at the second stage within the same production cycle and production stage may have the same production quantities under certain conditions. Based on the above theorem, a similar search-based algorithm, as with the single stage EPQ model, can be used to obtain the optimal new plan.

7.5.3 *Special cases for minor disruptions*

In this section, we discuss disruption management from minor disruptions that are characterized by situations in which only one parameter changes during the disruption period $[T_A, T_B]$. Each of these special cases is discussed separately.

Setup cost change

Setup cost could increase or decrease at both stages. If only one of the setup costs increases, then we have the following theorem.

Theorem 7.8 *Suppose there is a setup cost increase in the disruption period* $[T_A, T_B]$. *Then the optimal new plan is either the original plan or a new plan that has fewer setups than the original plan in* $[T_A, T_B]$. *Specifically, we have*
1) *if* S_1^p *increases, then the original plan remains optimal when production setup times are fixed;*
2) *if* S_1^p *increases and production setup times are flexible, then the optimal new plan is either the original plan or a new plan that has fewer production setups than the original plan in* $[T_A, T_B]$;
3) *if* S_1^o *or* S_2 *increases, then the original plan remains optimal when ordering setup times are fixed; and*
4) *if* S_1^o *or* S_2 *increases and ordering times are flexible, then the optimal new plan is either the original plan or a new plan that has fewer orders than the original plan in* $[T_A, T_B]$.

Based on Theorem 7.8, if the production (or ordering) setup times are fixed in the disruption management time window, the original plan is still the best plan when only the production (or ordering) setup cost increases. In addition, if the setup times are flexible, the search algorithm can be implemented more efficiently by adding an upper bound on the number of the production (or ordering) setups in $[T_A, T_B]$. Likewise, if only one of the setup costs decreases, we have the following theorem.

Theorem 7.9 *Suppose there is a setup cost decrease in the disruption period* $[T_A, T_B]$. *Then the optimal new plan is either the original plan or a new plan that has more setups than the original plan in* $[T_A, T_B]$. *Specifically, we have*
1) *if* S_1^p *decreases, the original plan remains optimal when production setup times are fixed;*
2) *if* S_1^p *decreases and production setup times are flexible, the optimal new plan is either the original plan or a new plan that has more production setups than the original plan in* $[T_A, T_B]$;
3) *if* S_1^o *or* S_2 *decreases, the original plan remains optimal when ordering setup times are fixed; and*
4) *if* S_1^o *or* S_2 *decreases and ordering times are flexible, the optimal new plan is either the original plan or a new plan that has more orders than the original plan in* $[T_A, T_B]$.

Holding cost change

If the holding cost in the first stage increases, the possible effect on the original plan is to increase the inventory cost in the first stage. As a result, there might be more production cycles in the new plan. This effect is similar to that of a decrease in the production setup cost. Likewise, if the holding cost in the second stage increases, the possible effect on the original plan is to increase the inventory cost in the second stage. Again, this might lead to more ordering cycles in the new plan. This effect is also similar to the effect of a decrease in the ordering setup cost. Consequently, the properties of Theorem 7.9 hold for the minor disruptions of holding cost increases. Similarly, the properties of Theorem 7.8 hold for the minor disruptions of holding cost decreases.

However, if the production and order setup times are fixed, a decision to produce/order more will generate more inventory holding cost; and a decision to produce/order less will create unsatisfied demand. Hence, the best course of action is to keep the original plan. More specifically, we have the following theorem.

Theorem 7.10 *Suppose there is a holding cost change during the disruption period $[T_A, T_B]$, then we have*
1) if H_1 changes, the original plan remains optimal when production and ordering setup times are fixed; and
2) if H_2 changes, the original plan remains optimal when ordering setup times are fixed.

Production cost change

When the production cost increases during the disruption, it is reasonable to consider the decision to produce less during the disruption period and produce more before so as to reduce the production cost. However, in-advance production will lead to larger inventory holding cost. So, there is a tradeoff between production and holding costs. We analyze this tradeoff in the following theorem.

Theorem 7.11 *Suppose there is a production cost increase in the disruption period $[T_A, T_B]$, then the optimal new plan has the following properties*

1) *it is either the original plan, or a new plan that produces more than the original plan in $[0, T_A]$ and produces less in $[T_A, T_B]$; and*
2) *if the production setup times are fixed, the production and inventory schedule of the production cycles in $[T_B, T_C]$ remains unchanged.*

When the production cost decreases, similar properties can be derived as stated below.

Theorem 7.12 *Suppose there is a production cost decrease in the disruption period $[T_A, T_B]$, then the optimal new plan has the following properties*
1) *it is either the original plan or a new plan that produces more than the original plan in $[T_A, T_B]$ and produces less in $[T_B, T_C]$; and*
2) *if the production setup times are fixed, the production and inventory schedule of the production cycles in $[T_0, T_A]$ remains unchanged.*

Production rate change

When the production setup times are fixed, if the new production rate R' is not lower than the demand rate D, producing more means accumulating more inventory and incurring a penalty for production quantity change while producing less means that we cannot satisfy all the demand. Thus, the best policy is to stick to the original plan. Yet, if the new production rate R' is lower than the demand rate D, then the new plan needs to produce more before the disruption period because the capacity is insufficient to satisfy the demand during the disruption period. Then, after the disruption period, the new plan will return to normal production. More specifically, we have the following theorem.

Theorem 7.13 *Suppose there is a production rate decrease in the disruption period $[T_A, T_B]$,*
1) *when the production setup times are fixed and the new production rate is not lower than the demand rate, it is optimal to keep the original plan; and*
2) *when the new production rate is lower than the demand rate, the optimal new plan is to produce more during the period $[0, T_A]$; furthermore, if the production setup times are fixed, the production and inventory schedule of the production batches in $[T_B, T_C]$ remains unchanged.*

Demand rate change

If the demand is changed and the setup times are fixed, then we have the following theorem:

Theorem 7.14 *Suppose there is a demand rate increase or decrease in the disruption period $[T_A, T_B]$. If the setup times are fixed, then the optimal new plan has the following properties*:
1) *if the demand rate increases by an amount $\delta_D > 0$, and $D + \delta_D \leq R$, then each ordering cycle orders an amount $Q_0(1 + \delta_D/D)$ and each production cycle produces an amount $n_0 Q_0(1 + \delta_D/D)$; and*
2) *if the demand rate decreases by an amount $\delta_D > 0$, then each ordering cycle orders an amount $Q_0(1 - \delta_D/D)$ and each production cycle produces an amount $n_0 Q_0(1 + \delta_D/D)$.*

Note that the above theorem is valid only for the case where the production rate is larger than the demand rate during the disruption period. If $D + \delta_D > R$, then the manufacturer will have to produce more quantities in the pre-disruption period to satisfy the increased demand during the in-disruption period.

If the demand rate changes when the setup times are flexible, then disruption management becomes critically dependent on the production and ordering policies. The optimal new plan depends on the relative values of D/R and n_0. In these settings, it is not clear in which direction the first stage inventory will change. This makes it difficult to obtain a general result on whether the number of setups for both stages will increase, decrease, or stay the same.

7.5.4 Two-stage model with multiple retailers

The above two-stage model can be further extended to the case with a single manufacturer in the first stage and multiple $m > 1$ retailers in the second stage. For example, we may have many retailers that are located in different cities and served by a single supplier. We study general disruptions of both fixed and flexible setup types as well as some special disruptions. It turns out that most of our previous results for the single-retailer case can be extended to the setting with multiple retailers.

Fixed setup times

Given an original plan, when all the setup times are fixed, the solution approach of Section 7.5.1 could be applied for the multiple-retailers setting. The objective function of each retailer is the same as the single-retailer case since with initial and end inventories, the holding cost can still be calculated from the area of the corresponding trapezoids. The first-stage inventory holding cost generally depends on the specific policy (exact or heuristic policies such as power of two) used.

However, if the first and the second stages exhibit special structure (e.g., the retailers having identical setup times), it is quite straightforward to write the expressions for the holding cost of the first stage, and the total cost for the two-stage system in our mathematical programming problem. The solution approach given in Section 7.5.1 can also be used here.

Flexible setup times

When the setup times are flexible, some retailers may want to increase their ordering sizes while others may wish to decrease their ordering sizes. The disruptions may make some retailers add cycles while causing other retailers to reduce ordering cycles. Thus, the optimal new production and inventory decisions of the first stage must account for the possible combinations among the retailers' ordering sizes, ordering times as well as the deviation penalties, which also depends on the types and the sizes of the disruptions. These complex disruption management problems are beyond the scope of the present research.

When all the retailers adopt a lot-for-lot size policy vis-a-vis the first stage, we have the following theorem that is similar to Theorems 7.6 and 7.7.

Theorem 7.15 *Given a disruption interval $[T_A, T_B]$, if all disrupted parameters $R'_i, H'_{1i}, S^{p'}_{1i}, S^{o'}_{1i}, C', D'_i, H'_{2j}$ and S'_{2j} are constants, $R'_i \geq \sum_{i=1}^{m} D'_i$, and if the ordering times are flexible, then all cycles in the optimal new plan in the interval, except those containing T_A and T_B, have the following properties:*
1) *an ordering cycle for each retailer starts only when its inventory level becomes zero;*

2) *all the ordering cycles for each retailer are of identical length;*
3) *a production cycle starts only at the time when the inventory level in the first stage is zero and the production of the first order can be completed just before its scheduled delivery; and*
4) *the production quantities for all production cycles are the same.*

Finally, we consider two special cases where (1) only a single retailer experiences a disruption, or (2) all the retailers face a disruption which is characterized by a change of a common parameter. It turns out that all our theorems in Section 7.5.3 still hold but the results for those two types of special disruptions have somewhat different effects on the first stage. Specifically, we have the following theorem.

Theorem 7.16 *When only one retailer experiences a disruption or all the retailers face a disruption with a common parameter, Theorems 7.8 through 7.13 still hold. While the general result of Theorem 7.14 also holds, the corresponding quantities need to be modified to fit with the multiple-retailers settings.*

7.6 Related Literature

There has been much research on how to revise the basic EPQ/EOQ model when system parameters change. Most concerns have been given to cases when the ordering price changes, for example, Lev *et al.*(1981), Taylor and Bradley (1985), Lev and Weiss (1990), Goyal (1992), Arcelus and Srinivasan (1995), Ardalan (1995), Tersine and Barman (1995), Chang and Dye (2000), and Huang *et al.*(2003). In other cases, researches on setup cost changes include Matsuyama (2001), on demand rate changes include Haneveld and Teunter (1998), and on production capacity uncertainty include Hariga and Haouari (1999). However, no deviation cost for revising the original schedule is included in the above research.

Our research is also relevant to the study of the finite horizon EPQ model since a disruption must be handled in a limited time period, existing research in this field includes Schwarz (1972), Lev and Sosyster (1979).

The two-stage EOQ/EPQ model belongs to the research on series inventory systems, the basic model of which was studied by Jackson et al.(1985), Roundy (1985,1986), Atkins and Sun (1995), etc.

Many theorems are provided without formal proofs in this chapter. The more detailed discussions on disruption management for EPQ models can be found in Xia et al.(2002,2004).

References

Arcelus, F.J. and G. Srinivasan (1995), Discount strategies for one-time-only sales, *IIE Transactions*, 27, 618-624.

Ardalan, A. (1995), A comparative analysis of approaches for determining optimal price and order quantity when a sale increases demand, *European Journal of Operational Research*, 84, 416-430.

Atkins, D. and D. Sun (1995), 98-percent-effective lot-sizing for series inventory systems with backlogging, *Operations Research*, 43, 335-345.

Chang, H.J. and C.Y. Dye (2000), An EOQ model with deteriorating items in response to a temporary sale price, *Production & Planning Control*, 11, 464-473.

Goyal, S.K. (1990), Economic ordering policy during special discount periods for dynamic inventory problems under certainty, *Engineering Costs and Production Economics*, 20, 101-104.

Haneveld, W.K.K. and R.H. Teunter (1998), Effects of discounting and demand rate variability on the EOQ *International Journal of Production Economics*, 54, 173-192.

Hariga, M. and M. Haouari (1999), An EOQ lot sizing model with random supplier capacity, *International Journal of Production Economics*, 58, 39-47.

Huang W., V. Kulkarni and J. Swaminathan (2003), Optimal EOQ for announced price increases in infinite horizon, *Operations Research*, 51, 336-339.

Jackson, P., W. Maxwell and Muckstadt (1985), The joint replenishment problem with a power-of-two restrictions, *IIE Transactions*, 17, 25-32.

Lev, B. and A.L. Sosyster (1979), An inventory model with finite horizon and price changes, *Journal of Operational Research Society*, 30, 43-53.

Lev, B., H.J. Weiss and A.L. Soyster (1981), Optimal ordering policies when anticipating parameter changes in EOQ systems, *Naval Research Logistics Quarterly*, 28, 267-279.

Lev, B. and H.J. Weiss (1990), Inventory models with cost increases, *Operations Research*, 39, 53-63.

Matsuyama, K. (2001), The EOQ-models modified by introducing discount of purchase price or increase of setup cost, *International Journal of Production Economics*, 73, 83-99.

Roundy, R.O. (1985), 98%-effective integer-ratio lot-sizing for one warehouse multiretailer systems, *Management Science*, 31, 1416-1430.

Roundy, R.O. (1986), A 98%-effective lot-sizing rule for a multiproduct, multistage production/inventory system, *Mathematics of Operations Research*, 11, 699-727.

Schwarz, L.B. (1972), Economic order quantities for products with finite demand horizon, *AIIE Transactions*, 4, 234-237.

Taylor, S.G. and C.E. Bradley (1985), Optimal ordering strategies for announced price increases, *Operations Research*, 33, 312-325.

Tersine, R.J. and S. Barman (1995), Economic purchasing strategies for temporary price discounts, *European Journal of Operational Research*, 80, 328-343.

Willem, K., K. Haneveld and R.H. Teunter (1998), Effects of discounting and demand rate variability on the EOQ, *International Journal of Production Economics*, 54, 173-192.

Xia, Y., X. Qi and G. Yu (2002), Real-time production and inventory disruption management under the continuous rate economic production quantity model, working paper, Department of Management Science and Information Systems, The Universoty of Texas at Austin.

Xia, Y., M.-H. Yang, B. Golany, S.M. Gilbert and G. Yu (2004), Real-time disruption management in a two-stage production and inventory system, *IIE Transactions*, 36, 111-125.

Chapter 8

Disruption Management for Discrete Production Planning Problems

8.1 Introduction

In this chapter, we study disruption management for a discrete production planning problem. Specifically, the problem has n discrete time periods, each of which has a known discrete demand, a production cost function, and an inventory cost function. We assume backlogging is allowed. The problem is to decide the production quantity and, hence, the inventory level for each period so that the total cost over the n periods is minimized.

This is a classical operations research problem. An optimal production/inventory plan can be easily obtained by a dynamic programming algorithm. The problem can also be viewed as a network flow model. When all production and inventory cost functions are linear, it is a linear min-cost network flow problem and can be solved in polynomial time. Other special cases have also been studied including convex cost functions and concave cost functions, and efficient algorithms exist for these cases.

After an optimal production/inventory plan is given, its execution, however, is subject to various disruptions. Demand change is probably the first that one can think of. When demand changes, the original plan may not remain optimal, and very probably become infeasible because the total production may be different from the total demand. Besides demand uncertainty, production and inventory cost functions may also change for some periods. When such cost disruption occurs, the original production plan is still feasible, but may become not optimal. In either case, a new production plan is needed to minimize total cost in the new environment. This is the disruption management problem we will study in this chapter.

With respect to modeling uncertainties, we will consider demand disruption and cost disruption, and give more emphasis on the cost disruptions. In fact, cost disruptions can model not only real cost changes but also a wide range of other disruptions, including but not limited to machine breakdowns, workers unavailability, inventory failures, supply shortages, etc. For example, machine breakdowns and workers unavailability may cause production capacity changes. Suppose period i has a limited production capacity. Then the production cost function can be set to be $+\infty$ when the production quantity is above the capacity. In this way, cost function change can also be used to model the production capacity change. Inventory capacity change can be modeled in the same way.

When generating the new production plan, we need to consider two types of costs. One is the pure production and inventory cost, i.e., the cost evaluated under the new production and inventory cost functions, as if we are solving a new production planning problem with these cost functions. The other is the deviation cost, i.e., the cost of switching from the original plan to the new plan. For example, if we need to produce more than what is planned, the part of the new production quantity can cause some extra costs.

In general, the deviation cost accounts for the adjustment the management, workforce, and its suppliers have to make to accommodate the change in plans, the extra communication and coordination costs incurred by the change, and probably the requirement that the new plan converges back to the original plan after the system-environmental changes incurred by the disruption has ebbed. For this last point, if it is required that the production and inventory level must return to the original plan beyond a specific number of periods, i.e., a time window, after a disruption occurs, we can use the deviation cost function to capture this requirement by setting the deviation penalty function beyond the time window to be $+\infty$. This forces the new plan to be the same as the original plan for periods beyond the time window.

By modeling the disruption management problem as minimizing the sum of production and inventory costs as well as their deviation costs, we will show that the disruption management problem is also a network flow problem with the same structure as the original planning problem. This suggests that the disruption management problem can be solved by using those existing known algorithms. In this regard, we will give a detailed implementation of a dynamic problem algorithm.

Moreover, we will show that for the disruption management there may exist more efficient algorithms than the existing ones. Because of the deviation cost, the new optimal plan will not be too far away from the original plan. Based on such a property, we will show how a local search algorithm can be used to find a new optimal plan. Moreover, we also show that the idea of greediness in the local search is actually the most efficient way to find the new optimal plan among all local search methods.

The structure of this chapter is organized as follows. In Section 8.2, we propose the mathematical formulation of the problem. In Section 8.3, we develop a dynamic programming algorithm to solve the problem, and in Section 8.4, we present and analyze a greedy local search algorithm for the special case of convex cost functions. Numerical examples and computational results are reported in Section 8.5, and related literature is given in the last section.

8.2 Problem Formulations

Initially, the manufacturer is to plan its production and inventory schedule for n time periods where the demand for each period i is known to be d_i's and the initial available and terminal required inventory levels are y_0 and y_n, respectively. For period i, we may denote the production costs by $c_i(x_i)$ where $x_i \geq 0$ is the production level for period i, and the inventory costs (either holding or backlogging) by $h_i(y_i)$ where y_i is the inventory level. In particular, $c_i(x_i)$ is increasing and $c_i(0) = 0$; while $h_i(y_i)$ is decreasing for $y_i < 0$, increasing for $y_i > 0$, and $h_i(0) = 0$. Then the production planning problem, referred to as the original problem (OP), can be formulated as follows.

$$(OP) \quad \min \sum_{i=1}^{n} c_i(x_i) + \sum_{i=1}^{n-1} h_i(y_i)$$

subject to

$$y_{i-1} + x_i - y_i = d_i \quad \forall i = 1, ..., n \quad (IA)$$

$$x_i \in \{0, 1, 2, ...\} \quad \forall i = 1, ..., n \quad (IB).$$

(OP) can also be regarded as a minimum cost network flow problem where x_i's are production flows, y_i's are inventory flows, and the corresponding arcs in the network are called production and inventory arcs, respectively. Then, Constraints (IA) are the flow conservation constraints, and Constraints (IB) specify the nonnegativity of production flows. Because of flow conservation, an n-dimensional integer vector $\mathbf{x} \equiv (x_1, ..., x_n)$ uniquely determines a feasible solution of (OP). The network representation of (OP) is in Fig. 8.1.

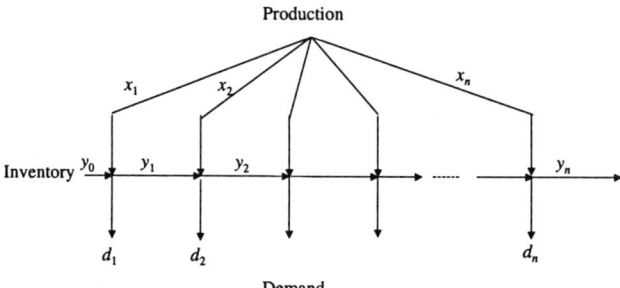

Fig. 8.1 Network flow model for the discrete time production/inventory problem

(OP) can be solved by a dynamic programming method which can be found in many operations research books. Suppose that $\mathbf{x}^*$ is an optimal solution for (OP). We now discuss how to model the disruption management problem when $\mathbf{x}^*$ have to be revised.

A disruption to (OP) can be either a demand change or a cost function change. In general, for any period i, we can denote the resolved real demand be $d_i + \Delta d_i$, the production and inventory costs be $c'_i(x_i)$ and $h'_i(y_i)$. To quantify the deviation cost with respect to the production plan change in period i, suppose the new production quantity is $x_i = x_i^* + \Delta x_i$. Then the function $\Delta c_i(\Delta x_i)$ can be used to capture the production deviation cost for period i. Similarly, the function $\Delta h_i(\Delta y_i)$ can be used to capture the inventory deviation cost. Note that the new inventory level for period i is $y_i = y_i^* + \Delta y_{i-1} + \Delta x_i - \Delta d_i$.

We can formulate the disruption management problem, denoted by (DM), of finding the new production plan to minimize the sum of production and inventory costs as well as their deviation costs as follows.

$$\min \sum_{i=1}^{n} \Big(c_i'(x_i^* + \Delta x_i) + \Delta c_i(\Delta x_i)\Big) + \sum_{i=1}^{n-1} \Big(h_i'(y_i^* + \Delta y_i) + \Delta h_i(\Delta y_i)\Big)$$

subject to

$$\Delta y_{i-1} + \Delta x_i - \Delta y_i = \Delta d_i \quad \forall i = 1, ..., n \quad (RA)$$

$$\Delta x_i \in \{-x_i^*, -x_i^* + 1, -x_i^* + 2, ...,\} \quad \forall i = 1, ..., n. \quad (RB)$$

Without loss of generality, we assume both Δy_0 and Δy_n are 0. For (DM), we see that $\Delta \mathbf{x}$ and $\Delta \mathbf{y}$ together form a new network flow model, where Constraints (RA) are about the flow conservation and Constraints (RB) specify the lower bound of the production deviation. The new network is shown in Fig. 8.2.

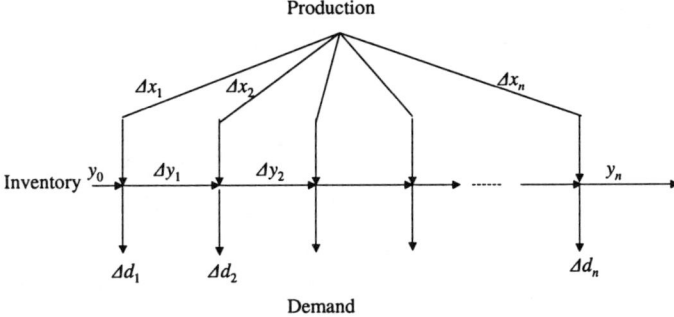

Fig. 8.2 Network flow model for disruption management

8.3 Dynamic Programming Algorithm

Because (DM) shares similar network structures with (OP), the algorithms developed for (OP) can also be used to solve (DM). For example, when all cost functions are linear, (DM) is a linear minimum cost network flow problem, and can be efficiently solved by linear programming. When the cost functions are of general forms, we demonstrate a dynamic programming algorithm that was originally in Florian et al.(1980) for solving (OP).

For $i, j = 1, 2, ..., n$ and $i \leq j$, define the following notation for the periods from i to j:

$X_{ij}^* \equiv \sum_{k=i}^{j} x_k^*$, total original production level,

$D_{ij} \equiv \sum_{k=i}^{j} d_k$, total original demand,

$D_{ij}' \equiv \sum_{k=i}^{j} d_k'$, total new demand,

$\Delta D_{ij} \equiv \sum_{k=i}^{j} \Delta d_k$, total demand difference,

$|\Delta D|_{ij} \equiv \sum_{k=i}^{j} |\Delta d_k|$, total absolute demand difference.

For the aim of simplicity, we assume that all the above terms are 0 for $i > j$. We also let $\overline{d} \equiv D_{1n}/n$ be the average initial demand per period, $\overline{d'} \equiv D_{1n}'/n$ the average new demand per period, and $\overline{|\Delta d|} \equiv |\Delta D|_{1n}/n$ the average absolute demand difference per period.

Let $F_i(\Delta y_{i-1})$ be the minimum cost of the subproblem of (DM) involving periods $i, i+1, ..., n$ when the change of the incoming inventory level from period $i - 1$ is Δy_{i-1}. Then for period i with the production level change Δx_i, the cost incurred in the current period is

$$F_i'(\Delta y_{i-1}, \Delta x_i) = c_i'(x_i^* + \Delta x_i) + \Delta c_i(\Delta x_i)$$
$$+ h_i'(y_i^* + \Delta y_{i-1} + \Delta x_i - \Delta d_i)$$
$$+ \Delta h_i(\Delta y_{i-1} + \Delta x_i - \Delta d_i).$$

To calculate $F_i(\Delta y_{i-1})$, we have to test all possible production levels for period i. This results in the following dynamic programming recursion

$$F_i(\Delta y_{i-1}) = \min_{\Delta x_i} \Big\{ F_i'(\Delta y_{i-1}, \Delta x_i) + F_{i+1}(\Delta y_{i-1} + \Delta x_i - \Delta d_i)|$$
$$\text{for } -x_i^* \leq \Delta x_i \leq \Delta D_{in} - \Delta y_{i-1} \Big\},$$

for $i = n-1, n-2, ..., 1$, $-X_{1,i-1}^* - \Delta D_{1,i-1} \leq \Delta y_{i-1} \leq X_{in}^* + \Delta D_{in}$, and for $i = 1$, $\Delta y_0 = 0$. We also have the initial conditions for period n such as for $-X_{1,n-1}^* - \Delta D_{1,n-1} \leq \Delta y_{n-1} \leq x_n^* + \Delta d_n$,

$$F_n(\Delta y_{n-1}) = c_n'(x_n^* + \Delta d_n - \Delta y_{n-1}) + \Delta c_n'(\Delta d_n - \Delta y_{n-1}).$$

The optimal objective function value of (DM) can be obtained from $F_1(0)$.

In the above dynamic programming algorithm, there are $O(n)$ stages. In each stage i, there are $O(X_{1n}^* + \Delta D_{1n}) \equiv O(n\overline{d'})$ different $F_i(\Delta y_{i-1})$'s; and each $F_i(\Delta y_{i-1})$ requires the comparison of $O(n\overline{d'})$ alternative terms. So the overall time complexity for the dynamic program is in $O(n^3 \overline{d'}^2)$ time.

8.4 Case for Convex Cost Functions

We now concentrate on the problem where all the involved costs are convex. The convex production cost, including the linear production cost, is very realistic and is commonly assumed in the production planning literature. The convex inventory holding-backlogging cost covers the case of linear holding and backlogging costs, and hence is very realistic as well. It is quite reasonable to assume the disruption costs $\Delta c_i(\cdot)$ and $\Delta h_i(\cdot)$ to be linear or quadratic over the absolute value to gauge the distance between the original plan and the new plan. So, it is also reasonable to assume that the disruption costs be convex. Now, $c_i(x_i^* + \cdot) + \Delta c_i(\cdot)$'s and $h_i(y_i^* + \cdot) + \Delta h_i(\cdot)$'s are all convex. When only the cost disruption is considered, (DM) is a convex minimum cost network flow problem (CMNF) with zero demand.

In the literature, people have developed many efficient algorithms for general CMNF problems. When used to solve our problem of

(DM), they are not the most efficient methods in that they all start from the scratch without using the knowledge about the initial optimal plan, thus much of the computation is wasted. In this section, we will introduce a greedy method which utilizes the knowledge about the original optimal plan with a running time being linearly dependent on the distance between the original plan and the new plan (to be defined).

In the following greedy algorithm, we assume the original solution $\mathbf{x}^*$ is still feasible to (DM), which is true when there is no demand disruption. When a demand disruption does occur, $\mathbf{x}^*$ may become infeasible in that the sum of production may not be still equal to the sum of all demand. This, however, can be easily handled by a preprocessing in which we adjust the production level by simply following the demand disruption for each period.

8.4.1 Preliminaries

We may use the following formulation (P) to unite our perceptions about (OP) and (DM). The network of (P) is in Fig. 8.3.

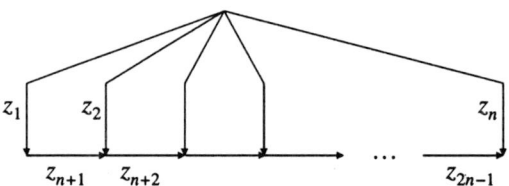

Fig. 8.3 Network flow model for the general problem

$$(P) \quad \min f(\mathbf{z}) \equiv \sum_{i=1}^{n} f_i^c(z_i) + \sum_{i=1}^{n-1} f_i^h(z_{n+i})$$

subject to

$$z_1 - z_{n+1} = 0 \quad (A1)$$

$$z_{n+i-1} + z_i - z_{n+i} = 0 \quad \forall i = 2, ..., n-1 \quad (A)$$

$$z_{2n-1} + z_n = 0 \quad (An)$$

Solving (OP) and getting an initial optimal solution $\mathbf{x}^*$ is equivalent to solving (P) with the cost functions

$$f_i^c(z) = \begin{cases} c_i(x_i^* + z) + \Delta c_i(z) & \text{if } z \geq -x_i^* \\ +\infty & \text{if } z \leq -x_i^* - 1 \end{cases}$$

$$f_i^h(z) = h_i(y_i^* + z) + \Delta h_i(z),$$

and getting an optimal solution $\mathbf{0}$. Solving (DM) and getting an optimal deviation solution $(\Delta \mathbf{x}^*, \Delta \mathbf{y}^*)$ is equivalent to solving (P) with the primed costs

$$f_i^{c\prime}(z) = \begin{cases} c_i'(x_i^* + z) + \Delta c_i(z) & \text{if } z \geq -x_i^* \\ +\infty & \text{if } z \leq -x_i^* - 1 \end{cases}$$

$$f_i^{h\prime}(z) = h_i'(y_i^* + z) + \Delta h_i(z),$$

and getting the optimal solution $\mathbf{z}^* \equiv (\Delta \mathbf{x}^*, \Delta \mathbf{y}^*)$.

Since the knowledge about the optimal original plan $\mathbf{x}^*$ has already been embedded in the cost functions, we cannot really solve (OP) by solving (P). Nevertheless, (P) is instrumental to our later presentations and derivations.

From now on, we call a $(2n-1)$-dimensional integer vector $\mathbf{z}$ a flow vector if it satisfies the n equations in (P). For the obvious reason, for $i = 1, ..., n-1$, we call z_i the flow on the ith production arc, and for $i = 1, ..., n-1$, we call z_{n+i} the flow on the ith inventory arc. Due to the independent equations that the z_i's have to follow, flows on the production arcs uniquely determine flows on the inventory arcs, and we still have $\sum_{i=1}^n z_i = 0$. Also, the sum or difference of two flow vectors remains to be a flow vector.

We may define operator $\| \cdot \|$ for every flow vector $\mathbf{z}$ such that $\| \mathbf{z} \| \equiv (\sum_{i=1}^n | z_i |)/2$. This $\| \cdot \|$ will serve as the distance operator for two different plans as will be seen later. We call a flow vector $\mathbf{s}$ a swap if $\| \mathbf{s} \| = 1$. Given swap $\mathbf{s}$, there must be $i, j = 1, ..., n$ and $i \neq j$, such that $s_i = 1$, $s_j = -1$, and $s_k = 0$ for $k = 1, ..., n$ and

$k \neq i, j$. The production arc in period i will be called s's starting arc and that in period j will be called s's ending arc. We call s counter-clockwise when $i < j$ and clockwise when $i > j$. A swap is a simple circuit in the production planning network, and it is the basic apparatus for our proofs.

We call an integer (not necessarily flow) vector **e** elementary if $e_i = -1, 0$, or $+1$ for every $i = 1, ..., 2n - 1$. A swap is an elementary flow vector with flows on exactly two production arcs. We say that elementary vector **e** does not cancel out integer vector **w** if for every $i = 1, ..., 2n - 1$, we have $w_i e_i \geq 0$. If, furthermore, we have that for every $i = 1, ..., 2n - 1$, $\mid w_i \mid \geq \mid e_i \mid$, then we say that **e** is compatible with **w**. Obviously, elementary vector **e** does not cancel out integer vector **w** if and only if **e** is compatible with the integer vector **w** + **e**.

Note that a swap in the production planning network is exactly a simple circuit defined in the more general network in Denardo (1982). We can prove one lemma related to the making of flow vectors by swaps that is similar to part of Theorem 5 in Denardo (1982). Due to the similarity, we omit the proof.

Lemma 8.1 *Suppose* $\mathbf{z}^1$ *and* $\mathbf{z}^2$ *are two flow vectors and denote* $\mathbf{z}^2 - \mathbf{z}^1$ *by* $\mathbf{z}$. *Then, we can find* $\| \mathbf{z} \|$ *swaps, all being compatible with* $\mathbf{z}$, *that add up to be* $\mathbf{z}$.

For convenience, for any two integer vectors **w** and **v**, we let $\delta(\mathbf{v}, \mathbf{w}) \equiv f(\mathbf{v} + \mathbf{w}) - f(\mathbf{v})$. The following lemma provides the logical source for all of our later results that rely on the convexity of $f(\cdot)$. We omit its proof because it is already embedded in the proof of Theorem 5 in Denardo (1982).

Lemma 8.2 *Suppose elementary vector* **e** *does not cancel out integer vector* **w**, *then for any integer vector* **v**,

$$\delta(\mathbf{v} + \mathbf{w}, \mathbf{e}) \geq \delta(\mathbf{v}, \mathbf{e}).$$

We say two elementary vectors **a** and **b** share no common arcs when $a_i b_i = 0$ for every $i = 1, ..., 2n - 1$. We say that a set of elementary vectors are independent when no two of them share common arcs. For two elementary vectors **a** and **b** and an integer vector **w**, by the definition of $\delta(\cdot, \cdot)$, the separability of $f(\cdot)$, and Lemma 8.2

(convexity of $f(\cdot)$), the following simple facts apply for the $\delta(\cdot,\cdot)$ operator.

1) $\delta(\mathbf{w}, \mathbf{a}+\mathbf{b}) = \delta(\mathbf{w}, \mathbf{a}) + \delta(\mathbf{w}+\mathbf{a}, \mathbf{b})$. Therefore, $\delta(\mathbf{w}+\mathbf{a}, -\mathbf{a}) = -\delta(\mathbf{w}, \mathbf{a})$.

2) When $\mathbf{a}$ and $\mathbf{b}$ share no common arcs, $\delta(\mathbf{w}+\mathbf{a}, \mathbf{b}) = \delta(\mathbf{w}, \mathbf{b})$ and therefore $\delta(\mathbf{w}, \mathbf{a}+\mathbf{b}) = \delta(\mathbf{w}, \mathbf{a}) + \delta(\mathbf{w}, \mathbf{b})$.

3) $\delta(\mathbf{w}+\mathbf{a}, \mathbf{a}) \geq \delta(\mathbf{w}, \mathbf{a}) \geq \delta(\mathbf{w}-\mathbf{a}, \mathbf{a})$.

Now, we can prove our first main theorem.

Theorem 8.1 *Given flow vector $\mathbf{z}^0$, suppose for any swap $\mathbf{s}$, we have $\delta(\mathbf{z}^0, \mathbf{s}) \geq 0$. Then, $\mathbf{z}^0$ is an optimal solution for (P).*

Proof. For any $\mathbf{z}'$ different from $\mathbf{z}^0$ that is feasible for (P), let $\mathbf{z}$ be $\mathbf{z}' - \mathbf{z}^0$. Due to Lemma 8.1, $\mathbf{z}$ is the sum of $m \equiv \|\mathbf{z}\|$ swaps, say $\mathbf{s}^1, ..., \mathbf{s}^m$, that are compatible with $\mathbf{z}$. Using Lemma 8.2 and the fact that $\delta(\mathbf{z}^0, \mathbf{s}^j) \geq 0$ for every $j = 1, ..., m$, we obtain

$$f(\mathbf{z}') - f(\mathbf{z}^0) = \delta(\mathbf{z}^0, \mathbf{z})$$
$$= \delta(\mathbf{z}^0, \sum_{j=1}^{m} \mathbf{s}^j)$$
$$= \sum_{j=1}^{m} \delta(\mathbf{z}^0 + \sum_{k=1}^{j-1} \mathbf{s}^k, \mathbf{s}^j)$$
$$\geq \sum_{j=1}^{m} \delta(\mathbf{z}^0, \mathbf{s}^j)$$
$$\geq 0.$$

Hence, $\mathbf{z}^0$ is an optimal solution for (P). ∎

Consider every move from a flow vector $\mathbf{z}$ to another flow vector $\mathbf{z} + \mathbf{s}$ where $\mathbf{s}$ is a swap as a local move, then Theorem 8.1 says that flow vector $\mathbf{z}$ is optimal if and only if there exists no improving local move from it. Also by Theorem 8.1, using any local descent method, where we move to a neighboring solution whenever there is a local improving move, will eventually let us converge to the optimal solution. Now, the problem is how fast a given local descent method converges.

Among all local descent methods, we suspect that a greedy algorithm where we choose the steepest descent move in each step will fare very well. Indeed, we will show that the greedy algorithm converges to the optimal point in the least number of possible steps for any local descent method. In the following, we may use the terms greedy and steepest interchangeably.

Before preceding to the next section, we list some simple facts about swaps that are to be used in the later proofs. The relationship between two swaps $\mathbf{s}^1$ and $\mathbf{s}^2$ are much simpler than the relationship between simple circuits in a general network. We can characterize the relationship into five mutually exclusive and complete categories.

1) $\mathbf{s}^1$ and $\mathbf{s}^2$ share no common arcs.

2) $\mathbf{s}^1$ and $\mathbf{s}^2$ completely cancel out each other when $\mathbf{s}^1 = -\mathbf{s}^2$.

3) $\mathbf{s}^1$ and $\mathbf{s}^2$ form one swap $\mathbf{s}$ when there are independent elementary vectors $\mathbf{a}$, $\mathbf{b}$, and $\mathbf{c}$ such that $\mathbf{s}^1 = \mathbf{a} + \mathbf{c}$, $\mathbf{s}^2 = \mathbf{b} - \mathbf{c}$, and $\mathbf{s} \equiv \mathbf{a} + \mathbf{b}$ is one swap.

4) $\mathbf{s}^1$ and $\mathbf{s}^2$ form two independent swaps $\mathbf{s}'$ and $\mathbf{s}''$ when there are independent elementary vectors $\mathbf{a}^1$, $\mathbf{a}^2$, $\mathbf{b}^1$, $\mathbf{b}^2$, and $\mathbf{c}$ such that $\mathbf{s}^1 = \mathbf{a}^1 + \mathbf{b}^1 + \mathbf{c}$, $\mathbf{s}^2 = \mathbf{a}^2 + \mathbf{b}^2 - \mathbf{c}$, and $\mathbf{s}' \equiv \mathbf{a}^1 + \mathbf{b}^2$ and $\mathbf{s}'' \equiv \mathbf{a}^2 + \mathbf{b}^1$ are two independent swaps.

5) $\mathbf{s}^1$ and $\mathbf{s}^2$ share same-direction common arcs when $s_i^1 s_i^2 \geq 0$ for every $i = 1, ..., 2n - 1$ and the inequality is strict for at least one i.

8.4.2 The greedy algorithm

Suppose we start a local descent method from an initial solution $\mathbf{z}^0$ and end with an optimal solution $\mathbf{z}^*$. Due to apparent reasons, the minimum number of steps this method has to take is $\| \mathbf{z}^* - \mathbf{z}^0 \|$. In this section, we will show that the greedy algorithm takes exactly this minimum number of steps to achieve optimality.

We begin with a simple lemma that will be used in the proofs of other theorems.

Lemma 8.3 *Suppose* $\mathbf{s}^1$ *and* $\mathbf{s}^2$ *are two consecutive steepest swaps during the greedy algorithm. Then, neither do these two swaps completely cancel out each other nor do they form one swap.*

Proof. Suppose the solution right before the selection of $\mathbf{s}^1$ is $\mathbf{z}$. When $\mathbf{s}^1$ and $\mathbf{s}^2$ completely cancel out each other, we have

$$\delta(\mathbf{z}, \mathbf{s}^1) + \delta(\mathbf{z} + \mathbf{s}^1, \mathbf{s}^2) = \delta(\mathbf{z}, \mathbf{0}) = 0.$$

Hence, $\delta(\mathbf{z}, \mathbf{s}^1)$ and $\delta(\mathbf{z}+\mathbf{s}^1, \mathbf{s}^2)$ cannot be negative at the same time, which is necessary for the two swaps to be consecutively steepest. When $\mathbf{s}^1$ and $\mathbf{s}^2$ form one swap, say $\mathbf{s}$, there must be independent elementary vectors $\mathbf{a}$, $\mathbf{b}$, and $\mathbf{c}$ such that $\mathbf{s}^1 = \mathbf{a}+\mathbf{c}$, $\mathbf{s}^2 = \mathbf{b}-\mathbf{c}$, and $\mathbf{s} = \mathbf{a}+\mathbf{b}$. Then, we have

$$\begin{aligned}
\delta(\mathbf{z}, \mathbf{s}) &= \delta(\mathbf{z}, \mathbf{a}+\mathbf{b}) \\
&= \delta(\mathbf{z}, \mathbf{a}) + \delta(\mathbf{z}, \mathbf{b}) \\
&= \delta(\mathbf{z}, \mathbf{a}) + \delta(\mathbf{z}, \mathbf{c}) + \delta(\mathbf{z}+\mathbf{c}, -\mathbf{c}) + \delta(\mathbf{z}, \mathbf{b}) \\
&= \delta(\mathbf{z}, \mathbf{a}+\mathbf{c}) + \delta(\mathbf{z}+\mathbf{a}+\mathbf{c}, \mathbf{b}-\mathbf{c}) \\
&= \delta(\mathbf{z}, \mathbf{s}^1) + \delta(\mathbf{z}+\mathbf{s}^1, \mathbf{s}^2).
\end{aligned}$$

For $\mathbf{s}^2$ to be a steepest swap at solution $\mathbf{z} + \mathbf{s}^1$, we must have $\delta(\mathbf{z} + \mathbf{s}^1, \mathbf{s}^2) < 0$. But this makes $\delta(\mathbf{z}, \mathbf{s}) < \delta(\mathbf{z}, \mathbf{s}^1)$, which renders $\mathbf{s}$ a better swap than $\mathbf{s}^1$ at $\mathbf{z}$. ∎

The following theorem shows that in the process of the greedy algorithm, the single-step improvements made, i.e., the magnitude of cost reduction, in later steps are no greater than those made in the earlier steps.

Theorem 8.2 *Suppose $\mathbf{s}^1$ and $\mathbf{s}^2$ are two consecutive steepest swaps during the greedy algorithm where the first swap starts at solution $\mathbf{z}$. Then, $\delta(\mathbf{z}, \mathbf{s}^1) \leq \delta(\mathbf{z} + \mathbf{s}^1, \mathbf{s}^2)$.*

Proof. By Lemma 8.3, we only have to consider three cases of the relationship between $\mathbf{s}^1$ and $\mathbf{s}^2$.

Case 1. $\mathbf{s}^1$ and $\mathbf{s}^2$ share no common arcs. Then,

$$\delta(\mathbf{z}+\mathbf{s}^1, \mathbf{s}^2) = \delta(\mathbf{z}, \mathbf{s}^2) \geq \delta(\mathbf{z}, \mathbf{s}^1).$$

Case 2. $\mathbf{s}^1$ and $\mathbf{s}^2$ form two independent swaps $\mathbf{s}'$ and $\mathbf{s}''$. Then,

$$\begin{aligned}
\delta(\mathbf{z}+\mathbf{s}^1,\mathbf{s}^2) &= \delta(\mathbf{z},\mathbf{s}^1+\mathbf{s}^2) - \delta(\mathbf{z},\mathbf{s}^1) \\
&= \delta(\mathbf{z},\mathbf{s}'+\mathbf{s}'') - \delta(\mathbf{z},\mathbf{s}^1) \\
&= \delta(\mathbf{z},\mathbf{s}') + \delta(\mathbf{z},\mathbf{s}'') - \delta(\mathbf{z},\mathbf{s}^1) \\
&\geq \delta(\mathbf{z},\mathbf{s}^1).
\end{aligned}$$

Case 3. $\mathbf{s}^1$ and $\mathbf{s}^2$ share same-direction common arcs. There are independent elementary vectors $\mathbf{a}$, $\mathbf{b}$, and $\mathbf{c}$ such that $\mathbf{s}^1 = \mathbf{a}+\mathbf{c}$ and $\mathbf{s}^2 = \mathbf{b}+\mathbf{c}$. Then,

$$\begin{aligned}
\delta(\mathbf{z}+\mathbf{s}^1,\mathbf{s}^2) &= \delta(\mathbf{z}+\mathbf{a}+\mathbf{c},\mathbf{b}+\mathbf{c}) \\
&= \delta(\mathbf{z},\mathbf{b}) + \delta(\mathbf{z}+\mathbf{c},\mathbf{c}) \\
&\geq \delta(\mathbf{z},\mathbf{b}) + \delta(\mathbf{z},\mathbf{c}) \\
&= \delta(\mathbf{z},\mathbf{s}^2) \\
&\geq \delta(\mathbf{z},\mathbf{s}^1).
\end{aligned}$$

∎

The next theorem is the key to our proof of the final theorem and it is, itself, a necessary condition for the latter.

Theorem 8.3 *If $\mathbf{s}^1$ is a steepest swap at solution $\mathbf{z}$ and $\mathbf{s}^2$ is a steepest swap at solution $\mathbf{z}+\mathbf{s}^1$, then $\mathbf{s}^1$ is a steepest swap at solution $\mathbf{z}+\mathbf{s}^2$.*

Proof. Let $\mathbf{s}^3$ be an arbitrary swap, our goal is to show that $\delta(\mathbf{z}+\mathbf{s}^2,\mathbf{s}^1) \leq \delta(\mathbf{z}+\mathbf{s}^2,\mathbf{s}^3)$. First, based on the assumptions, we can derive the following fact which will be often used later on.

$$\delta(\mathbf{z}+\mathbf{s}^2,\mathbf{s}^1) \leq \delta(\mathbf{z}+\mathbf{s}^1,\mathbf{s}^2) \leq \delta(\mathbf{z}+\mathbf{s}^1+\mathbf{s}^2,\mathbf{s}^3).$$

The first inequality is because that $\mathbf{s}^1$ is a steepest swap at solution $\mathbf{z}$ and the second inequality is due to Theorem 8.2. Then, we will prove the theorem in cases.

Case 1. $\mathbf{s}^1$ share no common arcs with $\mathbf{s}^3$. We have

$$\delta(\mathbf{z}+\mathbf{s}^2,\mathbf{s}^1) \leq \delta(\mathbf{z}+\mathbf{s}^1+\mathbf{s}^2,\mathbf{s}^3) = \delta(\mathbf{z}+\mathbf{s}^2,\mathbf{s}^3).$$

Case 2. $\mathbf{s}^1$ and $\mathbf{s}^3$ share opposite-direction common arcs, i.e., they form one or two independent swaps. Then, there must be independent elementary vectors such that $\mathbf{s}^1 = \mathbf{a} + \mathbf{c}$ and $\mathbf{s}^3 = \mathbf{b} - \mathbf{c}$. We have

$$\begin{aligned}
\delta(\mathbf{z} + \mathbf{s}^2, \mathbf{s}^1) &\leq \delta(\mathbf{z} + \mathbf{s}^1 + \mathbf{s}^2, \mathbf{s}^3) \\
&= \delta(\mathbf{z} + \mathbf{s}^1 + \mathbf{s}^2, \mathbf{b} - \mathbf{c}) \\
&= \delta(\mathbf{z} + \mathbf{s}^2, \mathbf{b}) + \delta(\mathbf{z} + \mathbf{c} + \mathbf{s}^2, -\mathbf{c}) \\
&\leq \delta(\mathbf{z} + \mathbf{s}^2, \mathbf{b}) + \delta(\mathbf{z} + \mathbf{s}^2, -\mathbf{c}) \\
&= \delta(\mathbf{z} + \mathbf{s}^2, \mathbf{s}^3).
\end{aligned}$$

Case 3. As shown in Fig.8.4, $\mathbf{s}^1$ and $\mathbf{s}^3$ share same-direction common arcs. For ease of presentation, we assume that both swaps are in the counter-clockwise direction. The case of both swaps being in the clockwise direction can be treated in a symmetric manner. Then, there are five elementary vectors $\mathbf{a}$, $\mathbf{b}$, $\mathbf{c}$, $\mathbf{d}$, and $\mathbf{e}$ such that
  1) $\mathbf{a}$, $\mathbf{c}$, and $\mathbf{d}$ are independent and $\mathbf{s}^1 = \mathbf{a} + \mathbf{c} + \mathbf{d}$,
  2) $\mathbf{b}$, $\mathbf{c}$, and $\mathbf{e}$ are independent and $\mathbf{s}^3 = \mathbf{b} + \mathbf{c} + \mathbf{e}$,
  3) $\mathbf{a}$ and $\mathbf{b}$ are to the left of $\mathbf{c}$ and $\mathbf{d}$ and $\mathbf{e}$ are to the right of $\mathbf{c}$.
Neither $\mathbf{a}$ and $\mathbf{b}$ nor $\mathbf{d}$ and $\mathbf{e}$ are identical. We say that $\mathbf{a}$ is to the left of $\mathbf{b}$ when the starting arc of $\mathbf{a}$ is to the left of that of $\mathbf{b}$, which happens to be the only arc where $\mathbf{b}$ has nonzero flow. Other symmetric cases are similarly defined.

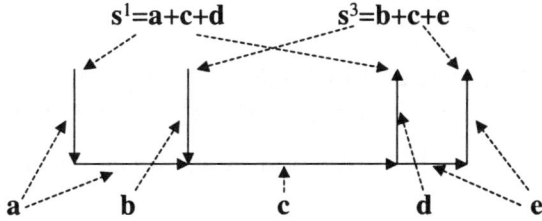

Fig. 8.4 Case 3 in the proof of Theorem 8.2

Later on, there will be several occasions where two elementary vectors, say $\mathbf{e}^1$ and $\mathbf{e}^2$, are decomposed into five elementary vectors, say **a**, **b**, **c**, **d**, and **e**, so that $\mathbf{e}^1 = \mathbf{a} + \mathbf{c} + \mathbf{d}$ and $\mathbf{e}^2 = \mathbf{b} \pm \mathbf{c} + \mathbf{e}$. Every time this occurs, the decomposition will be done in a similar fashion as in the above. We will not repeat the details any more.

Since

$$\delta(\mathbf{z}+\mathbf{s}^2, \mathbf{s}^1) = \delta(\mathbf{z}+\mathbf{s}^2, \mathbf{a}) + \delta(\mathbf{z}+\mathbf{s}^2, \mathbf{c}) + \delta(\mathbf{z}+\mathbf{s}^2, \mathbf{d}),$$
$$\delta(\mathbf{z}+\mathbf{s}^2, \mathbf{s}^3) = \delta(\mathbf{z}+\mathbf{s}^2, \mathbf{b}) + \delta(\mathbf{z}+\mathbf{s}^2, \mathbf{c}) + \delta(\mathbf{z}+\mathbf{s}^2, \mathbf{e}),$$

we need only to prove that

$$\delta(\mathbf{z}+\mathbf{s}^2, \mathbf{a}) \leq \delta(\mathbf{z}+\mathbf{s}^2, \mathbf{b}) \text{ and } \delta(\mathbf{z}+\mathbf{s}^2, \mathbf{d}) \leq \delta(\mathbf{z}+\mathbf{s}^2, \mathbf{e}).$$

Due to the apparent symmetry, both inequalities will be always true if the first one is always true. We set out to prove just that in the following.

In general, since $\mathbf{s}^1$ is a steepest swap at $\mathbf{z}$ and $\mathbf{b}+\mathbf{c}+\mathbf{d}$ is a swap, we can derive that

$$\delta(\mathbf{z}, \mathbf{a}) \leq \delta(\mathbf{z}, \mathbf{b}).$$

When $\mathbf{s}^2$ has no common arcs with either **a** or **b**, we have

$$\delta(\mathbf{z}+\mathbf{s}^2, \mathbf{a}) = \delta(\mathbf{z}, \mathbf{a}) \leq \delta(\mathbf{z}, \mathbf{b}) = \delta(\mathbf{z}+\mathbf{s}^2, \mathbf{b}).$$

In the following, we assume $\mathbf{s}^2$ has common arcs with at least one of **a** and **b**. Also, note that $\mathbf{s}^2$ and $\mathbf{s}^1$ do not completely cancel out each other or form one swap due to Lemma 8.3.

Case 3.1. **a** is to the left of **b** and $\mathbf{s}^2$ is in the counter-clockwise direction.

Case 3.1.1. As illustrated in Fig.8.5, $\mathbf{s}^2$ has common arcs with **a** but no common arcs with **b**. Let $\mathbf{a} = \mathbf{a}^1 + \mathbf{d}^1 + \mathbf{a}^2$ and $\mathbf{s}^2 = \mathbf{e}^1 + \mathbf{d}^1 + \mathbf{e}^2$.

From the fact that $\mathbf{s}^1$ is a steepest swap, we can easily verify that

$$\delta(\mathbf{z}, \mathbf{a}^1) \leq \delta(\mathbf{z}, \mathbf{e}^1).$$

Since $\mathbf{s}^2$ is a steepest swap at $\mathbf{z}+\mathbf{s}^1$ and $\mathbf{b} - \mathbf{a}^2 + \mathbf{e}^2$ is a swap, we can derive that

$$\delta(\mathbf{z}, \mathbf{e}^1) + \delta(\mathbf{z}+\mathbf{d}^1, \mathbf{d}^1) \leq \delta(\mathbf{z}, \mathbf{b}) + \delta(\mathbf{z}+\mathbf{a}^2, -\mathbf{a}^2) = \delta(\mathbf{z}, \mathbf{b}) - \delta(\mathbf{z}, \mathbf{a}^2).$$

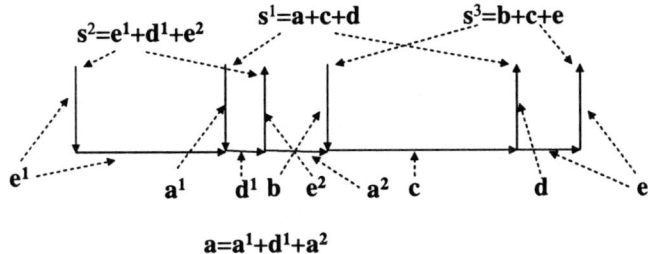

Fig. 8.5   Case 3.1.1 in the proof of Theorem 8.2

Then, we have

$$\begin{aligned}
\delta(\mathbf{z} + \mathbf{s}^2, \mathbf{a}) &= \delta(\mathbf{z} + \mathbf{s}^2, \mathbf{a}^1) + \delta(\mathbf{z} + \mathbf{s}^2, \mathbf{d}^1) + \delta(\mathbf{z} + \mathbf{s}^2, \mathbf{a}^2) \\
&= \delta(\mathbf{z}, \mathbf{a}^1) + \delta(\mathbf{z} + \mathbf{d}^1, \mathbf{d}^1) + \delta(\mathbf{z}, \mathbf{a}^2) \\
&\leq \delta(\mathbf{z}, \mathbf{e}^1) + \delta(\mathbf{z} + \mathbf{d}^1, \mathbf{d}^1) + \delta(\mathbf{z}, \mathbf{a}^2) \\
&\leq \delta(\mathbf{z}, \mathbf{b}) \\
&= \delta(\mathbf{z} + \mathbf{s}^2, \mathbf{b}).
\end{aligned}$$

Case 3.1.2. $\mathbf{s}^2$ has common arcs with both $\mathbf{a}$ and $\mathbf{b}$. Then, $\mathbf{s}^2$'s ending arc must be where $\mathbf{b}$ is. Using the same notation as Case 3.1.1, we have $\mathbf{a}^2 = \mathbf{0}$ and $\mathbf{e}^2 = -\mathbf{b}$. So $\delta(\mathbf{z} + \mathbf{s}^2, \mathbf{b}) = \delta(\mathbf{z} - \mathbf{b}, \mathbf{b}) = -\delta(\mathbf{z}, -\mathbf{b})$. Also, since $\mathbf{s}^2$ is a steepest swap at $\mathbf{z} + \mathbf{s}^1$, we can derive that

$$\delta(\mathbf{z}, \mathbf{e}^1) + \delta(\mathbf{z} + \mathbf{d}^1, \mathbf{d}^1) + \delta(\mathbf{z}, -\mathbf{b}) = \delta(\mathbf{z} + \mathbf{s}^1, \mathbf{s}^2) \leq 0.$$

Then,

$$\begin{aligned}
\delta(\mathbf{z} + \mathbf{s}^2, \mathbf{a}) &= \delta(\mathbf{z} + \mathbf{s}^2, \mathbf{a}^1) + \delta(\mathbf{z} + \mathbf{s}^2, \mathbf{d}^1) \\
&= \delta(\mathbf{z}, \mathbf{a}^1) + \delta(\mathbf{z} + \mathbf{d}^1, \mathbf{d}^1) \\
&\leq \delta(\mathbf{z}, \mathbf{e}^1) + \delta(\mathbf{z} + \mathbf{d}^1, \mathbf{d}^1) \\
&\leq -\delta(\mathbf{z}, -\mathbf{b}) \\
&= \delta(\mathbf{z} + \mathbf{s}^2, \mathbf{b}).
\end{aligned}$$

Case 3.1.3. s^2 has no common arcs with a. Then, s^2's starting arc must be the same as where b is. We have

$$\delta(z + s^2, a) = \delta(z, a) \leq \delta(z, b) \leq \delta(z + b, b) = \delta(z + s^2, b).$$

There are four other cases to be discussed. In the following, we only list those cases and sub-cases, but omit the discussion for each case because the arguments are similar.

Case 3.2. a is to the left of b and s^2 is in the clockwise direction.

Case 3.2.1. The starting arc of s^2 is the same as the starting arc of a.

Case 3.2.2. The starting arc of s^2 is to the right of the starting arc of a and the ending arc of s^2 is to the left of where b is.

Case 3.2.3. The ending arc of s^2 is where b is.

Case 3.3. a is to the right of b and s^2 is in the counter-clockwise direction.

Case 3.3.1. The ending arc of s^2 is the same as the starting arc of b.

Case 3.3.2. The starting arc of s^2 is the same as where a is.

Case 3.3.3. All other cases of 3.3 which are not included in 3.3.1 and 3.3.2.

Case 3.4. a is to the right of b and s^2 is in the clockwise direction.

Case 3.4.1. The starting arc of s^2 is the same as the starting arc of b.

Case 3.4.2. The starting arc of s^2 is neither the starting arc of b nor where a is.

Case 3.4.3. The starting arc of s^2 is the same as where a is.

Case 3.5. s^1 is counter-clockwise and s^3 is clockwise.

Case 3.5.1. s^2 is in the counter-clockwise direction.

Case 3.5.2. s^2 is in the clockwise direction. ∎

With Lemma 8.3 and the key theorem Theorem 8.3 handy, we can now take on our ultimate main theorem. The main idea is to use the exchangeability of consecutive steepest swaps.

Theorem 8.4 *Suppose we apply the greedy algorithm to an instance of (P) starting from an initial solution $\mathbf{z}^0$ and the method converges to an optimal solution $\mathbf{z}^*$. Then, the method should have taken exactly $\| \mathbf{z}^* - \mathbf{z}^0 \|$ steps to achieve optimality.*

Proof. Suppose the greedy algorithm takes t steps to reach optimality and the steepest swaps along the way are $\mathbf{s}^1, ..., \mathbf{s}^t$. Since $\mathbf{z}^* = \mathbf{z}^0 + \sum_{j=1}^{t} \mathbf{s}^j$, we need to prove that $\| \sum_{j=1}^{t} \mathbf{s}^j \| = t$. Since the left-hand side cannot be larger than the right-hand side, we prove that the left-hand side can be no smaller than the right-hand side by contradiction.

Suppose $\| \sum_{j=1}^{t} \mathbf{s}^j \| < t$, then there must be a $\tau = 1, ..., t-1$ such that $\mathbf{s}^\tau$ and $\mathbf{s}^t$ either completely cancel out each other or form one swap. When $\tau = t-1$, then by Lemma 8.3, this is impossible. Otherwise, for $j = \tau - 1, ..., t-1$, denote $\mathbf{z}^0 + \sum_{k=1}^{j} \mathbf{s}^k$ by $\mathbf{z}^j$. By induction, we can show that $\mathbf{s}^\tau$ is a steepest swap at solution $\mathbf{z}^k - \mathbf{s}^\tau$ for every $k = \tau + 1, ..., t-1$.

Recall that $\mathbf{s}^\tau$ is a steepest swap at solution $\mathbf{z}^{\tau-1}$ and $\mathbf{s}^{\tau+1}$ is a steepest swap at solution $\mathbf{z}^\tau$. By Theorem 8.3, $\mathbf{s}^\tau$ is a steepest swap at solution $\mathbf{z}^{\tau-1} + \mathbf{s}^\tau$. Suppose for some $k = \tau + 1, ..., t-2$, $\mathbf{s}^\tau$ is a steepest swap at solution $\mathbf{z}^k - \mathbf{s}^\tau$. We also have that $\mathbf{s}^{k+1}$ is a steepest swap at solution $\mathbf{z}^k$. According to Theorem 8.3, $\mathbf{s}^\tau$ is a steepest swap at solution $\mathbf{z}^{k+1} - \mathbf{s}^\tau$.

Finally, $\mathbf{s}^\tau$ is a steepest swap at solution $\mathbf{z}^{t-1} - \mathbf{s}^\tau$. But we also have that $\mathbf{s}^t$ is a steepest swap at solution $\mathbf{z}^{t-1}$. According to Lemma 8.3, $\mathbf{s}^\tau$ and $\mathbf{s}^t$ can neither completely cancel out each other nor form one swap. This is a contradiction. ∎

8.4.3 Solving original production planning problems

The above greedy algorithm can also be used to solve the original production planning problem (OP) itself. For simplicity, we assume that $y_0 = y_n = 0$ in the ensuing discussion.

There are two possible approaches to solve the original production planning problem. We may let the procedure start from initial solution $\mathbf{x}^1$ where $x_1^1 = n\bar{d}$ and $x_i^1 = 0$ for any $i = 2, ..., n$. Recall that

$\bar{d}$ is the average demand level. A simple application of Lemma 8.3 shows that only swaps starting from later periods and ending in period 1 can be the steepest swaps, and hence it takes only $O(n)$ time to complete each step in the procedure.

We may also let the procedure start from initial solution $\mathbf{x}^2$ where $x_i^2 = d_i$ for all $i = 1, ..., n$. In the worst case, $\mathbf{x}^2$ could be as away from the optimal solution $\mathbf{x}^*$ as $n\bar{d}$. But we guess that the average distance between $\mathbf{x}^2$ and $\mathbf{x}^*$ could be much smaller when the d_i's follow certain probabilistic laws. Simulation results in the next section confirms our guess.

In summary, there are three similar methods to solve (OP): the conventional incremental method always runs in $O(n^2\bar{d})$ time; the greedy algorithm starting from $\mathbf{x}^1$ in the worst case and most likely runs in $O(n^2\bar{d})$ time; while the greedy algorithm starting from $\mathbf{x}^2$ in the worst case runs in $O(n^3\bar{d})$ time and on average probably runs in much less time. When $\bar{d} \gg n$, we expect the third approach to take the least amount of time for most real-world cases.

8.5 Numerical Examples and Computational Experiments

8.5.1 *Numerical examples*

First we use a numerical example to illustrate our models of handling disruption in production planning. Suppose we have a manufacturer with two assembly lines. Line 1 has a production capacity of 50 items per day and a unit cost of $100 per item, and line 2 has a production capacity of 30 items per day and a unit cost of $120 per item. The manufacturer can indefinitely outsource its production with a unit cost of $200 per item. The holding cost is $10 per item per day and the backlogging cost is $20 per item per day. The manufacturer is to plan its production schedule for the next 10 days with the daily demand projected in the second row of Table 8.1 and with no initial and terminal inventories.

Table 8.1 Numerical Example: The Optimal Original Plan

Day i	1	2	3	4	5	6	7	8	9	10
d_i	75	90	65	55	70	80	85	100	75	65
x_i^*	80	80	70	65	80	80	80	80	80	65
y_i^*	5	-5	0	10	20	20	15	-5	0	

Table 8.2 Numerical Example: Deviation Costs

Day i	1	2	3	4	5	6	7	8	9	10
ΔC_i	15	15	15	10	10	10	10	5	5	5
ΔH_i	10	10	10	5	5	5	5	0	0	

From the given information, we have

$$c_i(x) = \begin{cases} 100x & \text{if } 0 \leq x \leq 50 \\ 120x - 1000 & \text{if } 51 \leq x \leq 80 \\ 200x - 7400 & \text{if } x \geq 81 \end{cases}$$

$$h_i(y) = \begin{cases} -20y & \text{if } y \leq -1 \\ 10y & \text{if } y \geq 0 \end{cases}$$

Also, $y_0 = y_{10} = 0$. For (OP), the optimal plan $\mathbf{x}^*$ costs \$82,100 and is displayed in the last two rows of Table 8.1.

For the deviation penalties, we assume that each $\Delta c_i(\cdot)$ is linear over the absolute value of its argument with coefficient ΔC_i and each $\Delta h_i(\cdot)$ is also linear over the absolute value of its argument with coefficient ΔH_i. We put the manufacturer's disruption cost coefficients in Table 8.2.

In the following, we consider several types of disruptions that can occur to the manufacturer, and compare three different solutions, keeping the original plan, an optimal plan $\mathbf{x}^c$ obtained by considering the deviation costs, and another "optimal" plan $\mathbf{x}^r$ which neglects the deviation costs.

Disruption 1. Line 2 has to be shut down for day one.

Now, we have

$$c_1'(x) = \begin{cases} 100x & \text{if } 0 \leq x \leq 50 \\ 200x - 5000 & \text{if } x \geq 51 \end{cases}$$

Table 8.3 Numerical Example: The Production Plans after Disruption 1

Day i	1	2	3	4	5	6	7	8	9	10
x_i^r	50	80	80	80	80	80	80	80	80	70
y_i^r	-25	-35	-20	5	15	15	10	-10	-5	
x_i^c	75	80	75	65	80	80	80	80	80	65
y_i^c	0	-10	0	10	20	20	15	-5	0	

Table 8.4 Numerical Example: The Production Plans after Disruption 2

Day i	1	2	3	4	5	6	7	8	9	10
x_i^r	75	75	50	80	80	80	80	80	80	80
y_i^r	0	-15	-30	-5	5	5	0	-20	-15	
x_i^c	80	80	50	80	80	80	80	80	80	70
y_i^c	5	-5	-20	5	15	15	10	-10	-5	

and every other cost functions remains the same as the counterpart. Had the manufacturer stuck to the initial plan, the cost would haven risen to $84,500.

Considering the changes to the initial plan, we obtain the optimal new plan $\mathbf{x}^c$ with a cost $84,400. Yet, without considering deviation penalty, the "optimal" plan $\mathbf{x}^r$ costs $83,550, but it actually costs $85,225 when evaluated with the deviation costs. In Table 8.3, we display both $\mathbf{x}^r$ and $\mathbf{x}^c$.

Disruption 2. Line 2 has to be shut down for the first three days.

In this case, the $c_i'(\cdot)$'s for $i = 1, 2, 3$ should be appropriately adapted from the corresponding $c_i(\cdot)$'s and all other primed costs remain the same as their non-primed counterparts. We list $\mathbf{x}^r$ and $\mathbf{x}^c$ in Table 8.4.

We see that the cost of keeping the original plan is $88,500, and the cost of the optimal plan $\mathbf{x}^c$ is $88,075. For $\mathbf{x}^r$, its cost is $87,000 without deviation cost, and the real cost is $88,425.

Disruption 3. Line 2 has to be shut down for the first three days and line 1 has to be shut down for the last two days. In addition, inventory levels can be no more than 10 after period 5 and before period 8.

Table 8.5 Numerical Example: The Production Plans after Disruption 3

Day i	1	2	3	4	5	6	7	8	9	10
x_i^r	75	80	50	80	80	80	80	95	75	65
y_i^r	0	-10	-25	0	10	10	5	0	0	
x_i^c	80	80	50	75	80	80	80	95	75	65
y_i^c	5	-5	-20	0	10	10	5	0	0	

Again, we need to first appropriately adapt the non-primed costs to the primed costs, which we omit showing here. Then, starting from $\mathbf{x}^*$, we may find both $\mathbf{x}^r$ and $\mathbf{x}^c$. The plans are displayed in Table 8.5.

Note that in this case, the initial plan $\mathbf{x}^*$ becomes infeasible after the disruption. So a new plan has to be generated. The cost for the optimal $\mathbf{x}^c$ is \$97,300. For $\mathbf{x}^r$, its cost is \$96,150 without deviation cost, and its real cost is \$97,325.

8.5.2 Computational experiments

Now we report our computational experiments in which some comparisons are made among the three alternative methods to solve (OP): the incremental method (ISM) in the conventional way, greedy algorithm starting from putting all production in the first period (SDM1), and greedy algorithm starting from producing what is immediately needed (SDM2). We let all three methods run over the same set of randomly-generated problem instances. To describe the generation of the random instances, given the number of periods n and the expected demand rate $\bar{d}$, we let the d_i's be independent Poisson random variables with mean $\bar{d}$. We also generate uniformly distributed random numbers θ which are used to construct the cost functions as follows.

For $i = 1, \ldots, n$, we let $c_i(0) = 0$,

$$c_i(x) = c_i(x-1) + \theta_{i0} + l \sum_{u=1}^{x-1} \theta_{iu} \text{ for } x = 1, ..., X,$$

and $c_i(x) = +\infty$ for $x \geq X + 1$. We also let $h_i(0) = 0$, and for $i = 1, ..., n$,

$$h_i(y) = h_i(y-1) + (\theta_{n+i,0} + l \sum_{v=1}^{y-1} \theta_{n+i,v})q \text{ for } y = 1, ..., Y,$$

$$h_i(y) = h_i(y+1) + (\theta_{n+i,Y} + l \sum_{v=1}^{-y+1} \theta_{n+i,Y+v})p \text{ for } y = -Y, ..., -1,$$

and

$$h_i(y) = +\infty \text{ for } y \leq -Y - 1 \text{ or } y \geq Y + 1.$$

In the above, X and Y are made large enough so that their finiteness does not affect our results; l, q, and p are nonnegative parameters, where l reflects how non-linear and convex the cost functions are, with the costs being linear when $l = 0$; q stands for the relative significance of the holding costs compared to the production costs; and p stands for the relative significance of the backlogging costs compared to the production costs. In all the experiments we fix $q = 0.1$ and $p = 0.2$.

For any combination of the parameters $(l, n, \bar{d})$, we generate 50 independent instances. We then run the three methods separately to each of the 50 instances and get the average steps taken and average elapsed running time (in seconds on a PC with a 1000MHz CPU) for all three methods. Throughout the study, we do verify that for each instance, all three methods always converge to solutions with the same cost.

First we report the case when the cost functions have large convexity, measured by $l = 0.1$. These results are in Tables 8.6 to 8.8. Each table contains two parts. The first part reports the computation time of the algorithms and the second part reports the steps used by the algorithms.

From Tables 8.6 to 8.8, we have the following observations:

Observation 1. SDM1 consistently takes slightly fewer number of steps than ISM and consumes slightly less time than the latter.

Table 8.6 Computation Time for $n = 30$ and $l = 0.1$

$\bar{d}$	100	200	300	400	500	600	700
ISM	0.03	0.05	0.08	0.11	0.13	0.16	0.18
SDM1	0.03	0.05	0.08	0.10	0.13	0.16	0.18
SDM2	0.02	0.03	0.04	0.04	0.06	0.07	0.07
ISM	2991	5967	8920	11972	14851	17826	20884
SDM1	2893	5769	8622	11569	14358	17225	20182
SDM2	144	198	259	265	353	469	412

Table 8.7 Computation Time for $n = 50$ and $l = 0.1$

$\bar{d}$	100	200	300	400	500	600	700
ISM	0.08	0.15	0.22	0.30	0.38	0.44	0.51
SDM1	0.08	0.15	0.22	0.29	0.37	0.44	0.50
SDM2	0.11	0.14	0.19	0.22	0.26	0.29	0.39
ISM	5027	10031	15017	20001	25002	29914	34562
SDM1	4925	9827	14715	19598	24516	29312	33856
SDM2	229	283	394	455	541	613	906

Table 8.8 Computation Time for $n = 100$ and $l = 0.1$

$\bar{d}$	100	200	300	400	500	600	700
ISM	0.30	0.61	0.92	1.24	1.55	1.86	2.25
SDM1	0.30	0.61	0.90	1.21	1.52	1.80	2.17
SDM2	0.93	1.32	1.59	1.81	2.11	2.45	3.32
ISM	10038	19917	29943	40052	49718	59706	68972
SDM1	9937	19719	29652	39614	49217	59109	68286
SDM2	458	657	790	889	1055	1226	1771

Observation 2. When demand rate increases, the computation times of ISM and SDM1 increase quickly than those of SDM2.

Observation 3. The computation time of SDM2 is less than that of ISM and SDM1 when n is small or $\bar{d}$ is large, or we may say when $\bar{d}/n$ is large.

Next we report in Tables 8.9 to 8.11 the case when the cost functions have small convexity, measured by $l = 0.01$.

The results in Tables 8.9 to 8.11 also support the three observations obtained from Tables 8.6 to 8.8. If we compare the results from the viewpoint of convexity, then we have further observations:

Observation 4. Neither ISM nor SDM1 is insensitive to the convexity of cost functions.

Table 8.9 Computation Time for $n = 30$ and $l = 0.01$

d	100	200	300	400	500	600	700
ISM	0.02	0.05	0.08	0.10	0.13	0.16	0.18
SDM1	0.02	0.05	0.07	0.10	0.12	0.15	0.18
SDM2	0.10	0.10	0.10	0.10	0.10	0.13	0.12
ISM	2991	5967	8920	11972	14851	17826	20884
SDM1	2888	5759	8620	11574	14344	17219	20168
SDM2	592	599	611	605	636	770	725

Table 8.10 Computation Time for $n = 50$ and $l = 0.01$

d	100	200	300	400	500	600	700
ISM	0.07	0.15	0.22	0.30	0.37	0.44	0.52
SDM1	0.07	0.15	0.22	0.29	0.36	0.43	0.50
SDM2	0.47	0.44	0.48	0.51	0.50	0.53	0.64
ISM	5027	10031	15017	20001	25002	29914	34562
SDM1	4900	9823	14696	19594	24517	29310	33855
SDM2	1001	939	1029	1100	1073	1086	1331

Table 8.11 Computation Time for $n = 100$ and $l = 0.01$

d	100	200	300	400	500	600	700
ISM	0.30	0.60	0.91	1.23	1.53	1.84	2.14
SDM1	0.30	0.60	0.90	1.21	1.50	1.79	2.08
SDM2	3.74	4.00	4.05	4.03	4.20	4.51	5.06
ISM	10038	19917	29943	40052	49718	59706	68972
SDM1	9936	19714	29662	39617	49210	59099	68269
SDM2	1922	2063	2097	2048	2211	2304	2542

Observation 5. When cost functions become less convex (l is small), SDM2 needs more time.

In summary, we can conclude that (1) SDM1 is an algorithm consistently a little superior to ISM and (2) SDM2 uses much less time than both ISM and SDM1 when $\bar{d}/n$ is large and the cost functions are more convex.

8.6 Related Literature

The convex minimum cost network flow problem (CMNF) has been extensively studied in the past decades. According to Ahuja *et* al.(1993), there are several pseudo-polynomial-time algorithms for the CMNF problem, such as the cycle-canceling algorithm and the incremental method (the successive shortest path algorithm in Veinott 1964 and Denardo 1982). The advantages of these algorithms are that they are easy to understand and implement. Given today's high speed computers, they are also very practical algorithms. In theory, however, polynomial-time algorithms exist for the CMNF problem, e.g., Minoux (1984), Minoux (1986) and Hochbaum and Shanthikumar (1990). These algorithms are based on the idea of capacity scaling which results in their time complexities being polynomially bounded by n, m, and $\log U$, where n is the number of nodes, m is the number of arcs, and U is the maximum capacity of the arcs. To our knowledge, for the CMNF problem, there is no strongly polynomial-time algorithm which is polynomially bounded only by n and m. More detailed results of this chapter can be found in Yang et al.(2001).

References

Ahuja, R.K., T.L. Magnanti and J.B. Orlin (1993), *Network Flows: Theory, Algorithms, and Applications*, Prentice-Hall, Upper Saddle River, New Jersey.

Denardo, E.V. (1982), *Dynamic Programming: Models and Applications*, Prentice-Hall, Englewood Cliffs, New Jersey.

Florian, M., J.K. Lenstra and A.H.G. Rinnooy Kan (1980), Deterministic production planning: Algorithms and complexity, *Management Science*, 26, 669-679.

Hochbaum, D.S. and J.G. Shanthikumar (1990), Convex separable optimization is not much harder than linear optimization, *Journal of ACM*, 37, 843-862.

Minoux, M. (1984), A polynomial algorithm for minimum quadratic cost flow problems, *European Journal of Operational Research*, 18, 377-387.

Minoux, M. (1986), Solving integer minimum cost flows with separable convex objective polynomially, *Mathematical Programming Study*, 26, 237-239.

Veinott, A.F. (1964), Production planning with convex costs: A parametric study, *Management Science*, 10, 441-460.

Yang, J., X. Qi and G. Yu (2001), Disruption management in production planning, working paper.

Chapter 9

Disruption Management for Supply Chain Coordination

9.1 Introduction

In this chapter, we demonstrate the application of disruption management in supply chain coordination . We start with a simple supply chain system with one supplier (referred to as she) and one retailer (referred to as he), both of whom are independent decision makers seeking to maximize their individual profit. Suppose the supplier makes a product, sells the product to a retailer at a wholesale price, and the retailer then sells it to customers at a retail price. We consider the case that the product is of a short life cycle such as fashionware, perishable foods, and news magazines. We also assume the market demand is a decreasing function of the retail price. The problem can be described as a Stackelburg game in which the supplier is the leader and the retailer follows the decision of the supplier.

The decision sequence is as follows. There are two time periods, the planning period followed by the selling period. In the planning period, the supplier first establishes a production plan based on a market forecast. When the selling period arrives, the actual demand is resolved. Then the supplier devises a wholesale price schedule for the retailer who then decides on the quantity of product to order from the supplier and sets the retail price for the purpose of maximizing his profit. Under the assumption of perfect information, for each wholesale schedule the supplier makes, she knows the best decision the retailer will make. So the supplier can maximize her profit by devising an optimal wholesale schedule.

In such a system, each person has an individual profit and the sum of the individual profit is called the supply chain profit. Note that the supply chain profit solely depends on the retailer's decision on the ordering quantity and the retail price, and the wholesale policy determines the profit allocation between the supplier and the retailer. When each person makes decisions separately, the maximum total supply chain profit may not be achieved. It can be shown that the retailer tends to order less and set a higher retailer price. This is the well-known double marginalization phenomenon. The basic purpose of supply chain coordination is to devise a mechanism that will induce the retailer to order the right quantity of product and set the right retail price so that the total profit of the supply chain is maximized. In most cases, both the supplier and the retailer can benefit from this type of coordination provided that there is an equitable distribution of the resulting profits.

The aim of this chapter is to study the impact on a two-period supply chain when the originally devised production plan needs to be changed. For products with short life cycles, a supplier often has to develop a production plan before the market demand is known for reasons such as capacity planning, the acquisition of raw materials, and capital budgeting. The situation is further complicated by the fact that the retailer, after observing the market demand, may place an order that is different from the supplier's production plan. If the order is to be satisfied, additional costs will be incurred, and sometimes these additional costs are significant. This is the deviation cost we need to capture in disruption management.

The rest of the chapter is organized as follows. In Section 9.2, we introduce a static model with a single time period and explain how the supply chain is coordinated. In Section 9.3, we analyze the case where a central decision maker faces a demand disruption and must develop a reactive plan, which is the goal that the coordination has to achieve. In Section 9.4, we show how the supply chain can be coordinated when the supplier and the retailer make decisions in an independent way. The above results are extended to the cases of nonlinear demand functions and two competitive retailers in the following two sections. A brief literature review is presented in Section 9.7.

9.2 Supply Chain Coordination without Disruptions

We begin with a supplier-retailer model in which the price-demand relationship is deterministic and known. The supplier makes a product that is purchased by the retailer who then sells it on the open market. The unit production cost, denoted by c, is fixed to the supplier, and her profit, denoted by $\bar{f}^s$, comes from the difference between the production cost and wholesale price. Meanwhile, the wholesale price determines the cost to the retailer, and his profit, denoted by $\bar{f}^r$, comes from the difference between the retail and the wholesale prices. Then the profit of the supply chain is $\bar{f}^{sc} = \bar{f}^s + \bar{f}^r$.

The game is played as follows. The supplier begins first by declaring a wholesale price policy. The retailer then reacts to that policy by deciding how much to order and what retail price to set. Once these decisions are made, the supplier must provide the quantity ordered to the retailer. We assume all information is available to both players.

Let the market demand be described by the relationship $d = \bar{D} - kp$, where $\bar{D}$ is the maximum possible demand or the market scale, p is the unit retail price, k is a price sensitive coefficient, and d is the demand under retail price p. In other words, when the retailer sets the retail price to be p, the market demand is d, which is the quantity that the retailer will order and the supplier must provide.

Given the retail price p, the supply chain profit is $f^{sc}(p) = (\bar{D} - kp)(p - c)$. It is easy to derive that the supply chain profit is maximized at $\bar{p} = (\bar{D} + kc)/(2k)$, which results in the maximum supply chain profit as $\bar{f}^{sc}_{max} = (\bar{D} - kc)^2/(4k)$, and the corresponding production quantity as $\bar{Q} = \bar{D} - k\bar{p} = (\bar{D} - kc)/2$.

To achieve the maximum supply chain profit $\bar{f}^{sc}_{max}$, a coordination scheme is needed between the supplier and the retailer. Formally, the supply chain coordination is a scheme that can induce the retailer to order $\bar{Q}$ and set the retail price at $\bar{p}$. The profit allocation between the supplier and the retailer is also determined by the coordination scheme. In the literature, people have proposed different ways to achieve coordination. Here we discuss the usage of an all-unit wholesale quantity discount policy.

An all-unit wholesale quantity discount policy is defined by three parameters q_0, w_1, and w_2 where $w_1 > w_2$. Let Q be the quantity that the retailer orders. If $Q < q_0$, the unit wholesale price is w_1. If the retailer orders $Q \geq q_0$, the unit wholesale price becomes w_2. So the cost to the retailer $C^r(Q)$ is given by

$$C^r(Q) = \begin{cases} w_1 Q & \text{if } Q < q_0 \\ w_2 Q & \text{if } Q \geq q_0 \end{cases}$$

We denote such a wholesale quantity discount policy as $AQDP(w_1, w_2, q_0)$.

For the supplier to make an $AQDP(w_1, w_2, q_0)$, she needs to set up a goal of profit, denoted by $\bar{f}^s$, that has to be achieved. Suppose $\bar{f}^s = \eta \bar{f}^{sc}_{\max}$, where $0 < \eta < 1$. Then by setting appropriate parameters for $AQDP(w_1, w_2, q_0)$ as determined in Lemma 9.1, the retailer will be induced to order $\bar{Q}$, the supplier will achieve $\bar{f}^s$, and the maximum supply chain profit will be realized.

Lemma 9.1 *For $\bar{f}^s = \eta \bar{f}^{sc}_{\max}$, $0 < \eta < 1$, the supply chain is coordinated under $AQDP(\bar{w}_1, \bar{w}_2, \bar{Q})$ with*

$$\bar{w}_1 > \frac{\bar{D}}{k} - \sqrt{1-\eta}\left(\frac{\bar{D}-ck}{k}\right), \quad \bar{w}_2 = c + \eta \frac{\bar{D}-ck}{2k}.$$

Proof. Note that the retailer either takes the unit wholesale price $\bar{w}_2$ or $\bar{w}_1$. If the retailer takes $\bar{w}_2$, he has to order at least $\bar{Q}$. His profit can be written as

$$f_1^r(Q) = Q\left(\frac{\bar{D}-Q}{k} - \bar{w}_2\right),$$

which is maximized at $\bar{Q}$ under the constraint of $\bar{Q} \leq Q$, and

$$f_1^r(\bar{Q}) = \bar{Q}\left(\frac{\bar{D}-\bar{Q}}{k} - \bar{w}_2\right) = (1-\eta)\bar{f}^{sc}_{\max}.$$

If the retailer takes the price $\bar{w}_1$, then his profit is

$$f_2^r(Q) = Q\left(\frac{\bar{D}-Q}{k} - \bar{w}_1\right),$$

which is maximized at $Q_2 = (\bar{D} - \bar{w}_1 k)/2 < \bar{Q}$ and $f_2^r(Q_2) = (\bar{D} - \bar{w}_1 k)^2/(4k)$. By assumption,

$$\bar{w}_1 > \frac{\bar{D}}{k} - \sqrt{1-\eta}\left(\frac{\bar{D}-ck}{k}\right),$$

so we have $(\bar{D} - \bar{w}_1 k)^2 < (1-\eta)(\bar{D} - ck)^2$, and

$$f_2^r(Q_2) = \frac{(\bar{D} - \bar{w}_1 k)^2}{4k} < (1-\eta)\frac{(\bar{D}-ck)^2}{4k} = (1-\eta)\bar{f}_{\max}^{sc} = f_1^r(\bar{Q}).$$

Therefore the retailer should order $\bar{Q}$ to maximize his own profit. Consequently, the supplier's profit goal, as well as the maximum supply chain profit, are achieved. ∎

Remark 1. Note that $AQDP(\bar{w}_1, \bar{w}_2, \bar{Q})$ is a feasible quantity discount policy only when $\bar{w}_1 > \bar{w}_2$ which can be guaranteed if

$$\frac{\bar{D}}{k} - \sqrt{1-\eta}\left(\frac{\bar{D}}{k} - c\right) > c + \eta\frac{\bar{D}-ck}{2k}. \qquad (9.1)$$

In fact, we see that (9.1) is equivalent to

$$\frac{\bar{D}-ck}{k} - \eta\frac{\bar{D}-ck}{2k} > \sqrt{1-\eta}\left(\frac{\bar{D}}{k} - c\right),$$

or $1 - \frac{\eta}{2} > \sqrt{1-\eta}$, which is true for all $0 < \eta < 1$.

Remark 2. Regarding the role of profit allocation, the $AQDP$ in Lemma 9.1 is devised from the supplier's point of view by setting a reserve profit $\bar{f}^s$ for the supplier. The same $AQDP$ can also be devised from the retailer's point of view by setting a reserve profit for the retailer. Suppose the minimum profit $\bar{f}^r$ is what the retailer has to earn in order to play the game. We can set $\bar{f}^s = \bar{f}_{\max}^{sc} - \bar{f}^r$ in Lemma 9.1.

9.3 Centralized Decision Making with Demand Disruptions

9.3.1 Modeling of disruption management

The above discussion assumes a deterministic and known demand-price function $d = \bar{D} - kp$, which may not be realistic because of uncertainties in practice. Uncertainty can be described and handled in different ways. In our proposed two-period model, there is a planning period followed by a selling period where the decision that needs to be made in the planning period is a production plan in terms of the product quantity. For a given estimated demand-price relationship $d = \bar{D} - kp$, such a plan can be made by using the model in the previous section to achieve the supply chain profit maximization. Note that each production plan is associated with a wholesale quantity discount policy to implement the supply chain coordination.

In the selling period, uncertainties are resolved, and the real demand-price function is observed. If it is the same as the estimated demand-price function, then the production and coordination plans that were made in the planning period can be executed without any difficulty. If it differs from what was supposed in the planning period, we call that a demand disruption occurs. It can be shown later that both the production and coordination plans need to be reconsidered in order to achieve the supply chain profit maximization after a demand disruption.

We assume a demand disruption can be captured by a market scale change, i.e., D becomes $\bar{D}+\Delta D$, which results in a new demand function $d = \bar{D} + \Delta D - kp$. For example, a publishing plan is made for a novel. Incidentally, the book becomes a best seller such that for the same retail price, there are more people willing to buy it than estimated.

In this section, we deal with such a demand disruption under the assumption that there is a central decision maker who seeks to maximize the total supply chain profit. This would be used as the goal for supply chain coordination when the supplier and retailer make decisions separately.

Let Q be the real demand under the resolved demand-price relationship, and p the new retail price, where $p = (\bar{D} + \Delta D - Q)/k$. Then we may have a production quantity deviation $\Delta Q = Q - \bar{Q}$. A deviation cost will be incurred for any $\Delta Q \neq 0$. For example, when $\Delta Q < 0$, there is leftover inventory in the amount of ΔQ either in the form of final product or work in process. Such inventory will have to be disposed of or possibly sold in a secondary market at a price far below p. When $\Delta Q > 0$, more product must be made to satisfy the newly emerged demand ΔQ. Such an unplanned demand, usually known as an emergency order, may require more expensive resources to produce. So the unit production cost will be more than the unit production cost c associated with the planned demand.

For a given real production quantity Q under a demand disruption, we assume the production quantity deviation cost is proportional to $\Delta Q = Q - \bar{Q}$. Let $\lambda_1 > 0$ and $\lambda_2 > 0$ be the marginal cost of the increase and decrease of production, respectively. Then the supply chain profit can be written as

$$f(Q) = Q(\frac{\bar{D} + \Delta D - Q}{k} - c) - \lambda_1(Q - \bar{Q})^+ - \lambda_2(\bar{Q} - Q)^+, \quad (9.2)$$

where $(x)^+ = \max\{x, 0\}$.

The meaning of λ_2 deserves more discussion. There are two cases. When $0 < \lambda_2 < c$, the model represents the case in which the leftover inventory $\bar{Q} - Q$ can be sold in a secondary market at a unit price less than c, say, $\bar{c}$. Thus, $\lambda_2 = c - \bar{c}$. When $c \leq \lambda_2$, the model represents the case in which a disposal cost of $\lambda_2 - c$ is incurred for each unit of the leftover inventory. In practice, the disposal cost is usually much less than the production cost so we assume that $\lambda_2 - c$ does not exceed c, or $\lambda_2 - c \leq c$.

Assumption 1 $\lambda_2 \leq 2c$.

9.3.2 *Optimal policies under a demand disruption*

Given the objective function $f(Q)$ in Eq. (9.2), the centralized decision maker needs to find a new optimal production quantity Q^* to maximize $f(Q)$. Intuitively, when market scale increases, the production level should also increase, and vice versa. Formally, we have the following lemma without detailed proof.

Lemma 9.2 *Suppose Q^* maximizes $f(Q)$ in (9.2). Then $Q^* \geq \bar{Q}$ if $\Delta D > 0$, and $Q^* \leq \bar{Q}$ if $\Delta D < 0$.*

From Lemma 9.2, when $\Delta D > 0$, the problem of maximizing $f(Q)$ reduces to maximizing the strictly concave function

$$f_1(Q) = Q(\frac{\bar{D} + \Delta D - Q}{k} - c) - \lambda_1(Q - \bar{Q}) \qquad (9.3)$$

subject to $Q \geq \bar{Q}$. Using the first order condition $f_1'(Q) = 0$ for an unconstrained problem, we have

$$f_1'(Q) = -\frac{2}{k}Q + \frac{1}{k}(\bar{D} + \Delta D) - c - \lambda_1 = 0.$$

Solving for Q gives

$$Q_1 = \frac{\bar{D} - ck}{2} + \frac{\Delta D - \lambda_1 k}{2}. \qquad (9.4)$$

We need to analyze Q_1 in Eq. (9.4) with respect to the constraint $Q \geq \bar{Q}$. There are two cases.

Case 1: $\Delta D \geq \lambda_1 k$. When this condition is true, Q_1 satisfies the constraint $Q \geq \bar{Q}$, implying that $f_1(Q)$ is maximized at Q_1. Let $Q^*_{\text{case1}} = Q_1$.

Case 2: $0 < \Delta D < \lambda_1 k$. When this condition is true, $Q_1 < \bar{Q}$ so Q_1 is infeasible to the optimization problem associated with (9.3). Thus $f_1(Q)$ is maximized at $\bar{Q} = (\bar{D} - ck)/2$. Let $Q^*_{\text{case2}} = \bar{Q}$.

In summary, we have

$$Q^* = \begin{cases} Q^*_{\text{case1}} = \frac{\bar{D}-ck}{2} + \frac{\Delta D - \lambda_1 k}{2} & \text{for Case 1} \\ Q^*_{\text{case2}} = \frac{\bar{D}-ck}{2} & \text{for Case 2} \end{cases}$$

Note that Case 1 represents a large market scale change while Case 2 represents a small market scale change.

Now we derive the corresponding optimal retail price p^*. We start with Case 2, where

$$p^*_{case2} = \frac{1}{k}(\bar{D} + \Delta D - Q^*_{case2}) = \frac{\bar{D}+ck}{2k} + \frac{\Delta D}{k} = \bar{p} + \frac{\Delta D}{k},$$

and the supply chain profit is

$$f^{sc}_{case2} = Q^*_{case2}(p^*_{case2} - c) = \frac{\bar{D}-ck}{2}\left(\frac{\bar{D}-ck}{2k} + \frac{\Delta D}{k}\right) = \bar{f}^{sc}_{max} + \Delta D \frac{\bar{Q}}{k}.$$

We see that when the market scale increases marginally, the maximum supply chain profit increases linearly with the market scale increase ΔD at a ratio of $\bar{Q}/k$.

For Case 1, we have

$$p^*_{case1} = \frac{1}{k}(\bar{D} + \Delta D - Q^*_{case1}) = \frac{\bar{D}+ck}{2k} + \frac{\Delta D + \lambda_1 k}{2k} = \bar{p} + \frac{\Delta D + \lambda_1 k}{2k}$$

with supply chain profit

$$\begin{aligned}
f^{sc}_{case1} &= Q^*_{case1}(p^*_{case1} - c) - \lambda_1(Q^*_{case1} - \bar{Q}) \\
&= \left(\frac{\bar{D}-ck}{2} + \frac{\Delta D - \lambda_1 k}{2}\right)\left(\frac{\bar{D}-ck+\Delta D + \lambda_1 k}{2k}\right) - \lambda_1 \frac{\Delta D - \lambda_1 k}{2} \\
&= \frac{(\bar{D}-ck)^2}{4k} + \frac{(\bar{D}-ck)(\Delta D + \lambda_1 k)}{4k} + \frac{(\Delta D - \lambda_1 k)(\bar{D}+\Delta D - ck - \lambda_1 k)}{4k} \\
&= \bar{f}^{sc}_{max} + \frac{(\bar{D}-ck)(2\Delta D)}{4k} + \frac{(\Delta D - \lambda_1 k)^2}{4k} \\
&= \bar{f}^{sc}_{max} + \Delta D \frac{\bar{Q}}{k} + f_{\Delta D}.
\end{aligned}$$

In the last expression, we use the notation $f_{\Delta D} = (\Delta D - \lambda_1 k)^2/(4k)$ which is a quadratic function of ΔD, showing that the supply chain profit increases quadratically with ΔD when ΔD is large enough. Using some algebra, f^{sc}_{case1} can be written alternatively as

$$f^{sc}_{case1} = \frac{(\bar{D} + \Delta D - (c+\lambda_1)k)^2}{4k} + \lambda_1 \bar{Q} \qquad (9.5)$$

where the first term can be interpreted as the profit that would result if the unit production cost was $c + \lambda_1$ for all items produced, and the second term as an adjustment, given that the unit production cost is actually c for the first $\bar{Q}$ products. This form will be used in the next section.

We now consider the case where $\Delta D < 0$ and assume that the resolved market scale $\bar{D} + \Delta D$ is still large enough so that a profit can be made, at least for the case when every decision is taken after observing the market, i.e.,

Assumption 2 $\bar{D} + \Delta D - ck > 0$.

Now the problem of maximizing $f(Q)$ in (9.2) reduces to maximizing

$$f_2(Q) = Q(\frac{\bar{D} + \Delta D - Q}{k} - c) - \lambda_2(\bar{Q} - Q) \qquad (9.6)$$

subject to $\bar{Q} \geq Q$. Similarly, we have two cases identified as Case 3 ($-\lambda_2 k \leq \Delta D < 0$) and Case 4 ($\Delta D < -\lambda_2 k$). Without going into the details, it can be shown that $f_2(Q)$ in (9.6) is maximized at

$$Q^* = \begin{cases} Q^*_{case3} = \frac{\bar{D} - ck}{2} & \text{for Case 3,} \\ Q^*_{case4} = \frac{\bar{D} - ck}{2} + \frac{\Delta D + \lambda_2 k}{2} & \text{for Case 4.} \end{cases} \qquad (9.7)$$

For Case 3, the optimal retail price is

$$p^*_{case3} = \bar{p} + \frac{\Delta D}{k} \qquad (9.8)$$

and the supply chain profit is $f^{sc}_{case3} = \bar{f}^{sc}_{max} + \Delta D \frac{\bar{Q}}{k}$.

For Case 4, the optimal retail price is

$$p^*_{case4} = \bar{p} + \frac{\Delta D - \lambda_2 k}{2k} \qquad (9.9)$$

and the supply chain profit is

$$f^{sc}_{case4} = \frac{(\bar{D} + \Delta D - (c - \lambda_2)k)^2}{4k} - \lambda_2 \bar{Q}$$

or
$$f^{\text{sc}}_{\text{case4}} = \bar{f}^{\text{sc}}_{\text{max}} + \Delta D \frac{\bar{Q}}{k} + \frac{(\Delta D + \lambda_2 k)^2}{4k}.$$

When $\Delta D < 0$, there might be concerns that the demand Q^*_{case4} given in (9.7) and the retail prices p^*_{case3} given in (9.8) and p^*_{case4} given in (9.9) could be negative, leading to an infeasible situation. However, this can be ruled out by Assumptions 1 and 2. We omit the detailed discussion on this.

It should be pointed out that the retail price p^* may be less than the production cost c when $\Delta D < 0$, implying the total profit of the supply chain becomes negative. This is unavoidable if the market scale is badly estimated or severely shrinks. For Case 3, a positive profit is equivalent to $p^* > c$, or $\bar{D} - kc + 2\Delta D > 0$. For Case 4, a positive profit means $f^{\text{sc}}_{\text{case4}} > 0$, which can be expressed as

$$(\bar{D} + \Delta D - ck)^2 + (\Delta D + \lambda_2 k)^2 > (\Delta D)^2.$$

Summarizing the above results, we have

Theorem 9.1 *Given a disruption in market demand ΔD, when the resolved demand function is $d = \bar{D} + \Delta D - kp$, the supply chain profit is maximized for the following values of the retail price p and the production order quantity Q.*

$$p^* = \begin{cases} \bar{p} + \frac{\Delta D - \lambda_2 k}{2k} & \text{if } \Delta D \leq -\lambda_2 k, \\ \bar{p} + \frac{\Delta D}{k} & \text{if } -\lambda_2 k \leq \Delta D \leq \lambda_1 k, \\ \bar{p} + \frac{\Delta D + \lambda_1 k}{2k} & \text{if } \lambda_1 k \leq \Delta D. \end{cases} \quad (9.10)$$

$$Q^* = \begin{cases} \bar{Q} + \frac{\Delta D + \lambda_2 k}{2} & \text{if } \Delta D \leq -\lambda_2 k, \\ \bar{Q} & \text{if } -\lambda_2 k \leq \Delta D \leq \lambda_1 k, \\ \bar{Q} + \frac{\Delta D - \lambda_1 k}{2} & \text{if } \lambda_1 k \leq \Delta D. \end{cases} \quad (9.11)$$

Theorem 9.1 implies that the original production plan $\bar{Q}$ has some robustness under a disrupted market scale. No change is required when the market scale is perturbed only slightly. In such circumstances, an adjustment in the retail price can be made to compensate for any deviation costs. Only when the market scale change exceeds the threshold given in Eq. (9.11), will it be necessary to change both the original production plan and retail price.

9.3.3 Value of disruption management

The importance of an appropriate response to a disruption can be evaluated by comparing the solution that keeps the original retail price $\bar{p}$ as if not knowing the disruption. When $\bar{D} + \Delta D - k\bar{p} > 0$, the amount of product that can be sold is $\hat{Q} = \bar{D} + \Delta D - k\bar{p}$, and the supply chain profit is

$$\hat{f}^{sc} = \hat{Q}(\bar{p} - c) - \lambda_1(\Delta D)^+ - \lambda_2(\Delta D)^-. \qquad (9.12)$$

When $\bar{D} + \Delta D - k\bar{p} \leq 0$, no product can be sold so the total profit is $\hat{f}^{sc} = -\lambda_2 \bar{Q}$, which is actually a pure loss. The profit difference, defined as $f^{sc}_{case_i} - \hat{f}^{sc}$, can be analyzed by the following cases.

(1) Case 1: $\Delta D > \lambda_1 k$. The profit difference is $\frac{(\Delta D - \lambda_1 k)^2}{4k} + \lambda_1 \Delta D$.
(2) Case 2: $0 < \Delta D \leq \lambda_1 k$. The profit difference is $\lambda_1 \Delta D$.
(3) Case 3.1: $-\lambda_2 k \leq \Delta D < 0$ and $\bar{D} + \Delta D - k\bar{p} > 0$. The profit difference is $-\lambda_2 \Delta D$
(4) Case 3.2: $-\lambda_2 k \leq \Delta D < 0$ and $\bar{D} + \Delta D - k\bar{p} \leq 0$. The profit difference is $\frac{(\bar{D} - ck)^2}{4k} + (\Delta D + \lambda_2 k)\frac{\bar{D} - ck}{2k}$.
(5) Case 4.1: $\Delta D < -\lambda_2 k$ and $\bar{D} + \Delta D - k\bar{p} > 0$. The profit difference is $\frac{(\Delta D + \lambda_2 k)^2}{4k} - \lambda_2 \Delta D$.
(6) Case 4.2: $\Delta D < -\lambda_2 k$ and $\bar{D} + \Delta D - k\bar{p} \leq 0$. The profit difference is $\frac{(\bar{D} + \Delta D - (c - \lambda_2)k)^2}{4k}$.

It is shown that our optimal disruption management policy always leads to greater profits when $\Delta D \neq 0$. Moreover, as the disruption grows larger, the profit difference increases quadratically with ΔD, as in cases 1 and 4, which highlights the importance of the disruption management model.

9.4 Decentralized Decision Making after Demand Disruptions

Now we discuss how the supplier and the retailer can make decisions jointly for a demand disruption. Recall that the supplier has planned to use a quantity discount policy to coordinate the supply chain for the estimated demand function. When a demand disruption occurs, we will show that the supplier can revise the planned quantity discount policy to induce the retailer to place the right order and set the right retail price. We discuss the problem for the above four cases.

9.4.1 Case 1 : $\Delta D \geq \lambda_1 k$

From (9.5), the total maximum supply chain profit under this case is

$$f_{\text{case1}}^{\text{sc}} = \frac{(\bar{D} + \Delta D - (c + \lambda_1)k)^2}{4k} + \lambda_1 \bar{Q}.$$

To achieve such a $f_{\text{case1}}^{\text{sc}}$, the retailer has to place an order of Q_{case1}^*. Suppose the profit that the supplier would like to earn is f^s. First, we consider the case where $f^s \geq \lambda_1 \bar{Q}$. This allows us to write supplier's profit goal as

$$f^s = \eta \frac{(\bar{D} + \Delta D - (c + \lambda_1)k)^2}{4k} + \lambda_1 \bar{Q} \tag{9.13}$$

where $0 \leq \eta < 1$ is a parameter specified by the supplier.

Theorem 9.2 *When $\Delta D \geq \lambda_1 k$ and $f^s \geq \lambda_1 \bar{Q}$, the supply chain can be coordinated under an all-unit quantity discount policy $AQDP(w_1, w_2, Q_{\text{case1}}^*)$ where*

$$w_1 > \frac{\bar{D} + \Delta D}{k} - \sqrt{1 - \eta}(\frac{\bar{D} + \Delta D}{k} - c - \lambda_1),$$

$$w_2 = c + \lambda_1 + \eta \frac{\bar{D} + \Delta D - (c + \lambda_1)k}{2k},$$

and η is defined in (9.13).

We omit the proof because it is similar to the proof of Lemma 9.1.

Now consider the case where $f^s < \lambda_1 \bar{Q}$. Let $f^s = \eta \lambda_1 \bar{Q}$ for $0 < \eta < 1$. Differently, a simple $AQDP$ cannot coordinate the supply chain in this case as shown in the following lemma.

Lemma 9.3 *When $\Delta D \geq \lambda_1 k$ and $f^s = \eta \lambda_1 \bar{Q}$ with $0 < \eta < 1$, the supply chain cannot be coordinated by an $AQDP(w_1, w_2, q_0)$.*

Proof. Suppose the supply chain could be coordinated for some $AQDP(w_1, w_2, q_0)$. Then the retailer should place an order of $Q^*_{case1} = (\bar{D} + \Delta D - (c + \lambda_1)k)/2$, and the profit of the supplier should be

$$f^s = \eta \lambda_1 \frac{\bar{D} - ck}{2}$$
$$= \frac{\bar{D} + \Delta D - (c + \lambda_1)k}{2} w_2 - c\frac{\bar{D} - ck}{2} - (c + \lambda_1)\frac{\Delta D - \lambda_1 k}{2}.$$

Solving for w_2 gives

$$w_2 = c + \lambda_1 + (\eta - 1)\frac{\lambda_1(\bar{D} - ck)}{\bar{D} + \Delta D - (c + \lambda_1)k}.$$

For this value of w_2, however, the profit of the retailer is maximized at $Q_2 = (\bar{D} + \Delta D - w_2 k)/2$. With some algebraic manipulation, it can be shown that $Q_2 > Q^*_{case1}$ which implies that the retailer will order Q_2 rather than Q^*_{case1}. Thus the supply chain is not coordinated. ∎

To develop a coordination mechanism, we introduce a *capacitated linear pricing policy* $CLPP(w, C)$ with the following characteristics. The unit wholesale price is w, but the retailer is restricted to ordering no more than the quantity C. This is equivalent to saying that the supplier has a production capacity of C, a common situation in practice.

Theorem 9.3 *When $\Delta D \geq \lambda_1 k$ and $f^s = \eta \lambda_1 \bar{Q}$ with $0 < \eta < 1$, the supply chain can be coordinated with a $CLPP(w, Q^*_{case1})$ for which*

$$w = c + \lambda_1 + (\eta - 1)\frac{\lambda_1(\bar{D} - ck)}{\bar{D} + \Delta D - (c + \lambda_1)k}.$$

Proof. From Lemma 9.3, the profit of the retailer is maximized at $Q_2 = (\bar{D}+\Delta D - wk)/2$, which is greater than the supplier's capacity Q^*_{case1}. Thus, simple calculus tells us that the retailer should order Q^*_{case1} to maximize his profit. As a consequence, the supply chain is coordinated. ∎

9.4.2 Case 2 : $0 < \Delta D \leq \lambda_1 k$

In this case, the maximum total supply chain profit is

$$f^{sc}_{\text{case2}} = \frac{(\bar{D}-ck)^2}{4k} + \Delta D \frac{\bar{D}-ck}{2k}$$

and the supply chain coordination implies that the retailer needs to order $Q^*_{\text{case2}} = \bar{Q} = (\bar{D}-ck)/2$. Suppose the supplier wants to obtain a profit of $f^s = \eta f^{sc}$. Similarly, there are two cases. When η is large, the supply chain is coordinated by an AQDP, and when η is small, the supply chain is coordinated by an CLPP.

Theorem 9.4 *For the case where $0 < \Delta D \leq \lambda_1 k$,*

1) when $\eta > 2\Delta D/(2\Delta D + \bar{D} - ck)$, the $AQDP(w_1, w_2, \bar{Q})$ can be used to coordinate the supply chain;

2) when $\eta \leq 2\Delta D/(2\Delta D + \bar{D} - ck)$, the $CLPP(w_2, \bar{Q})$ can be used to coordinate the supply chain, where

$$w_1 > \frac{\bar{D}+\Delta D}{k} - \sqrt{(1-\eta)(\bar{D}-ck)(\bar{D}-ck+2\Delta D)},$$

$$w_2 = c + \eta \frac{\bar{D}+2\Delta D - ck}{2k}.$$

Proof. When the retailer takes the wholesale price w_2, his profit can be written as $f_1^r(Q) = Q(\frac{\bar{D}+\Delta D - Q}{k} - w_2)$, which is maximized at $Q_1 = (\bar{D}+\Delta D - w_2 k)/2$.

(i) When $\eta > 2\Delta D/(2\Delta D + \bar{D} - ck)$, it can be shown that $Q_1 < \bar{Q}$. Under $AQDP(w_1, w_2, \bar{Q})$, the retailer has to order $\bar{Q}$ to maximize his profit.

(ii) When $\eta \leq 2\Delta D/(2\Delta D + \bar{D} - ck)$, $Q_1 > \bar{Q}$. Under $CLPP(w_2, \bar{Q})$, the retailer orders $\bar{Q}$ to maximize his profit.

In either case, the profit of the retailer is

$$f_1^r(\bar{Q}) = \bar{Q}(p^*_{case2} - w_2) = (1-\eta)\left(\frac{(\bar{D} - ck)^2}{4k} + \Delta D \frac{\bar{D} - ck}{2k}\right).$$

If the retailer takes the price w_1, his maximum profit would be $f_2^r = (\bar{D} + \Delta D - w_1 k)^2$. It can be shown that $f_2^r < f_1^r(\bar{Q})$ under the conditions of the theorem so w_2 yields a better result. ∎

In fact, when devising an $AQDP(w_1, w_2, q_0)$, once w_2 is specified, we can always find a w_1 large enough such that $w_1 > w_2$ and the retailer's profit is greater when the wholesale price is w_2 rather than w_1. For the sake of simplicity in what follows, we will only say that w_1 is large enough, rather than explicitly give a lower bound on its value.

9.4.3 Case 3 : $-\lambda_2 k \leq \Delta D < 0$

For this case, the maximum total supply chain profit is

$$f^{sc}_{case3} = \frac{(\bar{D} - ck)^2}{4k} + \Delta D \frac{\bar{D} - ck}{2k},$$

and the retailer should order Q^*_{case3} so that the supply chain is coordinated. Recall that the total supply chain profit is positive only when $\bar{D} + 2\Delta D > kc$. Suppose this is true and that the supplier wishes to achieve a profit of

$$f^s = \eta f^{sc}_{case3} = \eta\left(\frac{(\bar{D} - ck)^2}{4k} + \Delta D \frac{\bar{D} - ck}{2k}\right). \qquad (9.14)$$

Theorem 9.5 *For the case $-\lambda_2 k \leq \Delta D < 0$ and $\bar{D} + 2\Delta D > kc$, f^s defined in (9.14), $AQDP(w_1, w_2, \bar{Q})$ can be used to coordinate the supply chain, where w_1 is large enough, and*

$$w_2 = c + \eta \frac{\bar{D} + 2\Delta D - ck}{2k}.$$

However, the policy in Theorem 9.5 cannot be applied when $\bar{D} + 2\Delta D < kc$. This follows because

$$p^*_{\text{case3}} - w_2 = (1 - \eta)\frac{\bar{D} + 2\Delta D - ck}{2k} < 0,$$

which means that the retailer's profit is negative. In reality, the retailer has the option of not ordering any product if he cannot realize a profit. If no order is placed, the supplier will be forced to dispose of his entire production plan $\bar{Q}$ at a loss of $-\lambda_2 \bar{Q}$. To reduce this loss, the supplier needs to set a wholesale price policy that induces the retailer to order at least some amount of product. Although the supplier may sell the product at a wholesale that is lower than the production cost, it is still profitable to the supplier than disposing of all product. To devise an optimal wholesale price schedule, we must look at this situation from the retailer's point of view.

Suppose that the retailer must earn a profit of

$$f^{\text{r}} = -\mu f^{\text{sc}}_{\text{case3}} = -\mu\Big(\frac{(\bar{D} - ck)^2}{4k} + \Delta D \frac{\bar{D} - ck}{2k}\Big), \quad \mu > 0 \quad (9.15)$$

to participate in the game, where it is assumed that $f^{\text{sc}}_{\text{case3}} \leq 0$. Then the supplier's profit becomes

$$f^{\text{s}} = f^{\text{sc}} - f^{\text{r}} = (1 + \mu)\Big(\frac{(\bar{D} - ck)^2}{4k} + \Delta D \frac{\bar{D} - ck}{2k}\Big).$$

On the other hand, the supplier also has the option of not playing the game with the retailer if the retailer asks for too much, i.e., if μ is too large, because the supplier can minimize her losses by simply disposing of her entire lot $\bar{Q}$ and incurring a loss of $-\lambda_2 \bar{Q}$. To make it more attractive for the supplier, we need $f^{\text{s}} > -\lambda_2 \bar{Q}$, which is equivalent to $\mu < \mu_0$ where

$$\mu_0 = -\frac{\bar{D} - ck + 2(\Delta D + k\lambda_2)}{\bar{D} + 2\Delta D - ck}. \quad (9.16)$$

Defining

$$\mu_1 = -\frac{\bar{D} - ck}{\bar{D} - ck + 2\Delta D}, \quad (9.17)$$

we have that

Theorem 9.6 *For the case where* $-\lambda_2 k \leq \Delta D < 0$, $\bar{D} + 2\Delta D \leq kc$, f^r *in* (9.15), μ_0 *in* (9.16), *and* μ_1 *in* (9.17),

1) *when* $0 < \mu \leq \mu_1$, *the* $AQDP(w_1, w_2, \bar{Q})$ *can be used to coordinate the supply chain;*

2) *when* $\mu_1 < \mu < \mu_0$, *the* $CLPP(w_2, \bar{Q})$ *can be used to coordinate the supply chain; and*

3) *when* $\mu \geq \mu_0$, *it is optimal for the supplier to dispose of the entire production lot* $\bar{Q}$, *where*

$$w_2 = p^*_{case3} + \mu \frac{\bar{D} - ck + 2\Delta D}{2k} = \frac{\bar{D} + ck + 2\Delta D}{2k} + \mu \frac{\bar{D} - ck + 2\Delta D}{2k},$$

and w_1 *is large enough.*

Proof. If the retailer accepts the wholesale price w_2, his profit can be written as $f_1^r(Q) = Q(\frac{\bar{D}+\Delta D-Q}{k} - w_2)$, which is maximized at $Q_1 = (\bar{D} + \Delta D - w_2 k)/2$.

When $\mu \leq -(\bar{D} - ck)/(\bar{D} - ck + 2\Delta D)$, it can be shown that $Q_1 \leq \bar{Q}$. Under $AQDP(w_1, w_2, \bar{Q})$, the retailer has to order $\bar{Q}$ to maximize his profit. When $\mu > -(\bar{D} - ck)/(\bar{D} - ck + 2\Delta D)$, under $CLPP(w_2, \bar{Q})$, the retailer would order $\bar{Q}$ to maximize his profit.

In either case, it is best for the retailer to set the selling price at p^*_{case3}. Because $w_2 < p^*_{case3}$, it is to his advantage to place an order. ∎

9.4.4 Case 4 : $\Delta D < -\lambda_2 k$

Recall that the maximum supply chain profit for Case 4 is

$$f^*_{case4} = \frac{(\bar{D} + \Delta D - (c - \lambda_2)k)^2}{4k} - \lambda_2 \frac{\bar{D} - ck}{2}.$$

With respect to this value, suppose the retailer wishes to achieve a minimum profit of

$$f^r = \frac{(\bar{D} + \Delta D - (c - \lambda_2)k)^2}{4k} - \mu\lambda_2 \frac{\bar{D} - ck}{2}. \tag{9.18}$$

The supplier's profit is then $f^s = (\mu-1)\lambda_2 \frac{\bar{D}-ck}{2}$, and will be negative when the parameter $\mu < 1$. Whether positive or negative, though, to ensure that the supplier participates in the game, we must have $f^s > -\lambda_2 \bar{Q}$, or equivalently, $\mu > 0$. If this condition is not met, it is better for the supplier to dispose of her entire production lot $\bar{Q}$ in a secondary market rather than proposing a wholesale discount policy to induce the retailer to buy a portion of it.

Theorem 9.7 *For the case where $\Delta D < -\lambda_2 k$, when $\mu > 0$, we can use the $AQDP(w_1, w_2, Q^*_{case4})$ to coordinate the supply chain, where*

$$w_2 = c - \lambda_2 + \frac{\mu \lambda_2 (\bar{D} - ck)}{\bar{D} + \Delta D - (c - \lambda_2)k},$$

w_1 is large enough, and μ is defined in (9.18).

Proof. If the retailer takes the wholesale price w_2, then his profit can be written as $f^r(Q) = Q(\frac{\bar{D}+\Delta D - Q}{k} - w_2)$, which is maximized at $Q_1 = \frac{\bar{D}+\Delta D - w_2 k}{2}$. Because $w_2 > c - \lambda_2$, $Q_1 < \frac{\bar{D}+\Delta D - (c-\lambda_2)k}{2} = Q^*_{case4}$. So the retailer must order Q^*_{case4} to maximize his profit, and

$$f^r(Q^*_{case4})$$
$$= Q^*_{case4}(p^*_{case4} - w_2)$$
$$= \frac{\bar{D} + \Delta D - (c-\lambda_2)k}{2} \left(\frac{\bar{D} + \Delta D + (c-\lambda_2)k}{2k} - c + \lambda_2 - \frac{\mu \lambda_2 (\bar{D}-ck)}{\bar{D}+\Delta D-(c-\lambda_2)k} \right)$$
$$= \frac{(\bar{D}+\Delta D - (c-\lambda_2)k)^2}{4k} - \mu \lambda_2 \frac{\bar{D}-ck}{2},$$

which is just what the retailer desires. On the other hand, setting a very large wholesale price w_1 cannot lead to a greater profit than $f^r(Q^*_{case4})$. ∎

9.4.5 Impact of disruption management on supply chain coordination

To better understand the importance of disruption management in supply chain coordination, we compare the above policies under our disruption management model with the case when the supplier does not know the demand disruption and keeps the wholesale discount policy $AQDP(\bar{w}_1, \bar{w}_2, \bar{Q})$ originally developed in Section 9.2. From the perspective of the supplier, we are interested in determining whether her original profit goal can be achieved without knowing the real demand and, if so, whether she actually earns more than what is projected.

From the perspective of the retailer, he always knows the real demand, and makes his ordering decision based on it. In this sense, there is no disruption for the retailer because he is not involved in the planning period, but his profit is still affected by the supplier's decision. In comparison, we are interested in whether the retailer can earn more or less than what the supplier projected for him in the original plan.

Finally, for the supply chain as a whole, we discuss the conditions under which the maximum overall profit can be achieved.

Given the originally projected $AQDP(\bar{w}_1, \bar{w}_2, \bar{Q})$, the retailer's profit for wholesale price $\bar{w}_2$ is $f^r(Q) = Q(\frac{\bar{D}+\Delta D-Q}{k} - \bar{w}_2)$, which is maximized at $Q_1 = \bar{Q} + (\Delta D - \eta \bar{Q})/2$. Therefore, when $\Delta D > \eta \bar{Q}$, the retailer will order $Q_1 > \bar{Q}$ to maximize his profit. Recall that the supplier is obligated to provide this quantity to the retailer under the terms of the game. If $\bar{w}_2 > c + \lambda_1$, the supplier will earn more than $\bar{f}^s$ by selling the additional quantity $(\Delta D - \eta \bar{Q})/2$ to the retailer. The marginal profit will be $\eta(\bar{D} - ck)/(2k) - \lambda_1$. If $\bar{w}_2 < c + \lambda_1$, the supplier's projected profit $\bar{f}^s$ will be reduced by the amount $c + \lambda_1 - \bar{w}_2$ for each unit above $\bar{Q}$ that she provides. On the other hand, ordering more than $\bar{Q}$ is always beneficial for the retailer because the wholesale price is constant.

We now consider the coordination of the supply chain as a whole. By definition, coordination is achieved when the profits of both players are collectively maximized. This occurs only when the retailer places an order for the right quantity. If the demand disruption corresponds to Case 1 ($\Delta D \geq \lambda_1 k$), the retailer orders $Q^*_{\text{case1}} \geq \bar{Q}$; if the demand disruption corresponds to Case 2 ($0 < \Delta D < \lambda_1 k$), the retailer orders $Q^*_{\text{case2}} = \bar{Q}$. Because we are discussing the case where $\Delta D > \eta \bar{Q}$, we have $Q_1 > \bar{Q}$ as shown above. This corresponds to Case 1 so the supply chain is coordinated when $Q_1 = Q^*_{\text{case1}}$, or equivalently, when $\lambda_1 k = \eta \bar{Q}$.

When $\Delta D < \eta \bar{Q}$, assuming $\bar{w}_1$ is too large for the retailer to accept, the retailer then has two choices: he can either order $\bar{Q}$ when it is profitable to do so, or he can refuse to participate in the game. The hedging point at which the retailer makes a profit is where the retail price $\hat{p} = (\bar{D} + \Delta D - \bar{Q})/k$ is just greater than the wholesale price $\bar{w}_2$. It can be shown with some algebra that $\hat{p} > \bar{w}_2$ is equivalent to $\Delta D > (\eta - 1)\bar{Q}$. If the retailer orders $\bar{Q}$, then the supplier's target profit is achieved exactly because this is what she planned to sell before the disruption. When $\Delta D > 0$, there is some extra profit that goes to the retailer. When $\Delta D < 0$, the retailer's profit is less than what was projected. For the supply chain as a whole, coordination is achieved when $-\lambda_2 k \leq \Delta D \leq \lambda_1 k$. This corresponds to Cases 2 and 3 where the optimal order quantity is $\bar{Q} = (\bar{D} - kc)/2$.

In summary, the ability to react to the disruption has the following advantages. First, the supplier has a greater chance of increasing her profit. Recall that when the demand increase is sufficiently large, the total supply chain profit increases quadratically. If the supplier can dynamically change the discount policy, she can also increase her profit quadratically.

Not knowing of the disruption is likely to reduce the supplier's original profit (for the case where $\bar{w}_2 < c + \lambda_1$) even when $\Delta D > 0$. This situation can be avoided, though, if the disruption is handled properly. When $\Delta D > \eta \bar{Q}$ and $\bar{w}_2 > c + \lambda_1$, the supplier's marginal profit is positive so she can still benefit without knowing of the disruption. In fact, her profit grows linearly with ΔD, regardless of how large the market scale becomes.

On the other hand, the retailer is always better off when $\Delta D > 0$, and may even be able to increase his profit when the supply chain is not coordinated. Lack of coordination means that there is a gap between the maximum profit in the supply chain and the collective profits realized by the players. It may be possible for the retailer to exploit this gap.

When $\Delta D \leq (\eta - 1)\bar{Q}$, the retailer doesn't participate in the game and earns nothing, but the supplier suffers a significant loss $-\lambda_2 \bar{Q}$

because she has to completely dispose of her inventory. This case is partially avoidable when the supplier knows of the disruption and so can adjust her wholesale policy to induce the retailer to order some amount of product. In certain cases, the supplier may even earn a profit.

9.5 Extension to Nonlinear Demand Functions

All previous results are based on the assumption of a linear demand function $Q = D - kp$. In this section, we show that the above approach of modeling and analysis can be extended to some other cases. In this regard, we discuss the case of another commonly used nonlinear demand function $Q = Dp^{-k}$ with $k > 1$. We will outline the main results without detailed proof.

In the deterministic case, for the demand function $Q = \bar{D}p^{-k}$, it can be shown that the supply chain profit is maximized at

$$\bar{Q} = \bar{D}\left(\frac{k-1}{ck}\right)^k, \quad \bar{p} = \frac{ck}{k-1}, \quad \bar{f}_{\max}^{\mathrm{sc}} = \frac{\bar{D}}{k}\left(\frac{k-1}{ck}\right)^{k-1}.$$

The supply chain can be coordinated under the deterministic case by an $AQDP(\bar{w}_1, \bar{w}_2, q_0)$ where $\bar{w}_1$ is large enough, $\bar{w}_2 = c + \eta c/(k-1)$, $q_0 = \bar{Q}$, and η is the percentage of the total supply chain profit that the supplier wants to earn.

9.5.1 *Disruption management for centralized decision making*

Suppose a demand disruption occurs in the selling season and the resolved demand function is $Q = \delta \bar{D}p^{-k}$. When $\delta > 1$, the market scale is increased; and when $\delta < 1$, the market scale is decreased. To analyze the optimal reaction for a centralized decision maker, we assume the cost for deviating from the original production plan $\bar{Q}$ is a linear function to the magnitude of the deviation. Similar to Eq.(9.2), we have the objective function for disruption management as

$$f(Q) = Q\left(\left(\frac{\delta \bar{D}}{Q}\right)^{\frac{1}{k}} - c\right) - \lambda_1(Q - \bar{Q})^+ - \lambda_2(\bar{Q} - Q)^+. \quad (9.19)$$

To find the optimal Q^* that maximizes Eq.(9.19), there are four cases to be discussed:

Case 1: $\delta^{\frac{1}{k}} \geq 1 + \lambda_1/c$.

Case 2: $1 < \delta^{\frac{1}{k}} < 1 + \lambda_1/c$.

Case 3: $1 - \lambda_2/c \leq \delta^{\frac{1}{k}} < 1$.

Case 4: $\delta^{\frac{1}{k}} < 1 - \lambda_2/c$.

Parallel to Theorem 9.1, we have the optimal Q^* to maximize $f(Q)$ in Eq. (9.19) as follows:

$$Q^* = \begin{cases} Q^*_{\text{case1}} = \delta \bar{D}\left(\frac{k-1}{k(c+\lambda_1)}\right)^k, & \text{for case 1,} \\ \bar{Q} = \bar{D}\left(\frac{k-1}{ck}\right)^k, & \text{for cases 2 and 3,} \\ Q^*_{\text{case4}} = \delta \bar{D}\left(\frac{k-1}{k(c-\lambda_2)}\right)^k, & \text{for case 4.} \end{cases}$$

The corresponding optimal retail price is

$$p^* = \begin{cases} \frac{(c+\lambda_1)k}{k-1}, & \text{for case 1,} \\ \frac{ck}{k-1}\delta^{\frac{1}{k}}, & \text{for cases 2 and 3,} \\ \frac{(c-\lambda_2)k}{k-1}, & \text{for case 4.} \end{cases} \quad (9.20)$$

We see that even when the demand function becomes a nonlinear function, we can still observe similar managerial insights as we have obtained from Theorem 9.1 for the case of a linear demand function. Specifically, the production quantity will not change unless the magnitude of the demand disruption is large enough, and the retail price is always altered in order to respond to the demand disruption. This shows certain universality in the above approach of handling demand disruptions for a wide range of applications.

Moreover, we have found an interesting difference for the case of a nonlinear demand function. We see that the optimal retail price has both lower and upper bounds that are independent of the demand disruption δ. Compared with the linear demand model, the nonlinear demand model may better explain a practical phenomenon that the retail price cannot become arbitrarily high no matter how popular a product is. For the case of a decreased market scale, it is consistent with the fact that setting the retail price too low is less profitable than selling the product in a secondary market. Moreover, we do not need the assumption that $\lambda_2 \leq 2c$ as we did in the case of linear demand functions. When $\lambda_2 > 2c$, it can be correctly handled by Case 3.

9.5.2 Disruption management for supply chain coordination

We now discuss how the supply chain can still be coordinated when a demand disruption occurs. Suppose the profit that the supplier wants to earn is f^s.

Case 1: $\delta^{\frac{1}{k}} \geq 1 + \lambda_1/c$, where the total supply chain profit is

$$f^*_{\text{case1}} = \frac{\delta \bar{D}(c+\lambda_1)}{k-1} \left(\frac{k-1}{(c+\lambda_1)k}\right)^k + \lambda_1 \bar{D}\left(\frac{k-1}{ck}\right)^k.$$

When $f^s \geq \lambda_1 \bar{Q}$, f^s can be written as

$$f^s = \eta \frac{\delta \bar{D}(c+\lambda_1)}{k-1} \left(\frac{k-1}{(c+\lambda_1)k}\right)^k + \lambda_1 \bar{D}\left(\frac{k-1}{ck}\right)^k,$$

and the supply chain is coordinated by $AQDP(w_1, w_2, Q^*_{\text{case1}})$ where

$$w_2 = c + \lambda_1 + \eta \frac{c+\lambda_1}{k-1}.$$

When $f^s < \lambda_1 \bar{Q}$, f^s can be written as

$$f^s = \eta \lambda_1 \bar{D}\left(\frac{k-1}{ck}\right)^k.$$

In this case, if

$$\eta \geq 1 - \delta \frac{c+\lambda_1}{k-1}\left(\frac{c}{c+\lambda_1}\right)^k,$$

the supply chain is coordinated by $ADQP(w_1, w_2, Q^*_{case1})$, and if

$$\eta < 1 - \delta \frac{c+\lambda_1}{k-1}\left(\frac{c}{c+\lambda_1}\right)^k,$$

the supply chain is coordinated by $CLPP(w_2, Q^*_{case1})$ where

$$w_2 = \frac{k(c+\lambda_1)}{k-1} - (1-\eta)\frac{\lambda_1}{\delta}\left(\frac{c+\lambda_1}{c}\right)^k.$$

Case 2: $1 < \delta^{\frac{1}{k}} < 1 + \lambda_1/c$, where the maximum supply chain profit is

$$f^{sc}_{case2} = \bar{D}\left(\frac{k-1}{ck}\right)^k \left(\delta^{\frac{1}{k}}\frac{ck}{k-1} - c\right).$$

Suppose $f^s = \eta f^{sc}_{case2}$. Let

$$\eta_0 = 1 - \frac{\delta^{\frac{1}{k}}}{1 + k(\delta^{\frac{1}{k}} - 1)}.$$

When $\eta \geq \eta_0$, the supply chain is coordinated by an $AQDP(w_1, w_2, \bar{Q})$, and when $\eta < \eta_0$ the supply chain is coordinated by an $CLPP(w_2, \bar{Q})$, where

$$w_2 = c + \eta c\left(\delta^{\frac{1}{k}}\frac{k}{k-1} - 1\right).$$

Case 3: $1 - \lambda_2/c \leq \delta^{\frac{1}{k}} < 1$, where the maximum supply chain profit is

$$f^{sc}_{case3} = \bar{D}\left(\frac{k-1}{ck}\right)^k \left(\delta^{\frac{1}{k}}\frac{ck}{k-1} - c\right).$$

In this case, f^{sc}_{case3} is positive only when $\delta^{\frac{1}{k}} > 1 - 1/k$. Suppose this is true, and the supplier is asking for a profit of ηf^{sc}_{case3}. Then the supply chain is coordinated by an $AQDP(w_1, w_2, \bar{Q})$ with w_1 large enough and

$$w_2 = c + \eta\left(\delta^{\frac{1}{k}} \frac{ck}{k-1} - c\right).$$

When $1 - \lambda_2/c \le \delta^{\frac{1}{k}} \le 1 - 1/k$, the supply chain profit is nonpositive. Thus we have to devise the coordination from the viewpoint of the retailer. Suppose the retailer has a minimum desired profit of $f^{\mathrm{r}} = -\mu f^{\mathrm{sc}}_{\mathrm{case3}}$ with $\mu > 0$. Define

$$\mu_0 = -\frac{\delta^{\frac{1}{k}}}{\delta^{\frac{1}{k}} + 1 - k}, \text{ and } \mu_1 = -\frac{(\lambda_2 - 1)(k-1) + \delta^{\frac{1}{k}}}{\delta^{\frac{1}{k}} - c(k-1)}.$$

When $0 < \mu \le \mu_0$, the supply chain is coordinated by an $ADQP(w_1, w_2, \bar{Q})$; when $\mu_0 < \mu < \mu_1$, the supply chain is coordinated by an $CLPP(w_2, \bar{Q})$; and when $\mu \ge \mu_1$, the supplier would handle the whole production lot $\bar{Q}$ by herself with the cost of λ_2, where

$$w_2 = \delta^{\frac{1}{k}} \frac{ck}{k-1} + \mu\left(\delta^{\frac{1}{k}} \frac{ck}{k-1} - c\right).$$

Case 4: $\delta^{\frac{1}{k}} < 1 - \lambda_2/c$, with the maximum supply chain profit of

$$f^*_{\mathrm{case4}} = \frac{\delta \bar{D}(c - \lambda_2)}{k-1}\left(\frac{k-1}{(c-\lambda_2)k}\right)^k - \lambda_2 \bar{D}\left(\frac{k-1}{ck}\right)^k.$$

Suppose the minimum profit the retailer wants to earn is

$$f^*_{\mathrm{case4}} = \frac{\delta \bar{D}(c - \lambda_2)}{k-1}\left(\frac{k-1}{(c-\lambda_2)k}\right)^k - \mu \lambda_2 \bar{D}\left(\frac{k-1}{ck}\right)^k.$$

Define

$$\mu_3 = \frac{\delta \bar{D}}{k-1}\left(\frac{c}{\lambda_2} - 1\right)\left(\frac{c}{c-\lambda_2}\right)^k.$$

When $\mu \le 0$ or $\mu \ge \mu_3$, the supplier would process all production lot $\bar{Q}$ at the cost of λ_2, and when $0 < \mu \le \mu_3$, the supply chain is coordinated by $AQDP(w_1, w_2, Q^*_{\text{case4}})$, where

$$w_2 = c - \lambda_2 + \frac{\mu \lambda_2}{\delta}\left(\frac{c-\lambda_2}{c}\right)^k.$$

9.6 Extensions to a Supply Chain with Two Retailers

9.6.1 *Model description*

In this section, we discuss how to handle demand disruptions for the coordination of a supply chain with two competing retailers. In the system, each retailer has an opportunity to invest in demand promotion, such that the demand increases with the investment in demand promotion. As long as the extra profit brought by demand promotion can offset the investment, the total profit will increase. The question, then, is how much should be invested in demand promotion, and how the profit can be shared among the supplier and the two retailers.

Suppose the unit production cost of the supplier is a constant c. The retailers share a market with a constant retail price p, where $p > c$. Assume the total demand is given by

$$D(I_1, I_2) = \bar{D} + a(I_1 + I_2)^b,$$

and the demand for retailer i is

$$\frac{I_i}{I_1 + I_2} D(I_1, I_2), \quad \text{for } i = 1, 2,$$

where $I_i > 0$ is the investment of retailer i's sales promotion, $\bar{D}$ is the market size when neither retailers invests in sales promotion, $a > 0$ is the investment sensitivity coefficient and b is the investment-elasticity for the incremental demand. The total market demand increases with the investment in sales promotion. Further, we assume $0 < b < 1$, representing the marginal decrease of demand in investment.

To derive the optimal total supply chain profit, we first consider the centralized decision where the central decision-maker chooses investment I to maximize the following combined profit

$$\pi^c(I) = (p-c)(\bar{D} + aI^b) - I, \tag{9.21}$$

where I is the investment of the central decision-maker in sales promotion. It can be verified that $\pi^c(I)$ is a strictly concave function of I from the second-order condition. Hence, the investment I that satisfies the first-order condition is an optimal solution of maximizing Eq. (9.21). Thus, with the centralized decision, we have the following optimal investment for sales promotion,

$$I^c = \left(ab(p-c)\right)^{\frac{1}{1-b}}.$$

Now we discuss the case of decentralized decision making, i.e., how to implement supply chain coordination. We consider a contract in which the supplier offers both retailers an identical price-plus-subsidy rate contract (w, s), where w is a unit wholesale price, and s is a subsidy rate to encourage the retailer to invest for sales promotion, $c < w < p$, and $0 < s < 1$. More specifically, the supplier asks a wholesale price w per unit and offers retailer i a subsidy sI_i for his investment amount I_i. The profit functions of retailers 1 and 2 are respectively,

$$\pi_1(I_1; I_2, w, s) = (p-w)\frac{I_1}{I_1+I_2}\left(\bar{D} + a(I_1+I_2)^b\right) - (1-s)I_1,$$

$$\pi_2(I_2; I_1, w, s) = (p-w)\frac{I_2}{I_1+I_2}\left(\bar{D} + a(I_1+I_2)^b\right) - (1-s)I_2.$$

To derive the optimal investment for each retailer, we have the following lemma.

Lemma 9.4 *The profit function $\pi_i(I_i; I_j, w, s)$ of retailer i is a strictly concave function of I_i.*

Proof. Differentiate $\pi_i(I_i; I_j, w, s)$ with respect to I_i, we have

$$\frac{\partial \pi_i(I_i; I_j, w, s)}{\partial I_i} = \frac{\bar{D}(p-w)I_j}{(I_1+I_2)^2} + a(p-w)(I_1+I_2)^{b-2}(bI_i+I_j) - (1-s). \tag{9.22}$$

Take the second derivative, we have

$$\frac{\partial^2 \pi_i(I_i; I_j, w, s)}{\partial I_i^2} = -\frac{2\bar{D}(p-w)I_j}{(I_1+I_2)^3} + a(b-1)(p-w)(I_1+I_2)^{b-3}(bI_i+2I_j) < 0.$$

The above inequality follows from our assumptions that $p > w$, $0 < b < 1$ and $I_1 + I_2 > 0$. Thus, $\pi_i(I_i; I_j, w, s)$ is a strictly concave function of I_i. ∎

From Lemma 9.4, we can derive the following theorem.

Theorem 9.8 *There exists a unique symmetric Nash equilibrium for the two retailers' optimal investment that satisfies the following equation*

$$a(b+1)(p-w)(I_1^N + I_2^N)^b - 2(1-s)(I_1^N + I_2^N) + \bar{D}(p-w) = 0, \quad (9.23)$$

and

$$I_1^N = I_2^N > \frac{1}{2}\left(\frac{ab(b+1)(p-w)}{2(1-s)}\right)^{\frac{1}{1-b}}. \quad (9.24)$$

Proof. From Eq.(9.22), we know that the first-order condition of retailer 1's profit function is

$$\bar{D}(p-w)I_2 + a(p-w)(I_1+I_2)^b(bI_1+I_2) - (1-s)(I_1+I_2)^2 = 0, \quad (9.25)$$

and the first-order condition of retailer 2's profit function is

$$\bar{D}(p-w)I_1 + a(p-w)(I_1+I_2)^b(I_1+bI_2) - (1-s)(I_1+I_2)^2 = 0. \quad (9.26)$$

Subtract Eq. (9.26) from Eq. (9.25), we have

$$(I_2 - I_1)\left(\bar{D} + a(1-b)(I_1+I_2)^b\right)(p-w) = 0.$$

Since $p > w$, $0 < b < 1$, we must have $I_1^N = I_2^N$. Adding Eq. (9.26) to Eq. (9.25), we have

$$a(b+1)(p-w)(I_1^N + I_2^N)^b - 2(1-s)(I_1^N + I_2^N) + \bar{D}(p-w) = 0,$$

which should be satisfied for the Nash Equilibrium.

Let $f(I) = a(b+1)(p-w)I^b - 2(1-s)I + \bar{D}(p-w)$. Differentiate $f(I)$ with respect to I, we have

$$\frac{df(I)}{dI} = ab(b+1)(p-w)I^{b-1} - 2(1-s).$$

Furthermore, we follow from $0 < b < 1$ and $p > w$ that

$$\frac{d^2 f(I)}{dI^2} = ab(b+1)(b-1)(p-w)I^{b-2} < 0,$$

i.e., $F(I)$ is a strictly concave function of I. Hence, the root I^* of equation $df(I)/dI = 0$ maximizes $f(I)$, where

$$I^* = \Big(\frac{ab(b+1)(p-w)}{2(1-s)}\Big)^{\frac{1}{1-b}}.$$

We also know that $f(I)$ is a strictly increasing function of I when $0 \leq I \leq I^*$ and a strictly decreasing function of I when $I > I^*$. Note $f(0) = \bar{D}(p-w) > 0$. It follows that $f(I^*) > f(0) > 0$ and the root of equation $f(I) = 0$ must be more than I^*. So there is a big enough investment I such that $f(I) < 0$. According to the theorem for root existence, equation $f(I) = 0$ has a unique root I^{**} and $I^{**} > I^*$. ∎

From Theorem 9.8, we know that the two retailers' optimal investments are symmetric and larger than a positive constant. It is not clear whether the optimal total investment under the decentralized decisions is larger or smaller than that of the centralized decisions since the decentralized optimal total investment depends on the supplier's optimal wholesale price w and the subsidy rate s. Next, we will consider the coordination issue to realize the centralized solution under the decentralized setting.

9.6.2 Supply chain coordination

With a wholesale price w and a positive subsidy rate s, it is possible that the optimal supply chain profit is achieved under the decentralized decisions.

Theorem 9.9 *The centralized optimal supply chain profit could be realized if the price-plus-subsidy contract (w^*, s^*) satisfies*

$$s^* = 1 - \frac{p-w^*}{2(p-c)}\Big(\frac{b+1}{b} + \bar{D}(ab)^{-\frac{1}{1-b}}(p-c)^{-\frac{b}{1-b}}\Big),$$

and
$$\max\left\{c, p - \frac{2(p-c)}{\frac{b+1}{b} + \bar{D}(ab)^{-\frac{1}{1-b}}(p-c)^{-\frac{b}{1-b}}}\right\} < w^* < p.$$

Proof. The profit function of the supplier is
$$\pi_M(I_1, I_2; w, s) = (w-c)\left(\bar{D} + a(I_1+I_2)^b\right) - s(I_1+I_2),$$
the decentralized supply chain profit is
$$\Pi(I_1, I_2, w, s) = \pi_M(I_1, I_2, w, s) + \pi_1(I_1; I_2, w, s) + \pi_2(I_2; I_1, w, s)$$
$$= (p-c)\left(\bar{D} + a(I_1+I_2)^b\right) - (I_1+I_2).$$
So the supply chain coordination is achieved when $I_1^N + I_2^N = I^c$, i.e.,
$$I_1^N + I_2^N = I^c = \left(ab(p-c)\right)^{\frac{1}{1-b}}. \tag{9.27}$$
Inserting Eq.(9.27) into Eq.(9.23), we have
$$s^* = 1 - \frac{p-w}{2(p-c)}\left(\frac{b+1}{b} + \bar{D}(ab)^{-\frac{1}{1-b}}(p-c)^{-\frac{b}{1-b}}\right).$$
Since the second term is positive, we have $s^* < 1$. From $s^* > 0$, we follow that the wholesale price must satisfy the following inequality,
$$w > p - \frac{2(p-c)}{\frac{b+1}{b} + \bar{D}(ab)^{-\frac{1}{1-b}}(p-c)^{-\frac{b}{1-b}}}.$$
By our assumption $c < w < p$, we thus have
$$\max\left\{c, p - \frac{2(p-c)}{\frac{b+1}{b} + \bar{D}(ab)^{-\frac{1}{1-b}}(p-c)^{-\frac{b}{1-b}}}\right\} < w^* < p,$$
which proves Theorem 9.9. ∎

From Theorem 9.8 and Eq.(9.27), we derive

Corollary 9.1 *If the supply chain is coordinated, then the optimal investments of the two retailers are*
$$I_1^N = I_2^N = I^c/2 = \left(ab(p-c)\right)^{\frac{1}{1-b}}/2. \tag{9.28}$$

9.6.3 Centralized decision making for demand disruptions

In practice, there are many cases in which demand could change suddenly. With the unpredicted demand change, the supplier and the two retailers will make their decisions correspondingly. The supplier will adjust her production quantity and the wholesale price while the retailers adjust their original investment amounts. New contracts need to be considered to ensure that the supply chain's optimal solution is still realized. In the following, we use the notation with a tilde to denote the case under demand disruption. We assume that the investment sensitivity coefficient $\tilde{a}$ is $a + \Delta a > 0$, with a positive Δa representing an increased market demand, and a negative Δa representing a decreased market demand. Then the disrupted demand function is

$$\tilde{D}(\tilde{I}_1, \tilde{I}_2) = \bar{D} + (a + \Delta a)(\tilde{I}_1 + \tilde{I}_2)^b.$$

With the above demand function, a new plan that describes the wholesale price, the production quantity, and the investment amount is usually different from the original plan. There are deviation penalties associated with the difference. In this section, we assume a unit penalty cost c_u for the increased production and a unit penalty cost c_s for the decreased production quantity. For the centralized decision, the supply chain channel profit is

$$\tilde{\pi}^c(\tilde{I}) = (p-c)\left(\bar{D} + (a+\Delta a)\tilde{I}^b\right) - \tilde{I}$$
$$- c_u\left((a+\Delta a)\tilde{I}^b - a(I^c)^b\right)^+ - c_s\left(a(I^c)^b - (a+\Delta a)(\tilde{I})^b\right)^+,$$

where $\tilde{I}$ is the investment of the central decision-maker in sales promotion when the demand is disrupted. The first term represents the revenue of the investment in sales promotion and the second term is the investment amount for promotion, the third term represents the increased production quantity penalty, and the last term represents the decreased production quantity penalty.

To derive the optimal production quantity, we first assume that the unit penalty cost for extra production is less than the unit production profit, i.e., $c_u < p - c$, which means that the unit cost of the extra production is less than the unit retail price. Otherwise, there is no need to satisfy the extra demand since it is not profitable to produce.

Denote $\tilde{I}^* = \operatorname{argmax}_{\tilde{I}} \tilde{\pi}^c(\tilde{I})$. For convenience, we differentiate the supply chain profit function to two cases and discuss them separately. We assume that all the members in the supply chain know the relevant demand change. If $(a + \Delta a)\tilde{I}^b \geq a(I^c)^b$, maximizing $\tilde{\pi}^c(\tilde{I})$ is equivalent to maximizing

$$\tilde{\pi}_1^c(\tilde{I}) = (p-c)\left(\bar{D}+(a+\Delta a)\tilde{I}^b\right) - \tilde{I} - c_u\left((a+\Delta a)\tilde{I}^b - a(I^c)^b\right), \quad (9.29)$$

and if $(a + \Delta a)\tilde{I}^b \leq a(I^c)^b$, maximizing $\tilde{\pi}^c(\tilde{I})$ is equivalent to maximizing

$$\tilde{\pi}_2^c(\tilde{I}) = (p-c)\left(\bar{D}+(a+\Delta a)\tilde{I}^b\right) - \tilde{I} - c_s\left(a(I^c)^b - (a+\Delta a)\tilde{I}^b\right). \quad (9.30)$$

With $(a+\Delta a)\tilde{I}^b \geq a(I^c)^b$, Eq. (9.29) is a strictly concave function of $\tilde{I}$. Hence, the solution that satisfies the first-order condition is the optimal investment. Solving the first-order condition under the constraint $(a + \Delta a)\tilde{I}^b \geq a(I^c)^b$, we have

$$\tilde{I}^* = \begin{cases} \left((a+\Delta a)b(p-c-c_u)\right)^{\frac{1}{1-b}} & \text{for } \Delta a \geq a\left((\frac{p-c}{p-c-c_u})^b - 1\right), \\ \left(\frac{a}{a+\Delta a}\right)^{\frac{1}{b}} I^c & \text{for } -a < \Delta a < a\left((\frac{p-c}{p-c-c_u})^b - 1\right). \end{cases}$$

Without going into details, the optimal production quantity is

$$\tilde{Q}^* = \begin{cases} \bar{D} + (a+\Delta a)^{\frac{1}{1-b}}\left(b(p-c-c_u)\right)^{\frac{b}{1-b}} & \\ \qquad \text{for } \Delta a \geq a\left((\frac{p-c}{p-c-c_u})^b - 1\right), \\ \bar{D} + a\big(ab(p-c)\big)^{\frac{b}{1-b}} & \text{for } -a < \Delta a < a\left((\frac{p-c}{p-c-c_u})^b - 1\right). \end{cases}$$

Similarly, when $(a+\Delta a)\tilde{I}^b \le a(I^c)^b$, Eq.(9.30) is a strictly concave function of $\tilde{I}$, and we have the optimal $\tilde{I}^*$ as

$$\tilde{I}^* = \begin{cases} \left(\frac{a}{a+\Delta a}\right)^{\frac{1}{b}} I^c & \text{for } -a\left(1 - \left(\frac{p-c}{p-c+c_s}\right)^b\right) < \Delta a, \\ \left((a+\Delta a)b(p-c+c_s)\right)^{\frac{1}{1-b}} & \text{for } -a < \Delta a \le -a\left(1 - \left(\frac{p-c}{p-c+c_s}\right)^b\right), \end{cases}$$

and the optimal product quantity is

$$\tilde{Q}^* = \begin{cases} \bar{D} + a\big(ab(p-c)\big)^{\frac{b}{1-b}} & \text{for } -a\left(1 - \left(\frac{p-c}{p-c+c_s}\right)^b\right) < \Delta a, \\ \bar{D} + (a+\Delta a)^{\frac{1}{1-b}}\left(b(p-c+c_s)\right)^{\frac{b}{1-b}} & \text{for } \Delta a \le -a\left(1 - \left(\frac{p-c}{p-c+c_s}\right)^b\right). \end{cases}$$

9.6.4 Supply chain coordination with demand disruptions

Depending on the degree of the disruptions, we differentiate the coordination problem as follows. We provide main results without detailed proof.

Case 1. $\Delta a \ge a\left(\left(\frac{p-c}{p-c-c_u}\right)^b - 1\right)$.

In this case, the supply chain is coordinated if the contractual arrangement $(\tilde{w}^*_{\text{case1}}, \tilde{s}^*_{\text{case1}})$ satisfies

$$\tilde{s}^*_{\text{case1}} = 1 - \frac{p - \tilde{w}^*_{\text{case1}}}{2(p - c - c_u)}\left(\frac{b+1}{b} + \bar{D}\big((a+\Delta a)b\big)^{-\frac{1}{1-b}}(p-c-c_u)^{-\frac{b}{1-b}}\right),$$

and

$$\max\left\{c, p - \frac{2(p-c-c_u)}{\frac{b+1}{b} + \bar{D}\big((a+\Delta a)b\big)^{-\frac{1}{1-b}}(p-c-c_u)^{-\frac{b}{1-b}}}\right\} < \tilde{w}^*_{\text{case1}} < p.$$

Case 2. $-a\left(1 - \left(\frac{p-c}{p-c+c_s}\right)^b\right) < \Delta a < a\left(\left(\frac{p-c}{p-c-c_u}\right)^b - 1\right)$.

In this case, the supply chain is coordinated if the contractual arrangement $(\tilde{w}^*_{case2}, \tilde{s}^*_{case2})$ satisfies

$$\tilde{s}^*_{case2} = 1 - \frac{p - \tilde{w}^*_{case2}}{2(p-c)}\left(\frac{b+1}{b} + \bar{D}(ab)^{-\frac{1}{1-b}}(p-c)^{-\frac{b}{1-b}}\right)\left(1 + \frac{\Delta a}{a}\right)^{\frac{1}{b}},$$

and

$$\max\left\{c, p - \frac{2(p-c)}{\frac{b+1}{b} + \bar{D}(ab)^{-\frac{1}{1-b}}(p-c)^{-\frac{b}{1-b}}\left(1 + \frac{\Delta a}{a}\right)^{\frac{1}{b}}}\right\} < \tilde{w}^*_{case2} < p.$$

Case 3. $-a < \Delta a \leq -a\left(1 - \left(\frac{p-c}{p-c+c_s}\right)^b\right)$.

In this case, the supply chain is coordinated if the contractual arrangement $(\tilde{w}^*_{case3}, \tilde{s}^*_{case3})$ satisfies

$$\tilde{s}^*_{case3} = 1 - \frac{p - \tilde{w}^*_{case3}}{2(p-c+c_s)}\left(\frac{b+1}{b} + \bar{D}((a+\Delta a)b)^{-\frac{1}{1-b}}(p-c+c_s)^{-\frac{b}{1-b}}\right),$$

and

$$\max\left\{c, p - \frac{2(p-c+c_s)}{\frac{b+1}{b} + \bar{D}((a+\Delta a)b)^{-\frac{1}{1-b}}(p-c+c_s)^{-\frac{b}{1-b}}}\right\} < \tilde{w}^*_{case3} < p.$$

9.7 Literature Review

Supply chain coordination has gained new importance in recent years (see Cachon 2002 for a review). In what follows, we only discuss those factors that are closely related to our research. In the marketing literature, coordination schemes have mainly focused on the pricing decisions, with deterministic and known demand, for example, Jeuland and Shugan (1983), Moorthy (1987), and Ingene and Parry (1995).

In the operations research literature, most of the work on supply chain coordination has been confined to decisions related to the optimal reorder point and reorder quantity, e.g., Chen (1998), Cachon (2001), and Corbett (2001). More holistic efforts have been aimed at developing a single framework that combines the pricing, inventory, and production decisions, for example, Weng (1995a), Weng and Zeng (2001), Chen et al. (2001), Zhao and Wang (2002), and Boyaci and Gallego (2002).

When the supplier and the retailer act independently, an efficient mechanism is needed to handle the demand uncertainty, such as a return policy (Lau and Lau 1999), a flexible supply contract discussed in Tsay (1999) and Milner and Rosenblatt (2002). For a general discussion on wholesale quantity discount policy and its usage in supply chain coordination, please see Lee and Rosenblatt (1986), Dolan (1987), and Weng (1995a,b).

For relevant literature about demand promotions, we refer to Perry and Porter (1990), Iyer (1998), Tsay and Aggrawal (2000), Wang and Gerchak (2001), and Gilbert et al.(2002).

The main results for this chapter come from Qi et al.(2004), Xu et al.(2003) and Xiao et al.(2004).

References

Boyaci, T. and G. Gallego (2002), Coordinating pricing and inventory replenishment policies for one wholesaler and one or more geographically dispersed retailers, *International Journal of Production Economics*, 77, 95-111.

Cachon, G.P. (2001), Stock wars: Inventory competition in a two-echelon supply chain with multiple retailers, *Operations Research*, 49, 658-674.

Cachon, G.P. (2002), Supply chain coordination with contracts, to appear in Graves S, de Kok T, editors, *Handbooks in Operations Research and Management Science: Supply Chain Management*, North-Holland.

Chen, F. (1998), Echelon reorder points, installation reorder points, and the value of centralized demand information, *Management Science*, 44, S221-S234.

Chen, F., A. Federgruen and Y.-S. Zheng (2001), Coordination mechanisms for a distribution system with one supplier and multiple retailers, *Management Science*, 47, 693-708.

Corbett, C.J. (2001), Stochastic inventory systems in a supply chain with asymmetric information: Cycle stocks, safety stocks, and consignment stock, *Operations Research*, 49, 487-500.

Dolan, R. (1987), Quantity discounts: Managerial issues and research opportunities, *Marketing Science*, 6, 1-23.

Gilbert, S., Y. Xia and G. Yu (2002), Strategic interactions between channel structure and control of value-added services, working paper, Department of Management Science and Information Systems, The University of Texas at Austin.

Ingene, C. and M. Parry (1995), Coordination and manufacturer profit maximization: The multiple retailer channel, *Journal of Retailing*, 71, 129-151.

Iyer, G. (1998), Coordinating channels under price and non-price competition, *Marketing Science*, 17(4), 338-355.

Jeuland, A. and S. Shugan (1983), Managing channel profits, *Marketing Science*, 2, 239-272.

Lau, H.-S. and A.H.-L. Lau (1999), Manufacturer's pricing strategy and return policy for a single-period commodity, *European Journal of Operational Research*, 116, 291-304.

Lee, H. and M.J. Rosenblatt (1986), A generalized quantity discount pricing model to increase supplier's profits, *Management Science*, 32, 1177-1185.

Milner, J.M. and M.J. Rosenblatt (2002), Flexible supply contracts for short life-cycle goods: The buyers's perspective, *Naval Research Logistics*, 49, 25-45.

Moorthy, K. (1987), Managing channel profits: Comment, *Marketing Science*, 6, 375-379.

Perry, M. and R. Porter (1990), Can resale price maintenance franchise fees correct sub-optimal levels of retailer service, *International Journal of Industrial Organization*, 8, 115-141.

Qi, X., J.F. Bard and G. Yu (2004), Supply chain coordination with demand disruptions, *Omega*, 32, 301-312.

Tsay, A.A. (1999), The quantity flexibility contract and supplier-customer incentives, *Management Science*, 45, 1339-1358.

Tsay, A. and N. Aggrawal (2000), Channel dynamics under price and service competition, *Manufacturing & Service Operations Management*, 2(4), 372-391.

Wang, Y. and Y. Gerchak (2001), Supply chain coordination when demand is shelf-space-dependent, *Manufacturing & Service Operations Management*, 3(1), 82-87.

Weng, K. (1995a), Channel coordination and quantity discounts, *Management Science*, 41, 1509-1522.

Weng, K. (1995b), Modeling quantity discount under general price-sensitive demand functions: Optimal policies and relationships, *European Journal of Operational Research*, 86, 300-314.

Weng, K. and A.Z. Zeng (2001), The role of quantity discounts in the presence of heterogeneous buyers, *Annals of Operations Research*, 107, 369-383.

Xiao, T., Y. Xia, Z. Sheng and G. Yu (2004), Coordination of a supply chain with one-manufacturer and two-retailers under demand promotion and disruption management decisions, *Annals of Operations Research*, in press.

Xu, M., X. Qi, G. Yu, H. Zhang and C. Gao (2003), The demand disruption management problem for a supply chain system with non-linear demand functions, *Journal of System Science and System Engineering*, 12(1), 82-97.

Zhao, W. and Y. Wang (2002), Coordination of joint pricing-production decisions in a supply chain, *IIE Transactions*, 34, 701-715.

Chapter 10

Disruption Management for Project Scheduling

10.1 Introduction

We discuss disruption management for project scheduling in this chapter. In a project scheduling problem, there are multiple activities to be performed, and the project is completed only when all activities are completed. There are complex precedence and resource constraints among the activities. The problem is also known as the resource-constrained project scheduling problem (RCPSP).

In many cases, before a project is carried out, a schedule specifying the start and end times for each activity in the project must be developed, though there exist many uncertain factors such as unproven technologies, resource availability, team competence, and the commitment of upper management. As the project is being executed following the schedule, various disruptions such as activity durations and resource requirements begin to emerge. Depending on the magnitude of the disruption, the impact can vary widely. For small deviations, the initial schedule may still be followed with little or no adjustment. In other cases, the initial schedule may no longer be optimal with respect to the original objective, and may not even be feasible. Uncertainty is so prevalent in project scheduling that few projects finish without time or cost overruns (Pich et al. 2002). Disruption management for project scheduling is to study how to revise an initial project schedule to respond to different disruptions.

Although the original project scheduling problem and the disruption management problem share some similarities, there are significant differences between them. At the time of a disruption, certain new options may be available that were not feasible when the initial schedule was developed. The use of consultants or subcontractors, for example, may not have been considered initially because of company policies or pressure from upper management to use available staff. When disruptions occur, however, priorities may shift, opening the way for new options to be considered in the execution stage. There may also be new constraints and new commitments associated with activities in process, especially with respect to future activities, that were not anticipated when the original schedule was drawn up. These factors must all be considered when replanning.

Another important distinction comes from the deviation cost. Any schedule changes could have much wider implications than simply the need to increase the budget. The new objective must not only minimize the cost of the new schedule, but also minimize the deviation from the original schedule while getting back on track as soon as possible. In fact, modifying a schedule too much could turn a project with a promising return on investment into an outright failure when a full accounting of the deviation costs is made.

The rest of this chapter is organized as follows. In Section 10.2, we present a detailed discussion of disruptions in project scheduling, and develop an integer programming model to describe the problem. In Section 10.3, some special cases are addressed. In Section 10.4, we propose a hybrid mixed-integer programming/constraint programming (MIP/CP) procedure to solve the problem. An example is given in Section 10.5 followed by a summary of our computational results in Section 10.6. Related literature is given in the last section.

10.2   Modeling of Disruption Management for Project Scheduling

A project consists of n activities denoted by the set $\mathcal{A}$, where each activity needs to take a specific time and resources to be completed. A project schedule, specifying the start and end time for each activity, is assumed to minimize an objective function related to the completion times for the activities while satisfying the precedence and resource constraints specified in the problem statement. In studying disruption management for project scheduling, we assume an original schedule has been given.

A project may also have a number of milestones. Each milestone is associated with a set of activities, and the event time of a milestone is defined as the earliest time that all activities associated with the milestone have been completed. In addition to the real event time in a schedule, a milestone may also have a target time.

Sometimes, there are several different ways of performing an activity where it takes different time and resources in each different way. This is called the multi-mode resource-constrained project scheduling problem. In this case, a feasible schedule has to specify the implementation modes as well as the start and end times for all activities.

To formally describe a feasible schedule, we introduce the following notation.

Indices and sets

$\mathcal{A}$: set of all activities

i, j: activity indices; $i, j \in \mathcal{A} = \{0, 1, \ldots, n+1\}$, where 0 and $n+1$ are dummy activities indicating the start and completion of the project, respectively

$\mathcal{K}$: set of resources

$\mathcal{K}_r$: set of renewable resources; $\mathcal{K}_r \subseteq \mathcal{K}$

$\mathcal{K}_n$: set of non-renewable resources; $\mathcal{K}_n \subseteq \mathcal{K}$

k: index for resources; $k \in \mathcal{K} = \{1, \ldots, K\}$

$\mathcal{T}$: set of time periods

$\mathcal{T}_i$: set of time periods at which activity i can finish; $\mathcal{T}_i \subseteq \mathcal{T}$

t: time index; $t \in \mathcal{T} = \{0, 1, \ldots, T\}$, where T is an upper bound of the project completion time

Π_k: set of time slots on which resource k is constrained

π_k: index for time slots on which resource k is constrained; $\pi_k \in \Pi_k$, $\pi_k \subseteq \mathcal{T}$

$\mathcal{P}$: precedence set

(i, j): index for precedence relations; $(i, j) \in \mathcal{P}$ means that activity j can only start after activity i has finished

Θ: set of milestones

θ: index for milestones; $\theta \in \Theta$

$\mathcal{B}(\theta)$: set of activities whose completion defines milestone θ; $\mathcal{B}(\theta) \subseteq \mathcal{A}$, $\theta \in \Theta$

Parameters for activities and resources

$\bar{f}_i$: target finish time of activity i; $\bar{f}_i \in \mathcal{T}_i$

$\bar{t}_\theta$: target time of milestone θ

p_i: processing time (duration) of activity i; $p_0 = 0, p_{n+1} = 0$

r_{ik}: amount of resource k required by activity i per period

R_{π_k}: usage limit of resource k on time slot π_k

10.2.1 Types of disruptions

Disruptions can be captured by parameter changes. In the most general case, all parameters that define a project schedule may be disrupted. We divide the various types of disruptions into four categories, namely, (1) the project network, (2) activities, (3) resources, and (4) milestones.

Project network disruptions.

The structure of a project network is defined by the basic activities and the precedence relations among them. Precedence constraints specify the time order of the execution of activities and can be depicted in a directed network. A general precedence constraint can be written in the form of inequality on start/finish times of activities. A finish-start precedence constraint, which is the most common type, states that one activity can only start after another has finished.

During the execution of a project, it is possible that activities may be added or precedence relations revised. For example, engineering change orders from the customer may require that new activities be introduced into the schedule, while design mistakes may require the structure of the network to be changed.

New activity disruption $(\mathcal{A}_N, \mathcal{P}_N)$: A set of new activities $\mathcal{A}_N$ and corresponding precedence relations $\mathcal{P}_N$ need to be added to the project network.

Precedence disruption $(\mathcal{P}_A, \mathcal{P}_R)$: The project network for $\mathcal{A}$ needs to satisfy the additional precedence relations in $\mathcal{P}_A$, but no longer needs to satisfy the relations in $\mathcal{P}_R \subset \mathcal{P}$.

Activity disruptions.

An activity is said to be disrupted when either its duration or resource usage deviates from the scheduled values. For example, a duration change may be caused by technical difficulties or the need for rework; and more resource requirement may be due to specification changes.

Activity duration disruption δ_i: Activity $i \in \mathcal{A}$ takes δ_i more time to complete than initially planned.

Activity resource disruption γ_{ik}: Activity $i \in \mathcal{A}$ uses γ_{ik} more of resource k during its execution than planned.

Resource disruptions.

A resource constraint imposes a limit on resource usage in one or more time periods during the life of the project. Resources are classified into two types, renewable resources and non-renewable resources. Renewable resources are constrained in the number of units available in any time period, for example machine capacity and specialized personnel. Non-renewable resources are most often restricted in the total amount that can be used such as money and material.

Resource shortage is probably the most common type of disruption in project management. It may be caused by a variety of factors, such as machine breakdown, sudden loss of employees and resource overuse by other activities or projects. A resource disruption needs to be taken care of if it causes the schedule resource infeasible.

Resource disruption ρ_{π_k}: Limit of resource k to be used on time slot $\pi_k \in \Pi_k$ decreases by the amount of ρ_{π_k}.

Milestone disruptions.

Although a milestone disruption does not affect the feasibility of the on-going schedule, it may require that the schedule be revised to obtain a better objective measurement with respect to the new milestone.

Milestone disruption ϵ_θ: The target time of milestone θ changes from $\bar{t}_\theta$ to $\bar{t}_\theta \pm \epsilon_\theta$.

10.2.2 Options for disruption management

When a disruption occurs, there are different options as feasible decisions.

Mode alternative $m\,(i(m), p(m), r_k(m), c(m))$: Activity $i(m)$ is performed in mode m taking $p(m)$ time units to complete and requiring $r_k(m)$ resources, which is a different duration-resource usage combination than initially planned. Switching to this mode incurs a deviation cost of $c(m)$.

For each activity i, we define the set of all possible modes as $\mathcal{M}_i$. This set includes the mode in the original schedule (referred to as mode m_0) and the disrupted mode m_d if applicable.

Rescheduling $s\,(i(s), f(s))$: Activity $i(s)$ is rescheduled to finish at time $f(s)$.

Resource alternative $r\,(\pi_k(r), R(r), g(r))$: The use of resource k on time slot $\pi_k(r) \in \Pi_k$ increases to $R(r)$, incurring a cost of $g(r)$.

Corresponding to these options, we define the following decision variables.

x_{imt}: binary variable, $= 1$ if activity i is completed in mode m at time t

y_r: binary variable, $= 1$ if resource alternative r is selected

$t_\theta = \max\{\sum_m \sum_t t x_{imt} : i \in \mathcal{B}(\theta)\}$, event time of milestone θ in the new schedule

10.2.3 Objective function

The overall performance of a project is usually measured by three factors: time, cost and technical performance. A project schedule affects all of these factors in the specification of how and when the activities are performed and how resources are allocated. Therefore, a more general objective function than makespan is sometimes of interest.

The objective for the disruption management problem may be substantially different than the objective used to develop the original schedule. The new objective function must take into account the original schedule, the deviations resulting from the disruption, and the cost of getting back on track. These considerations lead to the following general form of the new objective which is to be minimized.

$$Q(\mathbf{x},\mathbf{y},\mathbf{t}) = \sum_{i,m,t} \alpha_{imt} x_{imt} \tag{10.1}$$

$$+ \sum_r g(r) y_r + \sum_{i,m} c_{im} \sum_t x_{imt} \tag{10.2}$$

$$+ \sum_i \left(\beta_i^1 \left[\sum_{m,t} t x_{imt} - \bar{f}_i \right]^+ + \beta_i^2 \left[\bar{f}_i - \sum_{m,t} t x_{imt} \right]^+ \right) \tag{10.3}$$

$$+ \sum_\theta \left(\lambda_i^1 [t_\theta + \epsilon_\theta - \bar{t}_\theta]^+ + \lambda_i^2 [\bar{t}_\theta - t_\theta - \epsilon_\theta]^+ \right), \tag{10.4}$$

where α, β and λ are given weights and $[z]^+ = max\{0, z\}$. The first term (10.1) measures the performance of the updated schedule, and may be related to the original objective function. Deviation costs associated with different mode alternatives and increasing resource usage are reflected in the second term (10.2). The penalty incurred for both earliness and tardiness deviations for each activity from the original schedule is represented by term(10.3), while term (10.4) captures the cost for milestone deviations. The weights α, β, and λ allow the user to specify the relative importance of each component of each term.

The components in square brackets in terms (10.3) - (10.4) are piecewise linear convex functions and can be easily linearized with the addition of one continuous variable and one constraint per function. With respect to (10.4), for example, the variable would represent the completion of milestone θ.

Note that in (10.1) we have used a general cost form for all activity completion times by specifying α_{imt} for each time point t. For example, the makespan of the project can be represented by the term $\sum_t t x_{n+1,0,t}$ where activity $n+1$ is the dummy activity indicating the completion of the project. Such a representation makes the input length of a problem instance in $O(nT)$ where n is the number of activities. The problem may also be encoded in a more succinct way for some special cases. More related discussions on this issue can be found in Möhring et al. (2001, 2003).

10.2.4 Disruption management time window

In addition to considering the deviation cost in the objective function, we can also limit the size of a deviation by introducing a constraint that places bounds on it. If a deviation becomes too large, its consequence may not be known. For example, we may want to resolve a delay of a critical activity within a few weeks because the competition already has a working system and too long a delay might jeopardize our market position.

To implement this idea, let T_0 be the current time and $[T_a, T_b]$ be the disruption management time window, where $0 \leq T_0 \leq T_a \leq T_b$. All activities whose finish time is outside of the time window will have the same schedule as originally planned. Let $\mathcal{A}_F$ be the set of activities outside the time window that are unfinished. For $i \in \mathcal{A}_F$ with planned finish time $\bar{f}_i$ and mode alternative m_0, the time window constraint can be written as

$$x_{im_0\bar{f}_i} = 1, \qquad \forall\, i \in \mathcal{A}_F. \tag{10.5}$$

For activities whose planned finish time falls within the time window, there also may be time window constraints. For example, if an activity has to be completed between t_1 and t_2, we have

$$\sum_m \sum_{t_1 \leq t \leq t_2} x_{imt} = 1. \tag{10.6}$$

10.2.5 ILP model

Based on the above discussion, we propose the following integer linear programming model to describe the disruption management for project scheduling.

$$(\text{RP}) \quad \min z = Q(\mathbf{x}, \mathbf{y}, \mathbf{t}) \tag{10.7}$$

subject to

$$\sum_{m\in\mathcal{M}_i}\sum_{t\in\mathcal{T}_i} x_{imt} = 1, \qquad i \in \mathcal{A} \cup \mathcal{A}_N \qquad (10.8)$$

$$\sum_{m\in\mathcal{M}_i}\sum_{t\in\mathcal{T}_i} tx_{imt} \leq \sum_{m\in\mathcal{M}_j}\sum_{t\in\mathcal{T}_i}(t-p_{jm})x_{jmt}, \; (i,j) \in \mathcal{P}_N \cup \mathcal{P}_A \cup (\mathcal{P} \setminus \mathcal{P}_R) \quad (10.9)$$

$$\sum_{t\in\pi_k}\sum_{i\in\mathcal{A}\cup\mathcal{A}_N}\sum_{m\in\mathcal{M}_i}\sum_{q=t}^{t+p_{im}-1} r_{imk}x_{imq} \leq R_{\pi_k} - \rho_{\pi_k} + y_{\pi_k}R(\pi_k), \pi_k \in \Pi_k, k \in \mathcal{K}$$
$$(10.10)$$

$$x_{im_0\bar{f}_i} = 1 \;\forall\; i \in \mathcal{A}_F \qquad (10.11)$$

$$\sum_{m\in\mathcal{M}_i}\sum_{t_1\leq t\leq t_2} x_{imt} = 1 \text{ for some } i \in \mathcal{A} \setminus \mathcal{A}_F \qquad (10.12)$$

$$\sum_{m\in\mathcal{M}_i}\sum_{t\in\mathcal{T}_i} tx_{imt} \leq t_\theta \;\forall i \in \mathcal{B}(\theta), \theta \in \Theta \qquad (10.13)$$

$$x_{imt} \in \{0,1\}, \qquad \forall\; i \in \mathcal{A} \cup \mathcal{A}_N, m \in \mathcal{M}_i, t \in \mathcal{T}_i \qquad (10.14)$$

$$y_{\pi_k} \in \{0,1\}, \qquad \forall\; \pi_k \in \Pi_k, k \in \mathcal{K} \qquad (10.15)$$

In the formulation, Eq. (10.8) guarantees that each remaining activity has a unique finish time; Eq. (10.9) ensures the precedence constraints; and Eq. (10.10) enforces resource constraints. Eq. (10.11) and (10.12) are about the time window $[T_a, T_b]$ constraints, and Eq. (10.13) determines the milestone time.

10.3 Some Special Cases

In this section, we study some special cases related to resource requirements.

10.3.1 *Resource-unconstrained case*

Without resource constraints, it is well known that the critical path method (CPM) can be used to solve the resultant problem when the objective is to minimize the makespan. In the case of a disruption, the cost associated with each affected activity may be a function of its completion time, such as earliness and tardiness deviation costs. So the CPM is no longer applicable.

Single mode case.

In this case, an activity or precedence relation is disrupted, but no mode alternatives are available for the activities. Thus, the objective value depends only on the start and finish times of the activities. This problem is called resource-unconstrained project scheduling with start time dependent costs.

An integer programming model for this problem can be obtained by removing the resource-related constraints and variables from model (10.7) - (10.15) and considering only the first term in the objective function of the general model. Using a tighter form of precedence constraints, we have

$$(P0) \quad \min \sum_{i \in \mathcal{A}} \sum_{t \in \mathcal{T}_i} \alpha_{it} x_{it} \qquad (10.16)$$

subject to

$$\sum_{t \in \mathcal{T}_i} x_{it} = 1, \qquad \forall \, i \in \mathcal{A} \qquad (10.17)$$

$$\sum_{l=t-p_j+1}^{T} x_{il} + \sum_{l=0}^{t} x_{jl} \leq 1, \qquad \forall \, (i,j) \in \mathcal{P}, t \in \mathcal{T} \qquad (10.18)$$

$$x_{it} \in \{0,1\}, \qquad \forall i \in \mathcal{A}, t \in \mathcal{T}_i. \qquad (10.19)$$

Note that the mode index m has been dropped from x_{imt} because each activity has only one mode. We call this problem (P0).

Theorem 10.1 *If each activity has only one mode, then the resource-unconstrained project scheduling problem with start-time dependent costs (P0) is polynomially solvable.*

(P0) has been long studied so we will not give a proof. For example, Möhring et al.(2001) showed that the LP relaxation of (10.16) - (10.19) is integral, implying that P0 is polynomially solvable. Moreover, Möhring et al. (2003) showed that P0 can be transformed into a minimum cut problem on a directed graph which can be solved in time $O(nmT^2 \log(n^2T/m))$, where n is the number of activities and m is the number of precedence constraints. Note that the polynomiality depends on our modeling approach where the input length of the problem is in $O(nT)$.

Multi-mode case.

Now we still consider the resource-unconstrained case, but allow an activity to have different durations, each incurring a different penalty cost in the objective function. This corresponds to the situation where there are tradeoff opportunities between an activity duration and its cost. Duration-cost tradeoffs are necessary if the disruption makes the current schedule infeasible. The ILP model for this problem can be written as

$$(P1) \quad \min \sum_{i \in \mathcal{A}} \sum_{m \in \mathcal{M}_i} \sum_{t \in \mathcal{T}_i} w_{imt} x_{imt} \qquad (10.20)$$

subject to

$$\sum_{m \in \mathcal{M}_i} \sum_{t \in \mathcal{T}_i} x_{imt} = 1, \qquad \forall\, i \in \mathcal{A} \qquad (10.21)$$

$$\sum_{m \in \mathcal{M}_i} \sum_{t \in \mathcal{T}_i} (t - p_{jm}) x_{jmt} - \sum_{m \in \mathcal{M}_i} \sum_{t \in \mathcal{T}_i} t x_{imt} \geq 0, \; \forall\, (i,j) \in \mathcal{P} \quad (10.22)$$

$$x_{imt} \in \{0, 1\}, \qquad \forall i \in \mathcal{A}, t \in \mathcal{T}_i. \qquad (10.23)$$

Theorem 10.2 *If each activity has at least two different modes, the resource-unconstrained project scheduling problem with start-time dependent costs* (P1) *is NP-hard.*

We refer the detailed proof to Zhu et al. (2003b).

If cost is only a function of the mode chosen for an activity, we have a minimum cost project crashing problem. This problem is very important in the context of disruption management because it resolves the disruption locally so no activities outside the disruption management time window are affected. When the time-cost tradeoff functions are linear and continuous, it is well known that the crashing

---

Algorithm 1: Heuristic for Project Crashing
input: $\mathcal{A}, \mathcal{P}, c_{im}, p_{im}, m \in \{1, \ldots, \mu_i\}, i \in \{1, \ldots, n\}$;
   and makespan limit L_0
output: Mode selection for all activities
begin
  Assign each activity the mode with the longest duration;
  Calculate makespan L
  if $L \leq L_0$, **then return**(current modes)
  while $L > L_0$ **do**
    begin
      when activity i on the critical path switches to mode m
        Let ΔL_{im} be the makespan decrease
        ΔZ_{im} be the cost increase
      Let $(\bar{i}, \bar{m}) = \arg\max\{\frac{\Delta L_{im}}{\Delta Z_{im}}\}$
      Set activity $\bar{i}$ to mode $\bar{m}$ and update L
    end
  while there exists a mode switch that can reduce the cost
    and satisfying $L \leq L_0$ **do**
    Make the mode switch with the largest cost reduction
  return(current modes)
end

---

problem can be formulated as an LP. For discrete time-cost tradeoffs, we are faced with an ILP.

One way to solve this problem is with an enumeration scheme based on branch and bound. In the search tree, each node would correspond to a subset of activities with fixed modes. Considering early time schedules only, a feasible solution is obtained when all activities are assigned modes and the makespan is within some predetermined limit. At each node we could calculate the lower bounds on crashing costs and the makespan. Given an incumbent, standard pruning rules would be used at each node to achieve some measure of efficiency.

Rather than developing an exact algorithm based on these ideas, we propose instead a heuristic to obtain quick solutions. Suppose a set $\mathcal{A}$ of n activities is constrained by precedence relations $\mathcal{P}$. Let activity i have μ_i crashing modes (including the original one), where mode m has duration p_{im} and crashing cost c_{im}. It is reasonable to assume that a longer duration will incur a smaller crashing cost for the same activity. The heuristic Algorithm 1 will give a feasible solution that is locally optimal with respect to mode change of a single activity.

This procedure is essentially a greedy heuristic. If the initialization process does not yield a feasible solution, we first try to attain feasibility by making the most cost-effective mode switches. We then try to reduce the crashing costs without violating the makespan limit. To allow for a greater exploration of the solution space, probabilistic sampling methods may be used at the mode selection step.

10.3.2 Case with one non-renewable resource

For a project, materials and budget can be viewed as non-renewable resource for which only the total amount of usage is limited. Instead of adding a penalty cost to the objective function as in problem (P1) to account for a disruption, we will impose a constraint on the availability of the resource in question. The ILP model for this case can be obtained by adding the following constraint to (10.20) - (10.23)

$$\sum_{i \in \mathcal{A}} \sum_{m \in \mathcal{M}_i} \sum_{t \in \mathcal{T}_i} r_{im} x_{imt} \leq R, \qquad (10.24)$$

where R is the resource limit and r_{im} is the resource requirement for activity i when mode m is selected. We call the augmented model (P2).

Theorem 10.3 *The multi-mode project scheduling problem* (P2) *with one non-renewable resource constraint is NP-hard.*

The proof is straightforward since (P1) is a special case of (P2).

Notice that the problem of finding a feasible solution to (P2) is the corresponding decision problem for (P1). Algorithm 1 can still serve as a heuristic for (P2) if we treat resource usage as a crashing cost. However, a feasible solution cannot be guaranteed.

10.3.3 Case with one renewable resource

We consider the case where each activity has only one mode. Because the amount of the resource that is available at time $t \in \mathcal{T}$ is fixed at R, the following constraint must be satisfied at each point in time.

$$\sum_{i \in A} \sum_{q=t}^{t+p_i-1} r_i x_{iq} \leq R, \qquad \forall\, t \in \mathcal{T} \qquad (10.25)$$

Combining constraint (10.25) with (10.16) - (10.19) gives an ILP model for the case with one non-renewable resource. We denote this problem as (P3).

Theorem 10.4 *Single mode project scheduling problem with one non-renewable resource* (P3) *is NP-hard.*

Proof. We identify several special cases of (P3) that are NP-hard. First, if every activity only uses one unit of the resource during its execution, we have a parallel machine scheduling problem, where each unit of the resource can be viewed as a machine. For a general linear objective function, the parallel machine scheduling problem is known to be NP-hard. An even simpler situation occurs when the resource limit is two and there are no precedence constraints. For makespan minimization, this is equivalent to a 2-partition problem, which is also NP-hard. ∎

This case corresponds to the basic RCPSP, which is known to be very difficult to solve, even when the objective is to minimize the makespan. Various heuristics and exact methods have been proposed for this version of the problem, but none seems to dominate.

10.4 A Hybrid MIP/CP Solution Approach

Mixed integer programming (MIP) and more recently, constrained programming (CP), are two popular ways of approaching general combinatorial optimization problems. They each decompose and search the solution space in different ways but similarly rely on some form of enumeration. Variants of branch and bound have proven quite effective in solving many routing and scheduling problems formulated as MIPs. In its simplest form, the most common approach is to begin by solving the LP relaxation to get a bound on the optimum. If the solution is not integral, the feasible region is partitioned in a branching step by fixing fractional variables to 0 or 1. A search tree is used for this purpose. In the extreme, all 0 and 1 combinations of the variables are investigated.

In contrast, CP was originally developed to solve constraint satisfaction problems (Baptiste et al. 2001). Constraint propagation is performed at each step in the enumeration process to reduce the domain of decision variables or to detect infeasibility caused by constraint conflicts. Branching is done by fixing the values of certain variables if no improvement results from the constraint propagation. Because CP only finds feasible solutions, it is necessary to solve a series of CP problems to bound the optimum.

The efficiency of MIP or CP in solving a combinatorial optimization problem is closely related to the nature of the constraints. Because the LP relaxation of the full model is solved at each iteration when the MIP approach is used, problems with a small number of *global* constraints and perhaps a large number of variables are most amenable. A problem with a non-trivial objective function may also be a good candidate for MIP because branching and fathoming are guided by objective function bounds. CP, on the other hand, is likely to perform better when the goal is to find good feasible solutions to problems with a large number of *local* constraints. This is due to the fact that constraint propagation is easier to perform on constraints with a small number of variables. Logic constraints, which usually cause trouble in MIP, can be handled efficiently in CP.

The disruption management problem for project scheduling has features that are difficult to handle with either MIP or CP individually. A complicated objective function that includes various costs and penalties makes the problem difficult for CP. Precedence constraints, though, only involve pairs of activities so CP should do well with them. Resource constraints can be either local or global depending on the resource type. Therefore, it is an open question as to how effective CP would be on problems that include both precedence and resource constraints. Nevertheless, the prospect of realizing the efficiencies of either approach motivated us to develop a hybrid MIP/CP procedure.

10.4.1 *Procedure*

There are mainly two ways of constructing a hybrid MIP/CP search tree (Rodšek et al. 1999). The first is based on the CP solver strategy. Within the CP search tree, LP relaxations are solved to obtain a lower bound at each node. The solution space is implicitly reduced by pruning infeasible or dominated nodes. The second way is to use the search strategy of an MIP solver. At each node, in addition to strengthening lower bounds with global cuts, constraint propagation is performed to reduce the number of variables. In fact, this procedure can be viewed as adding local cuts to the LP relaxations. Related work on hybrid modeling and constraint classification can be found in Bockmayr and Kasper (1998) and Jain and Grossmann (2001).

We follow the second strategy using branch and cut to construct the search tree and to tighten the LP relaxation of (10.7) - (10.15). Constraint propagation is used to reduce the domain of variables before the LPs are solved. This strategy allows us to take advantage of the special ordered sets (SOS) (10.8) and (10.12) when partitioning the solution space. SOS branching leads to a balanced search tree which, in turn, often increases the efficiency of the MIP solver. The general linear objective function (10.7) and the absence of logic constraints in the model also favor branch and cut as the primary analytic technique.

The main steps of the hybrid MIP/CP procedure are summarized below. Because violations of precedence constraints are mainly caused by SOS branching, we perform constraint propagation immediately before the new nodes are created rather than before the LP relaxation is solved.

Algorithm **2**: Hybrid MIP/CP Procedure
input: Problem instance and incumbent objective value $\bar{z}$, if available
output: Optimal objective function value z^* or "infeasible"
begin

Set $z^* = \min\{\bar{z}, \infty\}$.
Let Ω be the set of enumeration nodes to be explored.
Perform constraint propagation at the root node of the search tree.
if feasible **then**
    Add the root node to Ω.
while $\Omega \neq \emptyset$ **do**
    begin
    Select node $\omega \in \Omega$
    and solve the corresponding LP relaxation, $LP(\omega)$
    Resolve $LP(\omega)$ if new cuts are added.
    Let z^ω be the objective value.
    if $LP(\omega)$ is infeasible **or** $z^\omega \geq z^*$, **then**
        $\Omega = \Omega \setminus \{\omega\}$
    else
        if optimal solution of $LP(\omega)$ is integer **then**
            Set $z^* = \min\{z^*, z^\omega\}, \Omega = \Omega \setminus \{\omega\}$
        else
            begin
            if SOS branching to be performed **then**
                (S_1, S_2) = **call ConstraintPropagation**(ω)
                Create the first node by setting the upper bounds on variables in S_1 to 0.
                Create the second node by setting the upper bounds on variables in S_2 to 0.
            else
                Create two nodes by setting the branching binary variable to 0 and 1, respectively.
            Add the two created nodes to Ω.
            end
    end
    Report optimal solution z^* or "infeasible".
end

10.4.2 Branch and cut

Optimization problems can usually be formulated in different ways. Compact formulations have a small number of constraints, but often produce very weak LP relaxations. Yet, less efficient models can produce much tighter bounds but may require an exponential number of constraints. Different formulations of the traveling salesman problem illustrate this point.

When applying branch and cut, it is common to start with a compact model and solve the LP relaxation. If integrality is not achieved, then a "separation" problem is solved to identify valid inequalities (cuts) that are violated by the LP solution. These cuts are added to the model and the process is repeated. If no cuts are found or improvement is minimal, then the solution space is partitioned by selecting a variable for branching. Adding cuts to the model at each node in the search tree gives tighter LP bounds and hence may reduce the number of nodes that must be explored (see Bard et al. 2002 for an example).

For our problem, cuts can be developed from both the precedence and resource constraints. The latter (10.10) are in the form of knapsack constraints. Moreover, the variables that define the schedule for each activity i are divided into mutually exclusive special ordered sets. The cuts that can derived from these restrictions are called GUB cover cuts (Gu et al. 1998) and are generated automatically by CPLEX when requested.

Precedence cuts can be obtained by explicitly enumerating the possible finish times for activities with precedence relations. For example, if activity i precedes activity j, which has a duration of p_j, then we know that if activity i finishes at t activity j must finish after $t + p_j$. Each of the enumerated cases can be written in the form of a cut that can be used to tighten the LP bounds. For more detail, see Zhu et al. (2003a).

In standard branching, the bound on one variable at a time is fixed in the construction of the search tree. In SOS branching, the variables that make up each special ordered set are partitioned into two subsets, and all the variables in one subset are set to zero on each branch. This scheme can be exploited to great advantage during constraint propagation.

10.4.3 Constraint propagation

The purpose of constraint propagation in our approach is to fix the value of some variables before solving the LP relaxations. In particular, CP tries to tighten the finish time windows at each node in the search tree by maintaining the consistency of precedence constraints and by fixing variables in a way that excludes inferior (i.e., dominated) solutions. In the extreme case, if the finish time window for an activity is 0 at a certain node, we know that the corresponding problem is infeasible so the node can be fathomed.

Consistency of precedence constraints. In model (10.7) - (10.15), variables associated with activity i are defined on the subset $T_i = \{e_i, \ldots, l_i\}$, where the earliest finish time e_i and the latest finish time l_i are a function of the precedence relations and the makespan limit. At a node in the search tree, the time window in which activity i can finish $[\hat{e}_i, \hat{l}_i]$ is usually smaller than $[e_i, l_i]$. Due to precedence constraints, any change in the finish time window of one activity may affect the windows of both its predecessors and successors.

For $(i,j) \in \mathcal{P}$, the set of activities that are predecessors of j and successors of i, $\mathcal{A}_{ij} = \{\kappa : (i,\kappa) \in \mathcal{P}, (\kappa, j) \in \mathcal{P}\}$, can be viewed as a subproject. The minimum makespan of this subproject, call it d_{ij}, gives a lower bound on time (distance) between the finish of i and the start of j. We call the $(n+1) \times (n+1)$ matrix $D \equiv (d_{ij})$ the *distance matrix* for the project. We now define what we meant to be the consistency of precedence constraints at a node in the search tree.

Definition 10.1 Let $p_i^{\min}$ be the minimum possible duration of activity i and let T be an upper bound on the project makespan. A node in the search tree with finish time windows $[\hat{e}_i, \hat{l}_i] \; \forall \; i \in \mathcal{A}$, satisfies the consistency of precedence constraints if (1) $d_{ij} \geq d_{i\kappa} + d_{\kappa j} + p_\kappa^{\min}, \forall \; (i,\kappa) \in \mathcal{P}$ and $(\kappa, j) \in \mathcal{P}$, and (2) $\hat{e}_i \geq d_{0i} + p_i^{\min}$, $\hat{l}_i \leq T - d_{i,n+1} + 1, \forall \; i \in \mathcal{A}$.

The transitivity of the distance matrix D, which can be maintained through Algorithm 3, is given by condition (1) and is necessary for the satisfaction of the precedence constraints. Condition (2) ensures that the finish time window of each activity is consistent with the precedence constraints. At any node in the search tree, all variables associated with finish times outside of the window $[\hat{e}_i, \hat{l}_i]$ should be set to zero.

Algorithm 3: Update Distance Matrix
input: Distance matrix D; minimum durations of activities $p_i^{\min}, i \in \mathcal{A}$
output: Updated distance matrix D
begin
    for $\kappa = 2$ **to** $n+1$ **do**
        for $i = 0$ **to** $n+2-\kappa$ **do**
            for $j = i+1$ **to** $i+\kappa-1$ **do**
                if $(i,j) \in \mathcal{P}$ and $(j, i+\kappa) \in \mathcal{P}$ and $d_{i,i+\kappa} < d_{ij} + d_{j,i+\kappa} + p_\kappa^{\min}$ **then**
$$d_{i,i+\kappa} = d_{ij} + d_{j,i+\kappa} + p_\kappa^{\min}$$
end

In the disruption management model, there are two situations that may cause a violation of the consistency of precedence constraints. The first concerns branching on activity finish times. In SOS branching, the finish time window of an activity is divided in half to create two branches. One branch has a new e_i and the other has a new l_i. These changes can be propagated to reduce the finish time windows of other activities by maintaining consistency of precedence constraints.

The other situation arises when multiple resource modes exist. Here, distances between precedence constrained activities can only be bounded from below by the largest possible resource limit. Branching on the variables associated with the resource alternatives, though, leads to a reduction of the resource limit along the corresponding branch. This may allow us to increase some elements of the matrix D and hence reduce the finish time windows of other activities through propagation.

The procedure of maintaining consistency of precedence constraints was implemented as a callback function in CPLEX. The initial distance matrix D was obtained by finding the critical path in the unconstrained network, but any lower bounding method for minimum makespan problems could have been used.

The main steps of the procedure are presented in Algorithm 4. Constraint propagation is performed when SOS branching is applied. On each branch in the search tree, we identify the activity finish time windows and maintain the consistency of precedence constraints. As a result, additional variables are fixed to zero before the LP relaxations are solved. Using the incumbent objective function value $\bar{z}$, we also fix to zero those variables that cannot possibly produce a better solution. This is taken up next.

Algorithm 4: Constraint Propagation
input: Node in search tree and correspondig LP solution $\bar{x} = \{\bar{x}_{imt}\}$, upper bounds $u = \{u_{imt}\}$ on $x = \{x_{imt}\}$ at the current node
output: Two sets of variables (S_1, S_2) for creating two descendant nodes
begin
  let i_b = activity for which the variable set is selected for branching
  $p^{\min} = \{p_i^{\min}\}$, where $p_i^{\min} = \min\{p_{im} : m \in \mathcal{M}_i, \sum_t u_{imt} > 0\}$
  $t_b = \sum_{m,t} \bar{x}_{i_b mt}$
  let D = distance matrix corresponding to resource limits at the current node
  $\bar{D} = D; S_1 = \emptyset; S_2 = \emptyset$
  for $i = 1$ to $n+1$ do
    $\bar{D}(0, i) = \min\{t : \sum_{m \in \mathcal{M}_i} u_{im,(t+p_{im})} \geq 1\}$
  for $i = 1$ to n do
    $\bar{D}(i, n+1) = T - \max\{t : \sum_{m \in \mathcal{M}_i} u_{imt} \geq 1\}$
  $D_1 = \bar{D}; D_2 = \bar{D}$
  $D_1(i_b, n+1) = T - \lceil t_b \rceil$
  call **UpdateDistanceMatrix**$(D_1, p^{\min})$
  if an incumbent exists then
    call **ReductionOfDominatedSpace**
  for $i = 1$ to i_b do
    if $D_1(i, n+1) > T - l_i$ then
      add $\{x_{imt} : T - D_1(i, n+1) < t \leq l_i\}$ to S_1
  $D_2(0, i_b) = \lfloor t_b \rfloor - p_{i_b}^{\min}$
  call **UpdateDistanceMatrix**$(D_2, p^{\min})$
  if an incumbent exists then
    call **ReductionOfDominatedSpace**
  for $i = i_b$ to $n+1$ do
    if $D_2(0, i) > e_i$ then

    add $\{x_{imt} : e_i \leq t < D_2(0,i) + p_{im}\}$ to S_2
  return(S_1, S_2)
end

Dominated solution space. When the objective function consists of the schedule deviation term (10.3) only, we are able to estimate a lower bound on the finish time window for each activity $i \in \mathcal{A} \setminus \mathcal{A}_F$ at each node in the search tree. We can then compute a lower bound on the objective function, call it LB that can be used to fathom nodes when $LB \geq \bar{z}$.

Algorithm 5 provides the steps for removing dominated portions of solution space. For each activity, we enumerate possible finish times for the beginning and the end of finish time windows, and estimate the corresponding lower bounds. A finish time that leads to an inferior objective function value is excluded from the finish time window of the corresponding activity. The enumeration stops when we encounter an un-dominated lower bound.

Algorithm 5 Reduction of Dominated Space
input: Incumbent objective value $\bar{z}$, distance matrix D, finish time windows $[e_i, l_i], i \in \mathcal{A}$, disruption management time window $[T_a, T_b]$
output: New distance matrix D and finish time windows $[e_i, l_i]$
begin
  for activity i in the disruption management time window $[T_a, T_b]$ **do**
    begin
      for $t = e_i$ to l_i **do**
      begin
        $\hat{D} = D$, $\hat{d}_{0i} = t - p_i^{\min}$, $\hat{d}_{i,n+1} = T - t + 1$
        call **UpdateDistanceMatrix**$(\hat{D}, p^{\min})$
        $LB = \sum_{i \in \mathcal{A}} \left(\left[\hat{d}_{0i} + p_i^{\min} - \bar{f}_i\right]^+ + \left[\bar{f}_i - (T - \hat{d}_{i,n+1})\right]^+ \right)$
        if $LB < \bar{z}$ **then**
          $e_i = t$, $d_{0i} = t - p_i^{\min}$; **break** "for" loop
      end
      for $t = l_i$ to e_i **do**
      begin
        $\hat{D} = D$, $\hat{d}_{0i} = t - p_i^{\min}$, $\hat{d}_{i,n+1} = T - t + 1$
        call **UpdateDistanceMatrix**$(\hat{D}, p^{\min})$

$$LB = \sum_{i \in \mathcal{A}} \left(\left[\hat{d}_{0i} + p_i^{\min} - \bar{f}_i \right]^+ + \left[\bar{f}_i - (T - \hat{d}_{i,n+1}) \right]^+ \right)$$

      if $LB < \bar{z}$ **then**
          $l_i = t$, $d_{i,n+1} = T - t + 1$; **break** "for" loop
   end
end
call UpdateDistanceMatrix$(D, p^{\min})$
for activity i in the disruption management time window **do**
    if $e_i < d_{0i} + p_i^{\min}$, **then** $e_i = d_{0i} + p_i^{\min}$; **if** $l_i > T - d_{i,n+1} + 1$, **then** $l_i = T - d_{i,n+1} + 1$
end

10.5 Numerical Examples

In this section, we illustrate our disruption management modeling and solution procedure with a 10-activity project with one renewable resource. Each period, 10 units of the resource are available. The project network is shown in Fig. 10.1 along with activity durations and resource requirements. Fig. 10.2 depicts the original schedule which has a makespan of 32. The completion times indicated in the figure are target values and any deviation from them will incur a penalty that is a function of the option selected.

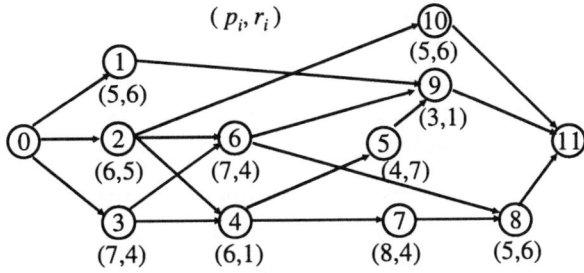

Fig. 10.1 Original project network

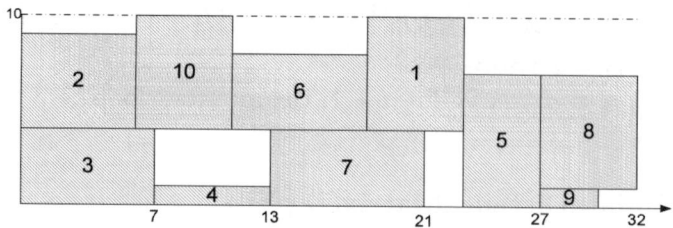

Fig. 10.2 Original schedule

Table 10.1 Mode alternatives

Activity	Target finish time	Mode	Duration	Resource usage	Mode cost
1	23	1	5	6	0
		2	4	7	5
		3	3	9	3
4	13	1	6	1	0
		2	4	3	6
		3	3	4	10
5	27	1	4	7	0
		2	3	8	9
		3	3	6	25
6	18	1	7	4	0
		2	5	6	6
		3	4	8	2
7	21	1	8	4	0
		2	6	5	4
		3	6	9	1
10	11	1	5	6	0

Furthermore, each activity has several different modes, each with a specific time duration and resource requirement. In Table 10.1, the alternative modes for some of the activities are listed where the mode used in the initial schedule is denoted as mode 1. In particular, the last column of the table is the deviation cost for switching to the mode in the new schedule.

Suppose that the schedule has been executed as planned up to time $t = 5$ when activity 2 is disrupted. An assessment of the situation indicates that 3 periods of rework are needed, thereby extending the duration of activity 2 from 6 to 9. This disruption causes all successors to be delayed, which further causes resource infeasibility. If we simply delay activities to make the schedule resource feasible,

Table 10.2 Initial distance matrix

$i \setminus j$	1	4	5	6	7	10	11	finish time window
0	5	9	12	9	12	9	32	-
1							5	[8, 27]
4			0		0		8	[12, 24]
5							5	[15, 27]
6							5	[13, 27]
7							5	[18, 27]
10							5	[14, 27]

most activities will deviate from their target finish times and the project will have a makespan of 35. To get back on track, we initiate a disruption management procedure with the objective of minimizing the deviations from the target finish times.

Regarding the disruption management time window, assume that we want the original schedule to be resumed at time 28, which means that everything after time 27 should be exactly the same as in the original schedule. Accordingly, we define the disruption management time window $[T_a, T_b]$ to be $[6, 27]$ and consider activities 1, 4, 5, 6, 7, 10 in the disruption management process.

To illustrate constraint propagation, we first construct the distance matrix for those activities in the disruption management time window as well as the two dummies 0 and 11. All other activities are fixed. Considering the precedence relations and the minimum duration of each activity, the initial distance matrix is given in Table 10.2. The corresponding finish time windows are also listed in the table.

We now discuss three possible cases for which constraint propagation can be used to tighten these windows.

Case 1 (Branching): Suppose the LP relaxation at the root node 0 gives fractional values for the variables that represent the finish time of activity 4. In particular, assume $\sum_{m,t} tx_{4,m,t} = 14.4$. If we partition on the finish time of activity 4 we have: branch 1 – activity 4 finishes before or at time 14, and branch 2 – activity 4 finishes at or after time 15. Based on the propagation of the precedence constraints for branch 2, activity 5 with duration 3 will now have a finish time window of $[18, 27]$ and activity 7 will have a finish time window of $[21, 27]$. The variables defined for activity finish times outside of these windows can be set to zero. No other activities are affected on branch 2. Also, no additional variables can be set to 0 in branch 1.

Case 2 (New incumbent solution): Suppose that each unit deviation from the target finish time for an activity incurs a cost of 5 and that we have a new incumbent solution with objective value $\hat{z} = 48$. All feasible solutions with $z > 48$ will be dominated so we only need to consider deviations that are $\leq \lfloor 48/5 \rfloor = 9$. In other words, any variable x_{imt} farther than 9 periods from its target finish will incur a cost greater than 48 and so can be set to 0. In the case of activity 1, which has a target finish time of 23, this means that we can reduce its original window [8, 27] to [14, 27]. Similarly, we have: activity 4 - [12, 22], activity 5 - [18, 27] and activity 10 - [14, 21].

Case 3 (Minimum duration change of an activity): Suppose that at some node in the search tree we observe that activity 5 has to be executed in mode 1, which has a duration of 4. Because the latest finish time of activity 5 is 27, this means that activity 4, which is an immediate predecessor of 5 and has duration 4, must finish no later than $27 - 4 = 23$. In general, an improved lower bound on the distance between a pair of activities (say, (i_1, i_2)), may be propagated to any pair (say, (i_0, i_3)) that has (i_1, i_2) between them. In this example, no further tightening is possible.

To show the effects of deviation penalties on the revised schedule, we now solve the problem with different penalty costs. Assume that each unit deviation from the target finish times, whether positive or negative, incurs a penalty of β [that is, $\beta_i^1 = \beta_i^2 = \beta$ in Eq. (10.3)]. The objective, which only includes the second term in Eq. (10.2) plus Eq. (10.3), can be written as

$$Q = \sum_{i \in \mathcal{A}, m \in \mathcal{M}_i} c_{im} \sum_{e_i \leq t \leq l_i} x_{imt}$$
$$+ \sum_{i \in \mathcal{A}} \beta \left(\left[\sum_{m \in \mathcal{M}_i, e_i \leq t \leq l_i} tx_{imt} - \bar{f}_i \right]^+ + \left[\bar{f}_i - \sum_{m \in \mathcal{M}_i, e_i \leq t \leq l_i} tx_{imt} \right]^+ \right)$$

where mode penalty c_{im} is listed in Table 10.1.

Table 10.3 Revised schedules

Activity	Target finish time	$\beta = 0$		$\beta = 3$	
		Finish time	Mode	Finish time	Mode
1	23	18	1	23	3
4	13	15	1	13	2
5	27	27	1	27	1
6	18	13	3	20	1
7	21	23	1	20	2
10	11	23	1	14	1
Optimal objective, z^*		2		31	
Total deviation		26		6	

Table 10.3 shows the revised schedules for $\beta = 0$ and $\beta = 3$. In the first case, shown in Fig. 10.3, the optimal objective value $z^* = 2$, while the total deviation is 26. When we penalize the deviation by setting $\beta = 3$, shown in Fig. 10.4, the total deviation is reduced to 6 and the optimal objective value increases accordingly to 31.

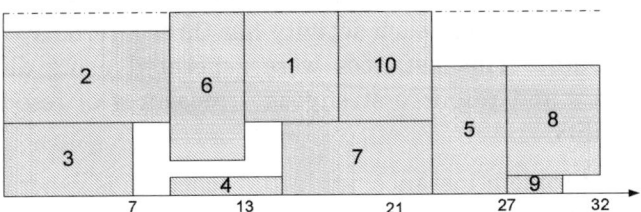

Fig. 10.3 Revised schedule with $\beta = 0$

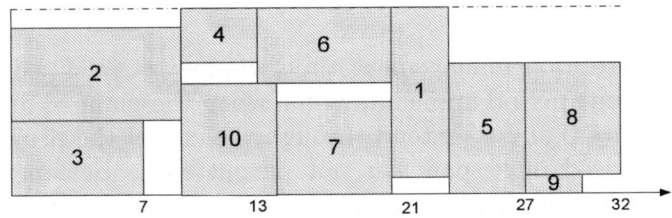

Fig. 10.4 Revised schedule with $\beta = 3$

Without explicitly considering deviation penalties ($\beta = 0$), the revised schedule is significantly different than the original. This is usually unacceptable in practice, hence the need for Eq. (10.3). To account for the relative importance of finish time deviations for each activity, different penalty coefficients can be assigned to the corresponding binary variables.

10.6 Computational results

Extensive computational experiment results are presented in Zhu et al.(2003b). Their main findings are summarized as follows.

The aims of the computational experiments are twofold. The first is to show the efficiency of the MIP/CP approach, and the second is to see how the initial schedule affects the disruption management process.

The hybrid MIP/CP procedure was tested over 554 instances of the 20-activity benchmark problem developed by Kolisch et al. (1995). Each instance has 20 activities, two renewable and two non-renewable resources, and each activity has three alternative duration-resource modes. The instances were generated using different resource factors and resource strengths – measures of resource usage and availability.

For each problem instance, an initial schedule is generated under the objective function of minimizing the makespan. All activities not on the critical path were left-shifted to obtain an early start version called the *baseline*. To create a disruption, the duration of activity 3 was extended by three time periods. In addition, the following conditions were imposed.

(1) The disruption management time window was defined to start at the time period immediately following the planned finish time of activity 3 and to extend through the end of the project.
(2) The revised makespan was not permitted to be more than 2 periods longer than the minimum makespan associated with the baseline schedule.
(3) Except for those activities already underway, any mode that was initially available for an activity could be selected.
(4) For each activity yet to be completed, the finish times in the baseline schedule were considered to be target finish times.

(5) The objective was to minimize the sum of deviations of all activities (i.e., unit penalty cost for all deviations).

In the first set of experiments, all 554 disruption management problems were solved starting with the minimum makespan solution for the RCPSP as the baseline. Both the MIP/CP procedure and the CPLEX MIP solver were applied and both found the optimal disruption management solution in all instances that were feasible. All codes were written in C++ and all computations were performed on a Linux workstation with a Xeon 1.7GHz processor.

For the problem instances, on average each problem has 367 variables and 125 constraints. The average CPU time for the MIP/CP procedure is 6.68 seconds, while that for the CPLEX MIP solver is 9.25 seconds, which shows the MIP/CP approach is more efficient.

In the second set of experiments, two candidates as the initial schedules are considered: (1) the schedule that actually minimizes the makespan (referred to above as the baseline), and (2) the schedule obtained by running a genetic algorithm (GA), also with a minimum makespan objective. Of course, the two schedules could be the same if the GA finds the optimum.

To see how the initial schedule affects the disruption management problem, the same disruption scenario was used but starting with the schedule provided by the GA instead of with the MIP/CP procedure. In 461 out of the 554 instances, the GA found the minimum makespan so only 93 instances are relevant.

Out of the 93 instances, eight were infeasible when the disruption management process started with the GA schedules compared to 40 when the optimal initial schedules were used. It is also found that the average CPU time for the GA schedules is 7.39 seconds, while the CPU time is 14.93 seconds for the optimal initial schedule.

The results raise a number of questions about constructing an initial schedule. If there is no uncertainty, starting with the minimum makespan would, of course, be best as long as the computational effort to find it is reasonable. When disruptions occur, however, the disruption management problem may be harder to solve when we start with an optimal schedule rather than with a "good" schedule.

Our computations also show that an optimal initial schedule is more likely to lead to an infeasible disruption management problem than a heuristic initial schedule. This is primarily due to the slack that exists in a non-optimal schedule. By implication, then, it may be desirable to sacrifice a bit on makespan to gain some flexibility for dealing with disruptions.

10.7 Literature Review

Due to the increased interest over the past decade, a large amount of literature on the resource-constraint project scheduling problem (RCPSP) has appeared. Most existing algorithms for minimizing the makespan of an RCPSP fall into one of the following categories: priority rule-based sequencing heuristics, metaheuristics, and sequence enumeration based branch-and-bound. Work on variations or combinations of these methods can also be found. For a review of models, algorithms, classification schemes, and benchmark problems, we refer to the survey papers by Bottcher *et al.* (1999), Herroelen *et al.* (1998) and Kolisch and Padman (2001).

The typical way project managers address uncertainty is with parametric analysis supplemented by risk assessment (e.g., Chapman 1997). The general idea is to identify and evaluate the uncertainty associated with different aspects of the project and to take precautionary steps to reduce their impacts. Historical data are used to gain statistical insights and to assess the consequences of unplanned outcomes.

Using stochastic networks to represent resource-unconstrained projects is an alternative approach that has been studied for a long time (Elmaghraby 2000). In contrast to CPM, classical PERT (program evaluation and review technique) identifies a critical path in the project network by replacing activity durations with their expected values. A criticality index, the probability that an activity is on a critical path, is then computed and used to allocate resources. Slightly more sophisticated methods like Q-GERT have also been developed. What is missing are comparable methods for analyzing the RCPSP in the presence of uncertainty.

The main content of this chapter is from Zhu et al.(2003b). Some other efforts in discussing disruption and delays in project scheduling can be found in Howick and Eden (2001), Eden et al.(2002), and Howick (2003).

References

Baptiste, P., C. Le Pape and W. Nuijten (2001), *Constraint-based scheduling: Applying constraint programming to scheduling problems*, Kluwer Academic Publishers, Boston, MA.

Bard, J.F., G. Kontoravdis and G. Yu (2002), A branch-and-cut procedure for the vehicle routing problem with time windows, *Transportation Science*, 36(2), 250-269.

Bockmayr, A. and T. Kasper (1998), Branch and infer: A unifying framework for integer and finite domain constraint programming, *INFORMS Journal on Computing*, 10(3), 287-300.

Bottcher, J., A. Drexl, R. Kolisch and F. Salewski (1999), Project scheduling under partially renewable resource constraints, *Management Science*, 45, 543-559.

Chapman, C. (1997), Project risk analysis and management - PARM the generic process, *International Journal of Project Management*, 15(5), 273-281

Eden, C., T. Williams, F. Ackermann and S. Howick (2002), On the nature of disruption and delay (D&D) in major projects, *Journal of the Operational Research Society*, 51, 291-300.

Elmaghraby, S.E. (2000), On criticality and sensitivity in activity networks, *European Journal of Operational Research*, 127(2), 220-238.

Gu, Z., G.L. Nemhauser and M.W. Savelsbergh (1998), Lifted cover inequalities for 0-1 integer programs: Computation, *INFORMS Journal on Computing*, 10(4), 427-437.

Herroelen, W., B. De Reyck and E. Demeulemeester (1998), Resource-constrained project scheduling: A survey of recent developments, *Computers & Operations Research*, 25(4), 279-302.

Howick, S. (2003), Using system dynamics to analyse disruption and delay in complex projects for litigation: Can the modelling purposes be met? *Journal of the Operational Research Society*, 54, 222-229.

Howick, S. and C. Eden (2001), The impact of disruption and delay when compressing large projects: going for incentives? *Journal of the Operational Research Society*, 52, 26-34.

Jain, V. and I.E. Grossmann (2001), Algorithms for hybrid MILP/CP models for a class of optimization problems, *INFORMS Journal on Computing*, 13(4):258-276.

Kolisch, R., A. Sprecher and A. Drexl (1995), Characterization and generation of a general class of resource-constrained project scheduling problems, *Management Science*, 41(10), 1693-1703.

Kolisch, R. and R. Padman (2001), An integrated survey of deterministic project scheduling, *OMEGA*, 29(3), 249-272.

Möhring, R.H., A.S. Schulz, F. Stork and M. Uetz (2001), On project scheduling with irregular starting time costs, *Operations Research Letters*, 28, 149-154.

Möhring, R.H., A.S. Schulz, F. Stork and M. Uetz (2003), Solving project scheduling problems by minimum cut computations, *Management Science*, 49(3), 330-350.

Pich, M.T., C.H. Loch and A. De Meyer (2002), On uncertainty, ambiguity, and complexity in project management, *Management Science*, 48(8), 1008-1023.

Rodosěk, R., M.G. Wallace and M.T. Hajian (1999), A new approach to integrating mixed integer programming and constraint logic programming, *Annals of Operations Research*, 86, 63-87.

Zhu, G., J.F. Bard and G. Yu (2003a), A branch-and-cut procedure for multi-mode resource constraint project scheduling problem, working paper, Department of Management Science and Information Systems, The University of Texas, Austin.

Zhu, G., J.F. Bard and G. Yu (2003b), Disruption management for resource-constraint project scheduling, working paper, Department of Management Science and Information Systems, The University of Texas, Austin.

Chapter 11

Conclusion

This book is about disruption management. As a means of dealing with uncertainty, the emphasis of disruption management is to dynamically and efficiently revise a published operational plan in its execution period. The major steps in doing this are to identify and model the various types of disruptions, to develop and justify the criteria used to evaluate the results, and to devise efficient and effective solution schemes to respond to disruptions.

We have studied several disruption management problems in airlines, manufacturing systems, logistics, and supply chains as well as demonstrated the significant values of successful disruption management applications. From our research experience in this field, we have found some common issues that exist in disruption management.

With respect to modeling, it is important to recognize the deviation cost, i.e., the cost of switching from the original plan to the new plan. Depending on the situation, the deviation cost may be in different forms. It can be measured by the completion time difference of a job or an activity, as in the machine scheduling and project scheduling models. It can also be the change of production and inventory level, as in the production planning problem and the supply chain coordination problem. Moreover, it can also be something new that does not exist in the original plan, such as the job movement between different facilities in logistics scheduling problems. Usually, the disruption management problem itself is a bicriteria optimization problem, with one criterion associated with the deviation cost and the other associated with the original objective. In most cases, we can use the approach of assigning each criterion a weight and optimizing a single objective that is the weighted sum of the two sub-criteria.

With regard to the solution approaches to disruption management problems, there are three cases. Sometimes the solution techniques used to handle the original problem still work with certain modifications. For example, in rescheduling aircraft and crews in airlines, we use the time-space network flow models that are similar to the models in traditional aircraft and crew scheduling problems. For the discrete production planning problem in the general case, we present a dynamic programming algorithm which is essentially the same as the one in the literature used to solve the original problem. In the supply chain problem, the supply chain can be coordinated after demand changes by the same wholesale quantity discount policy, but with new parameters.

In the second case, there exists an efficient algorithm for the disruption management problem, though the algorithm for the original problem still works. One example is the discrete production planning problem with convex costs. The greedy algorithm developed for disruption management is shown to be more efficient than the general convex network flow algorithm.

With the last case, the solution schemes for the original problem are no longer valid, and new algorithms are needed. Several examples of this case arise in machine scheduling for predictive disruption management. While the original problems are easy and can be solved with the SPT rule, they become NP-hard after a disruption. Thus simple rules are no longer optimal. In the EPQ models, while it is easy to derive the optimal policy for the classical EPQ problem, it becomes much more difficult for the disruption problems.

Observing the new plan after a disruption occurs, we find that very often it is not too different from the original plan under certain circumstances. For the machine scheduling problem we studied, the new schedule is also in SPT sequence in some form. For the supply chain problem, we find that the optimal production quantity is to keep the original plan when the demand disruption is smaller than some threshold value. In the discrete production planning problem, the efficiency of the greedy algorithm derives from the small distance between the new optimal solution and the original optimal solution. In the EPQ models, the new plan still follows the equal-batch pattern in most time intervals.

In these cases, this similarity of the new plan and the original plan can be partially explained in two ways. Mathematically, the deviation cost has a large influence. A reasonable consequence of reducing the deviation cost is that the new plan will not be too different from the original plan. This is also consistent with the fact the managers do not want to see totally different plans when disruptions occur. For example, there may be other organizational units whose plans depend on the execution of the disrupted plan. If we change the original plan dramatically, then the ripple effect throughout the organization may be very difficult to estimate and control.

Disruption management is a new and promising research area with both theoretical and practical values. In addition to the work presented in this book, there is much more room for research and application in virtually all sectors of the economy.

Index

activity disruption, 261
aircraft scheduling, 51

branch and bound algorithm, 87
branch and cut, 272

constrained programming, 270
constraint propagation, 275
Continental Airlines case, 3
convex minimum cost network flow, 197
crew node, 82
crew pairing, 80
crew scheduling, 79

deadhead, 82
delay arc, 59
demand disruption, 224
deviation cost, 23
disruption management time window, 24
dynamic programming, 110, 112, 130, 140, 143, 149, 152, 196

EDD schedule, 118, 145
efficient solution, 35
EOQ, 157
EPQ, 157

flight node, 82
flight scheduling, 51

goal programming, 32
greedy algorithm, 198

hybrid MIP/CP solution approach, 270

job disruption, 103

legality check, 89
lexicographic structure, 34
local search method, 45
logistics scheduling, 135
LP relaxation, 66, 95, 266

machine disruption, 102
machine scheduling, 47, 101
milestone disruption, 261
milestone of a project, 259
minimum cost network flow, 194
multi-mode project scheduling, 267
multiple solutions, 25, 35, 66, 91

Nash equilibrium, 247
Nokia and Ericsson case, 2

pairing generation/modification, 88
parallel machine scheduling, 124, 135
Pareto optimal, 36
partial solution, 25, 34, 91
post-disruption management, 103
predictive disruption management, 103

production planning, 191
project network disruption, 260
project scheduling, 257
protection arc, 59

reserve node, 83
resource disruption, 261
return node, 83
robust optimization, 20

sales promotion, 245
scenario-based model, 40
set packing model, 73
shortest path problem, 36
SPT schedule, 105
Stackelburg game, 219
supply chain coordination, 219
swap, 199

time band model, 70
time-space network, 57, 82
traveling salesman problem, 49
two-stage EPQ model, 176

wholesale quantity discount, 221